THE CREATIVE MOMENT

ALSO BY JOSEPH SCHWARTZ

Einstein for Beginners (with Michael McGuiness)

THE CREATIVE MOMENT

How Science Made Itself Alien to Modern Culture

JOSEPH SCHWARTZ

HarperCollins*Publishers*

HarperCollins books may be purchased for educational, business, or sales promotional use. For information, please call or write: Special Markets Department, HarperCollins Publishers, Inc., 10 East 53rd Street, New York, NY 10022. Telephone: (212) 207-7528; Fax: (212) 207-7222.

FIRST EDITION

Designed by Alma Hochhauser Orenstein

Library of Congress Cataloging-in-Publication Data

Schwartz, Joseph, 1938–
The creative moment: how science made itself alien to modern culture / Joseph Schwartz.
p. cm.
Includes bibliographical references and index.
ISBN 0-06-016788-2
1. Creative ability in science. 2. Creative ability in technology. 3. Science—Social aspects. 4. Science and civilization. I. Title.
Q172.5.C74S34 1992
500—dc20 91-59933

---

92 93 94 95 96 MAC/HC 10 9 8 7 6 5 4 3 2 1

To the memory of Luis Alvarez
who taught all of us

"Can you become a star overnight?"
"Sure. It takes about twenty years."

—ANON.

In the early 1960s, flushed with youthful excitement about high-energy physics at Berkeley, I went home to Los Angeles to visit my family. My grandmother, born in the little town of Chudnov near Kiev, a radical, an atheist, a survivor of the 1905 Russian revolution, asked my mother: *"Vos ist dos azoins physik? Vos er tut undzer Joe?"*

I really couldn't think of a way to explain it to her. Finally I said something like, Well, it's about what things are made of. My mother translated. *"S'iz vegn vi zachn veren tzunoifgeshelt."*

My grandmother looked at my mother. *"Vi zachn zeinen tzunoifgeshelt? Un du farshteist dos?"* My mother shrugged. So did my grandmother. *"Azoins. Ker er farichten mein TV?"* My mother laughed. "Mama wants to know if you can fix her TV set. Can you?"

I couldn't. It bothered me.

Contents

Acknowledgments

A book like this cannot be made without readers to comment critically on it as it is produced. Mine were David Albury, Steve Bernow, Chuck Elliot, Terry Karten, Caradoc King, Bob Lapides, Andy Metcalf, and Susie Orbach. I am grateful to them for the time they took to give the material their serious attention. Their responses were not always pleasant to read but they always made me think about the material more carefully.

Preface

This book is an endeavor to present what I consider to be a more mature way of thinking about science. I want to show that it is possible to respond critically to a work of science in the same way that we respond critically to a movie, to show that it is possible not only to evaluate the work—good, bad, overrated, indifferent—but also to interpret it. Why here? Why now? What assumptions about the world did it express? Are those assumptions valid today?

I hope to accomplish three things with this critical approach. First, by analyzing selected creative moments in Western science, I hope to bring the meaning and significance of certain scientific classics into common currency. Everyone is entitled to understand the main outlines of Newton's achievement, to understand the beautiful arguments of the second law of thermodynamics that reveal the inherent limitations of heat engines, to understand Einstein's contribution. Second, I want to comment critically on aspects of science in the 1990s—chaos theory, superconductivity, AIDS research, the origins of human intelligence, the superconducting supercollider—to evaluate the work and to explore what it says about our present condition. And third, I want to show, by taking the creative moments of Western science in historical sequence, that our present fear and awe of science—a recent phenomenon, less than one hundred years old—is a symptom of a serious structural problem in the West with ramifications in every area of cultural life.

* * *

When I wrote *Einstein for Beginners* in 1979, I wanted to show writers and readers that a different kind of writing about science was possible. I chose the theory of relativity as a subject for a popular book because I felt sure that by setting the scene properly, one could show that the astonishing results of relativity, generally considered to be impossible to understand, were a consequence of a simple physical fact: there were no instantaneous interactions across a distance. As a physicist I knew that the theory of the stability of a bicycle was actually more complicated than the theory of relativity.

Einstein for Beginners raised questions. What was going on that relativity had become so mystified? How had Einstein, whose work in physics was characterized by simplicity, clarity, and directness, become such a symbol of incomprehensibility to the outside world? And what about his worldwide popularity? How could one account for the incredible hero worship that followed the verification of the general theory of relativity in 1919?

These questions fed into questions that had long bothered me. Why was our science journalism so banal? What did it mean that politicians from right to left shared equally in a view of science as a golden goose that could be simply harnessed for progress? What did it mean that our philosophers seemed to write about science so unrecognizably? What lay behind the blank stares I received whenever I told anyone I was a physicist? Why did my continuing interest in how things worked seem to make me stand out as a freak in my social circle?

On one level these questions are expressions of what the British novelist C. P. Snow described in 1958 in his theory of two cultures. Physicists and other scientists are members of a scientific subculture that has become increasingly isolated from the mainstream. Snow named the problem. The question is how to understand it. What does it mean that Western civilization is divided in this way?

To understand the two cultures and the scientific revolution, one needs a way to look beneath surface appearances to get at the underlying meanings. Science is an accumulation of written narratives about our relationship to nature. It is no accident that this repository is called the scientific literature. The scientific literature consists of narratives, stories of how we have understood our experiences of the natural world. And like other narratives, they can be analyzed critically to uncover their unstated assumptions and hidden meanings.

We are quite accustomed to critical comment and analysis in the arts. No major exhibition is complete without commentaries that situate and analyze the work on view and relate its meanings to the human condition. The same can be done for science. The complex meanings contained in the scientific literature have as much to tell us about ourselves as do the meanings contained in our art because both are human constructions of reality.

Almost everything written today about science is hopelessly out of date. Do scientists seek the truth? No. It is far more accurate to say that they seek understanding. Is science about objectivity? No. It is about evidence, argument, persuasion, and ultimately about power. Is science about numbers? Not really. It is about relationships. Was Einstein a genius? Genius is the mystification of accomplishment.

Our ideas about science are dated because we are so out of touch with it. The clichés cited originated a century ago when science was an integral part of the culture of Western Europe. From the Great Exhibition of 1851 to the beginning of the First World War science was the pride of Europe commanding audiences and participation. The city of Leeds had six societies devoted to amateur microscopy alone. The way we have understood science has not advanced since the Victorians. Our times call for different interpretations, for a critical appraisal in the light of the experience of the twentieth century.

A plan of the book may be helpful.

The creative moment is celebrated in Western culture as the apex of individual accomplishment. However, it takes nothing away from the achievements of a Beethoven or an Einstein to note that their creative moments were in fact complex social events. The creative moment as we idealize it today is an illusion, something we tend to celebrate in others, not in ourselves. As such it represents an externalization of our human powers, both individual and collective, onto cultural icons who more often than not are confused and bewildered by the fame thrust upon them. As Einstein once said: "You know, I don't wear socks."

Creative moments are not mysterious products of genius but represent the conjunction of complex social events. I have structured each chapter to demonstrate this fact. The reader will see what was happening in a particular society during the period in question and understand the contributions of some of the great names of science. The chapters will show it is possible to evaluate what was accomplished, to understand its meanings, both manifest and latent.

Chapter 1 is a presentation and analysis of aspects of the work of Galileo and Newton. The setting is 17th century revolutionary Europe. The tensions of the transformation from a static absolutist feudalism to a dynamic mercantilism are expressed in both art and science. We see how Western science became mathematized, how the mathematical language of science that is so off-putting to the untrained person today was an outcome of the conflict between the secular and ecclesiastical worldviews and was largely designed to do just that.

Chapter 2 presents some famous results from the understandings of nature created as part of the industrial revolution. The centerpiece is Albert Einstein's theory of relativity because, like Beethoven's symphonies, the theory of relativity is one of the most significant markers of the cultural development of the West.

Chapter 3 analyzes the building of the atomic bomb. The U.S. military command knew as early as 1942 that the Nazis would never get the bomb but withheld that information to manipulate the physicists into building a weapon for use in the post-war period. And the circumstances that threw European physicists and U.S. generals together arose in Europe of the interwar years when the future direction of the industrial revolution was in balance.

Chapter 4 is a presentation and analysis of the spectacular successes of molecular biology in the 1950s and early 1960s. The meaning of the successes in understanding fundamental life processes has not been properly integrated into our intellectual culture. We are left stranded with unimaginative research strategies and an outmoded nineteenth century vision of genetically determined human capabilities.

Chapter 5 discusses issues in elementary particle physics, the world of quark, strangeness, charm, and string to show that like most Hollywood movies of the last two decades, these inventions are derivative and escapist. The point is not to express dissatisfaction about what has or has not been produced but to show that our physics no less than our movies expresses ideas about ourselves and our possibilities.

Chapter 6 addresses the question of why we are afraid of science. The division of labor and corresponding division of interest that we now experience in the West as Snow's two cultures is a particular outcome of industrialization: instead of the miracle of mass production making possible increased democratic involvement in all of culture including science, our relationships to nature and to each other have become superficial and unknowing, the province of specialists rather than the material of life.

Taken in historical sequence, the creative moments of Western science tell a story of the rise and present stagnation of the West. The industrial revolution has failed to materialize the hopes of universal emancipation raised by the promise of material abundance. Instead of global plenty and of the creative engagement of the human being with all aspects of culture that was envisaged by the scientific romantics of the nineteenth century, the human race is trapped in a web of exploitative relationships, with nature and with each other, which produces a dazzling culture of consumption for a minority in the North and a culture of acute poverty for the majority in the South. But at the same time our science, more than any other single human activity, shows clearly that we as a species have the capacity to create our world. The promise is still there.

Science is not a royal road to truth. It is not particularly objective. It does not necessarily bring out the best in people. Science is a human construction. It is what happens when human beings together try to make sense of their experience of nature. Works of science are ways of understanding created through human effort which, like works of art, can be interrogated for what they say about ourselves and our development. By finding out about our science we find out about ourselves.

CHAPTER 1

Florence 1623/Cambridge 1687

Today the great Copernican controversy of the sixteenth and seventeenth centuries is largely a footnote in history. The battle between the scientific and religious cosmologies symbolized by the trial of Galileo for advocating a sun-centered picture of planetary motion has long since been won by science. In spite of rearguard action by religious fundamentalists around the world, modern science is the new voice of authority. Science is no longer embattled. Its leading practitioners are honored participants in the highest councils of state.

The story of Galileo as victim told by Sir David Brewster in 1835 was important for the early Victorian scientists. They had ample reason for attacking the regressive role the Church was still playing in the development of science. But it is not important for us. The contemporary problem of science is not its conflict with religion but its lack of accessibility. For us today, the story of Galileo is not the familiar story of the suppression of truth by repressive authority but the far more important story of how the subversive clarity of physics came to be expressed in its present inaccessible mathematical language.

Galileo Galilei was born in 1562 in Pisa. He was the first of seven children of Vincenzio Galilei, a musical theorist and cloth merchant, and Giulia Ammannati, a member of the Pisa nobility. The Galilei family had been prominent in liberal Tuscan society since the thirteenth century. Vincenzio Galilei was a leading member of the Florentine intelligentsia of the period. He was contemporaneous with Michelangelo, Titian, and Tintoretto. Copernicus, who was educated in law at Ferrara, in medicine at Padua, and in astronomy at Bologna, published his heliocentric theory when Vincenzio Galilei was twenty-three years old.

The period is one of decline for Italian cultural preeminence achieved in the Renaissance, the decline of Spain as a world power and the shift of the center of gravity of European development northward from Italy, first to Holland and then to England. Elizabeth I was excommunicated in 1571; the Spanish Armada was defeated in 1588 by the abler and more highly motivated English seamen; the Dutch burghers of Holland and Zeeland declared their independence from Spain in 1581 by rejecting the royal authority of Philip I. By the end of the sixteenth century the Dutch had achieved world leadership in commerce, manufacture, and finance, a triple hegemony that was to last for over a century.

It is a period when the cracks in the medieval fortress split wide open and through them ran the merchants, manufacturers, and bankers of the new Europe. The Catholic Church, reeling under the pressures of the Protestant reformation, founded the College of Jesuits in 1560 to lead the intellectual and cultural forces of the Counter-Reformation.

Within this larger context of revolt against the domination of Spain and the domination of the Catholic Church came the movement in every social sphere that signifies a major historical transformation. Secular painting, a new way of seeing; opera, a new way of singing; machine technology, a new way of producing; observational science, a new way of understanding—all these arose in opposition to established civil and ecclesiastical authorities.

Galileo was born into a family that was centrally involved in one of the major disputes between the new and the old European sensibilities. His father, a principal figure in the development of opera, was also a principal theorist in the development of the Western musical scale. The dispute over the musical scale pitted the practical sensibility of the men of the New Music, who sought methods that would permit the words and emotions of a text to be expressed clearly, against the classical sensibility of an old guard who sought to preserve the musical theory and practice of the ancient Greeks. The problem attracted the attention of the leading intellectuals of the period, among them Kepler, Mersenne, and Descartes. The English revolutionary poet John Milton was a critical follower of the Italian musical scene.

As a youth, Galileo alarmed his father by his rejection of the liberal values of patrician Florence. An excellent student at the church school at Vallembrosa, Galileo declared his intention to enter the monastery there. Vincenzio would not have it. Instead he forced Galileo to enter the University of Pisa to study medicine.

The young Galileo, already an accomplished lutenist with an extensive knowledge of music and painting as well as a flair for mathematics, was still in rebellion against his father. He dropped out of the University of Pisa two years later to study mathematics with Ostilio Ricci, a student of the famous Tartaglia. Again Vincenzio intervened. Classical mathematics was another trap he wished his son to avoid.

Chastened, Galileo left the university in 1585 without a degree and went to Florence. This time, more to his father's liking, he studied Euclid and Archimedes, supporting himself by giving private mathematics lessons. He made experiments in hydrostatics, met with the leading Jesuit mathematicians in Rome, and angled for a university appointment as a mathematician.

In 1588 he lectured to the Florentine Academy on the geography of Dante's *Inferno* "treated mathematically." His intellectual orientation was still far from clear. Would he dedicate himself to the scholastic traditions of the Church, or would he follow his father's lead in searching for new forms of expression to express the new social sensibilities?

The following year, in 1589, Vincenzio published his *Discorso intorno all'opere di messer Gioseffo Zarlino da Chioggia,* a polemical attack on the musical theories of his former teacher Gioseffo Zarlino. Zarlino had proposed a modification of the Pythagorean musical scale using a theory of consonance based on the presumed existence of so-called sonorous numbers, 2, 3, 4. The idea was that the consonance a listener experienced when strings divided in the ratios of 3:2 or 4:3 were sounded together was due to properties of the numbers 2, 3, and 4. Vincenzio showed experimentally that strings hung with weights in the ratio of 9:4 or 16:9 were just as consonant when sounded together as strings of lengths in the ratio 3:2 or 4:3. Pythagoras was wrong. Consonance lay not in numbers in and of themselves but in the human response to the physical properties of stretched strings.

The *Discorso* was decisive for Galileo. Impressed by his father's use of experience to settle theoretical questions, Galileo began what was to be a lifelong critique of established practice. The polemical style he had learned from his father was to be put to use attacking rather than defending the old system.

In following his father Galileo became a man of technique and observation. From his first instrument designs in 1586 to his detailed proposals for the draining of the Pontine marshes, his career—like the careers of the other leading physicists of the sixteenth and seventeenth centuries—was closely tied to technical developments. (Among his credits are the invention of the cantilever, his discovery that a catenary curve distributes the stress equally in an arch—a result used extensively by Christopher Wren in his design of St. Paul's Cathedral—and his analysis of the strength of building materials showing that large ships have to be disproportionally larger than small ships to withstand the structural stresses their larger size brings.)

In 1589, Galileo obtained a chair in mathematics at his old university, Pisa, where he immediately began to denounce Aristotle to his students. He angered members of the faculty by ridiculing the tradition of academic robes and he angered the authorities in Florence by denouncing an unworkable plan to dredge the harbor in Livorno. After three years of agitation in Pisa, he was lucky to get a six-year contract at the University of Padua, a world-class public university in the Republic of Venice.

At Padua he came into his own. He made friends. He attracted competent students, including Gianfresco Sagredo, who was to become the central character in his *Dialogue on the Two World Systems* written thirty years later. He lectured on the Greek classics as well as on fortifications, military engineering, and hydraulic engineering. His lectures on mechanics were widely circulated in manuscript form throughout Europe. He continued to work on the problems of land drainage and the associated problems of dike construction, retaining walls, diversionary banks, and bank erosion. In 1594 he applied to the government of Venice for a patent on a water-raising machine.

When he first arrived in Padua, the university where Copernicus had been educated in medicine, he looked into Copernican theory. As he described it: "[I] checked the Copernicans to see if they were masters of the arguments on the other side and such was the readiness of their answers that I was satisfied that they had not taken up this opinion from ignorance or vanity."

But the times seemed not right for strong public statements on astronomical questions. In 1597 Kepler wrote Galileo asking him to take a stand in favor of Copernicus. Galileo declined.

> Like you I accepted the Copernican position several years ago.... I have written up many reasons and refutations on the subject, but I have not dared bring them into the open being warned by the fortunes of Copernicus himself, our master, who procured for himself immortal fame among a few but stepped down among the great crowd (for this is how foolish people are numbered) only to be derided and dishonored. I would dare publish my thoughts if there were many like you but since there are not I shall forbear.

Galileo lectured at Padua for eighteen years, achieving an international reputation. He was an enormously popular teacher, attracting up to one thousand students to his lectures. He lived a bohemian life-style with Marina Gamba and their three children, Virginia, Olivia, and Vincenzio, a relationship sufficiently scandalous for one Signore Fabbroni to testify in 1598 before the Venetian Senate that Galileo "was living in illicit intercourse with Marina Gamba." Until the year 1609 Galileo continued to avoid cosmological questions.

In April 1609, on one of his frequent trips to Venice, he and his friend Paolo Sarpi heard rumors of a "Dutch trunk," a tube with two lenses that had the effect of making distant objects seem near.

Sarpi wrote to Giacomo Badovere, a former student of Galileo who was living in Paris, asking for confirmation. Badovere sent what details he could while Sarpi persuaded the Senate that it should not purchase the Dutch instrument but should wait for Galileo to build one.

Alive to the commercial possibilities of the telescope, Galileo taught himself to grind glass and by August he had constructed a device three times as powerful as the Dutch instruments then being offered for sale in Venice. Galileo's idea was to mount a converging lens in the front end of the tube. The converging lens formed an image of the distant object inside the tube. He then used a second, diverging lens to magnify the image produced by the converging lens. The curved surface of the glass lenses acted to spread apart the narrow bundle of light rays coming from a distant source, thus rendering it larger. Galileo's design is still in use today in the manufacture of two- and three-power opera glasses.

By the winter of 1609 Galileo had constructed an improved thirty-power instrument. Here was a way to settle theoretical questions in astronomy. Direct observation, the method used by his father to settle theoretical questions in music would take the place of reason and refutation. He would explore the sky to see what the evidence of his senses would bring.

The brightest object in the evening sky in Padua in January 1610 was the planet Jupiter, then at its closest approach to the earth. On January 7 at 1:00 A.M. he observed "three stars near Jupiter, two to the east and one to the west." The following night the stars had moved: "all three were on the west side of Jupiter." Two nights later, they had moved again.

Galileo had observed three of the moons of Jupiter: Io with a period of revolution about Jupiter of 1.8 days, Europa with a period of 3.6 days and Ganymede with a period of 7.2 days. On January 13 he observed a fourth moon, Calisto, with a period of 16.8 days. In March he rushed into print with his book *The Sidereal Messenger,* a popular account of what he had seen. He concluded his description of the motion of Jupiter's satellites with strong words: "I therefore concluded and decided unhesitatingly that these three stars in the heavens were moving about Jupiter."

The Sidereal Messenger caused a sensation throughout Europe.

Direct observation had shown that it was possible for heavenly bodies to move around centers other than the earth. A critical argument against Copernicus had been removed. The observations were the talk at the tables of the nobility and the bars of the fishmongers. Kepler wrote to him: "My dear Galileo, I must tell you what occurred the other day. My friend the Baron Wakher von Wachenfels drove up to my door and started shouting excitedly from his carriage: 'Is it true? Is it really true that he has found stars moving around stars?' I told him that it was indeed so, and only then did he step into the house."

A new world had been brought into view. In addition to the moons of Jupiter, Galileo had seen mountains on the moon, he had resolved the Milky Way into "at least eighty and possibly one hundred separate stars," and in subsequent observations he saw the phases of Venus and a definite if poorly resolved image of Saturn's rings. The heavenly bodies had a rich physical structure that could be determined only by observation, not by deduction from ancient tests and Holy Scriptures.

It was at this point that Galileo began his twenty-year walk along the tightrope of the Inquisition. Tired of the duties of academic life in the Republic of Venice, he maneuvered successfully to get an easier job at the Medici court in his native Florence. He was to be chief philosopher and mathematician to the Medicis, with no official duties except for occasional lectures to sovereign princes and instruction to the prince's children.

The move alienated his entire social circle. His friend Gianfresco Sagredo tried in vain to dissuade him: "Where will you find the same liberty as here in Venetian territory where a contract makes you the master of those who command?… You may be harried by court life…. Also your being in a place where the authority of the [Jesuits] stands high gives me great cause for worry." Marina Gamba broke off her relationship with him. She stayed behind with the three children in Venice, getting married two years later to Giovanni Bartoluzzi, a carpenter employed by the Delfino family. Many of his friends and colleagues broke with him as well, angry because he had cast his lot with the Florentine nobility instead of remaining with them in republican Venice.

Cesare Cremonini, a rival of Galileo in Padua but a staunch

defender of the university against the incursions of the Jesuits, who twice had been challenged by the Inquisition, met Paolo Galdo, a friend of Galileo, in the street. In a discussion of the telescope he said: "Enough, I don't want to hear any more about it. But what a pity that Mr. Galileo has gotten involved in these entertainment tricks and has forsaken our company and his safe haven of Padua. He may come to regret it."

The fears were real enough. After traveling throughout Europe to avoid persecution for advocating Copernican views, Giordano Bruno had returned to Italy only to be burned to death in 1600. But then Bruno was an outsider, an eccentric, not part of the ruling elite.

Closer to home was the case of Paolo Sarpi, Galileo's friend and colleague. Sarpi had been friendly with Pope Sixtus V and with Cardinal Robert Bellarmine, the leading Jesuit theologian. But he had broken with them over the question of Venetian sovereignty. An outspoken opponent of Church interference with the Venetian State, he was excommunicated and, in 1607, agents of the Vatican dragged him into a Venetian alleyway and stabbed him nearly to death. "I recognize the stylus of the Holy Office," Sarpi said after the attack.

Galileo was not Sarpi. Instead of siding once and for all with the Republic of Venice and the new Europe of commerce and manufacture, his patrician background and intimate knowledge of church politics made him feel that with the protection of the liberal nobility of Florence he would be able to continue the success of *The Sidereal Messenger* in reaching receptive but classically uneducated men of affairs throughout Italy. He wrote to Paolo Gualdo in May 1612: "These people, while provided with a good intelligence, yet, because they cannot understand what is written in [learned language] retain through life the idea that these big folios contain matters beyond their capacity which will forever remain closed to them. I want them to realize that nature, as she has given them eyes to see her works, has given them a brain apt to grasp and understand them."

At first all went well. The Jesuit astronomers in Rome confirmed his observations. He was feted at a massive party in the Quirinal gardens of Cardinal Bandini, and made a member of the

Lincean Academy, Rome's most prestigious scientific society. The Pope received him. He wrote home to his friend Filippo Salviati of the Florentine banking family: "I have been received and feted by many illustrious cardinals, prelates, and princes of this city who wanted to see the things I have observed and were much pleased."

In 1613, encouraged by his reception in Florence and Rome, Galileo published his *Letters on Solar Spots* under the sponsorship of the Lincean Academy. The telescope had shown that the solar spots were in fact attached to the sun and that they moved. Thus the sun rotated and was not a perfect immutable celestial sphere. He wrote to a friend: "This novelty may well be the funeral or rather the last judgment of philosphy."

But in the meantime the lower echelons of the Church had been active against Galileo. Galileo had written to Benedetto Castelli, who had succeeded him as professor of mathematics in Pisa, saying that the Scriptures may have not been literally correct when they asserted that Joshua had made the sun stand still. The letter passed into the hands of Niccolo Lorini, a Florentine Dominican priest. On February 5, 1615, Lorini sent a copy of the letter to Rome, denouncing Galileo for "wanting to set forth Holy Scripture in his own fashion and contrary to the common interpretation of the Holy Fathers."

In spite of opposition in high places to the attack, the charges were too serious to ignore. On March 19, 1615, the Holy Office of the Inquisition granted a request to hear Father Thomas Caccini "concerning the errors of Galileo." On December 3, 1615, Galileo set off for Rome to face the Inquisition for the first time.

The Church was prepared to admit the heliocentric universe as a mathematical convenience. But it could not permit the Scriptures to be contradicted. On April 12, 1615, Cardinal Bellarmine had written an explication of the official Church view to Father Paolo Foscarini, head of the Carmelite Order in Calabria, professor of theology at the University of Messina, and an author of a recent book defending Galileo.

> To say that on the supposition of the Earth's movement and the Sun's quiescence all the celestial appearances are explained bet-

> ter than by the theory of epicycles is to speak with excellent good sense and to run no risk whatsoever. Such a manner of speaking is enough for a mathematician. But to want to affirm that the Sun, in very truth, is at the center of the universe and only rotates on its axis without going from east to west, is a very dangerous attitude and one calculated not only to arouse all Scholastic philosophers and theologians but also to injure our holy faith by contradicting the Scriptures.

Galileo felt confident that he could convince the leaders of the Church to resist pressures from below and to accept the reality of the heliocentric theory. He campaigned through society Rome with zest, debating guests at dinner parties with a skill that delighted his audiences. As one society observer wrote: "We have here Sig. Galileo, who often in gatherings of men of curious mind bemuses many concerning the opinion of Copernicus.... Monday in particular, in the house of Federico Guisilieri, he achieved wonderful feats; and what I liked most was that before answering the opposing reasons, he amplified them himself with new grounds, which appeared invincible so that in demolishing them subsequently he made his opponents look all the more ridiculous."

It was to no avail. On February 25, 1616, the theological experts of the Holy Office submitted a recommendation of censure to the General Congregation of the Inquisition. On the same day the Pope ordered Cardinal Bellarmine to instruct Galileo to abandon his opinion that the earth moves and the sun is stationary, to abandon his opinion that the earth rotates, and to "abstain altogether" from teaching, discussing, or defending this opinion. If he did not agree he was to be imprisoned. Galileo agreed.

On March 5, 1616, the decree "suspending" Copernicus was published and sent to all offices of the Inquisition. The decree was read from all the pulpits, books were confiscated, and a Neapolitan printer, Lazzaro Scorrigio, was jailed for printing a pro-Copernican pamphlet. The fight was over. The balance of forces tipped toward a renewed fundamentalism.

To a certain extent Galileo had been taught his lesson. His hopes for persuading the liberal higher authorities had not materialized. He had narrowly avoided prosecution himself and all that his campaign had accomplished was to have Copernican writings placed on the Index. In the seesaw battle for the control of the Church, the fundamentalists of the lower orders had won the day.

Stubbornly Galileo stayed on in Rome against the advice of experienced observers of the Rome scene. On June 30 the Grand Duke ordered him to return home: "You have got out of this honorably. You can let the sleeping dog lie and return here. There are rumors going around that we do not like, and the monks are all powerful."

Perhaps Galileo at this point could have gone back to Venice to join those who were committed to break the institutional power of the Church. He would have had to accept excommunication as his friend Paolo Sarpi had done in order to be able to write as he pleased about the new cosmology.

But Galileo felt the problem was the frightened closed minds of the monks of the lower orders and the superstitious, gullible people whom they led. Not for him was a sharp break with the liberal Renaissance world that had nurtured him. He was a good Catholic. It was only his father that had kept him from pursuing a career in the Church.

He returned to Florence to work on other projects. He spent two years on one of the most famous problems of the seventeenth century—the determination of the longitude at sea—compiling precise tables of the recurrent positions of the moons of Jupiter that could serve as the much-needed clock to determine the time at sea with respect to the time in Florence. He corresponded with his students, particularly Bonaventura Cavalieri, who were developing their ideas on the infinitesimal quantities necessary to describe accelerated motion. Cavalieri's book, *The Geometry of Indivisibles,* became a standard text for the next two generations of mathematicians. Leibniz used it in his subsequent invention of calculus as did Isaac Barrow, Newton's predecessor at Cambridge. He wrote a carefully worded treatise on the causes of the tides at the request of the Archduke Leopold of Austria covering his back against prosecution by writing: "I consider this treatise which I send you to be merely a poetical conceit, or a dream."

But the analysis of the spectacular comets of 1618 by the Jesuit astronmers infuriated Galileo. Marginal notes in Galileo's copy of a Jesuit discussion of the phenomenon—a talk given by Father Horatio Grassi to the Collegio Romano—are filled with expletives.

Galileo prepared a reply. His *Discourse on Comets* appeared in June 1619. The Church prepared a counter polemic. The liberal intelligentsia felt that Galileo should continue to respond, but carefully. Carmine Stelluti, a friend from the Lincean Academy, wrote to him: "To take on the Fathers would mean never to see the end of it, for there are so many that they could face the whole world and even if they are in the wrong they will never admit to defeat."

With Federico Cesi, Giovanni Ciampoli, and Virginio Cesarini, all leading figures in the Lincean Academy, providing editorial support, and with the enthusiastic backing of liberal aristocratic Rome, Galileo set to work to make a definitive reply to the fundamentalism of the lower-ranking monks in the Church orders. And here is where the deal got made.

Still smarting from his failure in Rome three years ago, Galileo decided to give up the plain language of *The Sidereal Messenger* and to house his argument in the only social institution feared by the Church. That institution was the ancient institution of mathematics.

Cardinal Robert Bellarmine, the leading Jesuit intellectual, against whom the English king, the French parliament, and the Venetian senate railed for his sophisticated advocacy of papal supremacy, had taken great pains throughout his career to avoid antagonizing the mathematicians. Here is Bellarmine instructing a parish priest that on the question of the reality of events on the Day of Judgment, the mathematicians had more powerful arguments than those of the Bible and that only actual events could prove the Scriptures right.

> ... if, swayed by the authority of the Gospel, we dare to affirm that the stars will really fall from heaven on the Last Day, we are immediately confronted by a mighty mob of mathematicians, out of whose hands there is no means of escape. They will vociferate and clamor in our ears, just as if they themselves had mea-

> sured the size of the stars, that it is impossible for the stars to fall upon the Earth, for even the least of the fixed stars is so much bigger than the Earth, that the Earth could not possibly receive it if it were to fall.
>
> To these asseverations of the mathematicians we might oppose the opinion of St. Basil the Great, St. John of Chrysostom, St. Ambrose, the most learned St. Augustine and very many others, who hold that with the single exception of the Sun, the Moon is bigger than any of the stars, from which it follows that the Earth must be bigger than any of them, for even the mathematicians admit that the Moon is much smaller than the Earth.
>
> Still such an argument would not keep the mathematicians quiet, and, as we have no wish to be drawn into a dispute with them we give as our opinion ... that the problem cannot be solved until the signs actually appear.

Galileo's experience of the last ten years had shown him that arguments in plain language using the evidence of the senses were not enough to win. Finally, the Church must be told hands-off. A way to accomplish that might be to appeal to the well-accepted countervailing authority of mathematics. In 1621 Galileo began work on *Il Saggiatore,* the document that was to become the most often quoted manifesto of the scientific method in the following four centuries.

In August 1623 the liberals in the Vatican defeated the conservatives by electing Maffeo Barberini to be Pope. That October Galileo published *Il Saggiatore.* Translated, the title page read:

The Assayer
by Galileo Galilei
Lincean Academician
Chief Philosopher and Mathematician
to the Most Serene Grand Duke of Tuscany

Written in the form of a letter to the
most illustrious and reverend
Sig. Don Virginio Cesarini
Lincean Academician
Lord Chamberlain to His Holiness

Using the full force of cultivated wit, Galileo attacked the slavish devotion of his less-educated opponents to ancient texts. But the key statement, the statement that made his project safe in the eyes of the Holy Office, was the famous statement that the book of the universe was written in mathematical symbols.

The full passage shows Galileo's determination to swat down the Jesuit gnats once and for all by appealing to the authority of mathematical argument.

> Possibly [Sarsi] thinks that philosophy is a book of fiction created by some man, like the *Iliad* or *Orlando Furioso,* books in which the least important thing is whether what is written in them is true. Well, Sig. Sarsi, that is not the way matters stand. Philosophy is written in this grand book—I mean the universe—which stands continuously open to our gaze, but it cannot be understood unless one first learns to comprehend the language and interpret the characters in which it is written. It is written in the language of mathematics and its characters are triangles, circles, and other geometrical figures, without which it is humanly impossible to understand a single word of it; without these one is wandering around in a dark labyrinth.

Triangles and circles indeed. Galileo had written up his observations of the moons of Jupiter without any mathematics at all. And as for the geometrical figures, Galileo was struggling, not with Euclidean geometry, but with the subtleties of the infinitely small subdivisions of time and distance that were to become, forty years later, the new mathematics of calculus. Triangles and circles referred to the well-established canon of Euclid. Galileo's appeal to the authority of the mathematics of ancient Greece was designed to shut up the opposition. The trick worked.

Barberini liked *Il Saggiatore* so much he had it read to him over meals. To the head of the Lincean Academy he asked eagerly: "Is Galileo coming? When is he coming?" From now on no more easily accessible nonmathematical writing. Galileo had seen the light. The new physics was acceptable to the Church provided it was couched as a mathematical hypothesis and not as a direct representation of reality. Barberini gave his approval for Galileo to write a new book on the Copernican system, the only condition being that he present the opposing arguments fairly.

As it turned out, the liberal forces in the Vatican could not hold their ground. Barberini, the son of a Florentine merchant family, dreamed of recapturing the achievements of the Renaissance. But eight years later, when Galileo had his new dialogue ready for publication, Barberini's hopes for a liberal, revitalized Church had not materialized. The Protestant Dutch were firmly the dominant commercial, financial, and military power in Europe, the Thirty Years' War was causing mass disruption and the crisis accompanying the social changes sweeping Europe was expressing itself in the persecution of women. Between 1600 and 1700 over 100,000 people, 85 percent of them women, were accused of being witches. Kepler's mother was one of the accused. Mass trials were held. Fifty thousand women were convicted and burned at the stake. In 1609 the entire town of Navarre in France was declared witches. In 1623–24 600 women were burned in Bamberg. In 1628 158 women were burned at Wurzburg.

In the political climate of the times the liberal papacy could not hold. After intense politicking within the Vatican, the fundamentalists had their way. In 1632 Galileo was forced to make his famous recantation after which he lived out the remaining nine years of his life under house arrest in Arcetri on the outskirts of Florence.

The writing on the wall was clear. If physics were to survive in a socially divided Europe, it had to be well hidden. In July 1633, Descartes, having decided against publication of his cosmology *Le Monde*, wrote to Mersenne from the safety of Holland:

> I was intending to send you my *Monde* ... but I must tell you now that recently in both Leiden and Amsterdam, I have been questioned as to whether the world system of Galileo is included in the book. I hear that Galileo's own book has been printed, but that all the copies have been burned in Rome and that he has been condemned to some punishment. This seems to me so astonishing that I am half resolved to burn all my papers, or at least allow them to be seen by nobody.

But *Il Saggiatore* had established a framework for the possibility of a final compromise between the new and old cosmologies. Educated Europe watched and learned. The message was: keep it quiet, keep it obscure and keep it mathematical.

Fifty years later a prudent Newton adopted the strategy of *Il Saggiatore* in his composition of *Principia,* thereby setting in stone the compromise that gave us the mathematized physics we have today.

In England, Elizabeth I and her father, Henry VIII, before her had succeeded in disarming the feudal nobility and weakening the Catholic Church through the sale of its properties, removal of its privileged immunities, and the authorization of an English translation of the Bible that effectively gave the Protestant minority a revolutionary handbook. By the turn of the century the Puritans were a leading social force and England was the most powerful Protestant country in Europe.

James I and his son Charles I sought to reverse the accomplishments of Elizabeth by attempting to move the English state toward a form of royal absolutism then evolving in France. In 1628 William Laud, a high Anglican appointee of Charles, installed the ecclesiatical Star Chamber and imposed a rigid censorship of press and pulpit. Parish churches were closed to public meetings of any kind. Strict uniformity of church ritual was imposed from above. Protestants throughout England felt the country was on its way to a renewed Catholicism. The 102 signers of the Mayflower Compact were among the 20,000 Puritans who risked the three-month Atlantic crossing to America in the decades leading up to the English Civil War.

On June 18, 1640, Charles rejected the Nineteen Propositions demanded by Parliament. In August he declared war on Parliament from his base in Nottingham. In an atmosphere of extreme tension, the famous Long Parliament of November 1640 was convened. Mass demonstrations at Westminster supported Parliament. A plot organized by Lord Strafford to arrest leading members of the Commons was discovered. In March 1641 Strafford was impeached for high treason, and on May 12 he was beheaded before a crowd of 200,000. On July 5, 1641, the Commons abolished the Privy Council, the Star Chamber, and the High Commission. Ecclesiatical censorship was ended, ecclesiastical control of education was ended, church lands were sold, and the bishops and church courts were abolished. The Church bureaucracy had been dismantled.

Between 1642 and 1649 Crown fought Parliament for control of England. For the Crown were the nobility, most of the gentry, and their tenants. For Parliament were the townsmen, merchants, craftsmen, independent farmers, and some gentry. Within Parliament were further divisions between Presbyterians, those who wanted an accommodation with the king, and the Independents, those who wanted to abolish the monarchy altogether.

The mass mobilization organized by Puritan forces with modern military organization provided by Cromwell and the New Model Army proved decisive. The king's forces were defeated by Cromwell's red-shirted cavalry at the battles of Marston Moor (1644) and Naseby (1645). In April 1646 Charles fled to Newcastle and surrendered to the Scots. From Newcastle he attempted to exploit divisions in the Commons.

On January 4, 1649, with Presbyterian sympathizers of the king excluded from Parliament, the Independents declared Parliament "the supreme power in this nation." The House of Lords was abolished. All lands belonging to the Crown and Royalists were confiscated and sold. A commission was established to try the king for treason. On January 30, 1649, Charles was beheaded as a "public enemy to the good people of this nation." On May 19, 1649, a republic was proclaimed.

Newton was born on December 25, 1642, the year Galileo died and the year the English Civil War began. His father died before he was born and he was raised primarily by his grandmother in rural Lincolnshire, a Puritan, pro-Parliamentary stronghold. He was educated in the radical Puritan tradition at a grammar school in Grantham. He grew up in the 1650s in the period of progressive disillusionment with the Puritan political experiment of Cromwell's republic.

In 1660 Charles II, son of the beheaded Charles I, was returned to the English throne. The eleven-year period of Commonwealth

England was over. Ireland had been colonized. Scotland had been reconquered. The Dutch had been defeated both commercially and militarily. Jamaica had been brought into the English fold. Foreclosures of Royalist estates had destroyed the power and prestige of the nobility. Radical elements in the army and among the Levellers had been suppressed. Independents now joined with Presbyterians and Royalists to install a new state apparatus.

The House of Lords was reinstated. Peers of the realm were exempted from arrest for debt and regained the right to be tried by one another. The bishops were reinstalled. The Clarendon Code excluded nonconformists from local government office. The educational reforms of Commonwealth England were reversed. Censorship was reinstated and Oxford and Cambridge were purged. Newton, then nineteen years old, had just gone up to Cambridge. He watched as John Wilkins, the master of his college, was dismissed against the wishes of the faculty. Wilkins had been Cromwell's brother-in-law and had been appointed warden of Wadham College by the Parliamentarians. Perhaps as many as twenty physicists in all were purged from the Cambridge and Oxford colleges.

The physicists regrouped in London under Wilkins's leadership and succeeded with effort in forming a Royal Society under the patronage of Charles II. The nucleus of the Royal Society was formed by men who had owed their appointments in Oxford to the Parliamentary Commissioners. John Wallis had been the cryptographer for the Long Parliament. Jonathan Goddard had been army physician for Cromwell in Ireland and Scotland. Thomas Sydenham had been an official in the New Model Army, Sir William Petty a surveyor of Ireland under Cromwell's Protectorate. Henry Oldenburg, the second secretary of the society, had been a strong Cromwell supporter, describing him in 1654 as "the greatest hero of the century."

Bending to the new realities, the organizers gave the entire nobility the honor of automatic fellowship in the society while political unreliables like Thomas Hobbes and Samuel Hartlib were excluded. Shunning "politicks of any kind," the society pledged itself to the pursuit of useful knowledge for the "Encrease of Commerce," and pledged its support in "securing the foundations of religion against all attempts of mechanical atheism." The pursuit of physics was to be confined to "men of freer lives" for "if mechanics alone were to make a philosophy they would bring it all into their shops and force it wholly to consist of springs and wheels and weights."

Even with these concessions the Royal Society remained under attack throughout the early years of its existence. In 1667 Oldenburg, whose exchanges with European physicists significantly contributed to the development of both calculus and mechanics, was arrested on suspicion of treasonable correspondence. In 1669, in a direct slap at the Royal Society, Cambridge University entertained Cosimo de' Medici with a disputation on the subject of experimental philosophy and "a condemnation of the Copernican system." Also in 1669, at an official Oxford ceremony, the Puritan turncoat Robert South attacked "Cromwell, fanatics, the Royal Society and the new philosophy." And in 1671 Henry Stubbe attacked Baconian experiential philosophy as being a primary cause of "contempt of the ancient ecclesiastical and civil jurisdiction and the old government as well as governors of the realm."

Newton reacted to the conflicts of the times differently from Galileo. In 1665, four years after he had gone up to Cambridge, he completed most of the work for which he is now celebrated—development of the calculus, the equations of motion, and the theory of gravitation. But Copernicus was still on the Index. Descartes was on the Index and had fled to Holland. Newton had been refused a senior fellowship at Cambridge because of his nonconformist ideas about the Holy Trinity.

Newton was not a patrician. In the words of Christopher Hill, he was a Puritan but at a lower temperature. His stepfather and his maternal uncle had been Lincolnshire rectors. Like Descartes, he kept his thinking to himself. It took twenty years for Edmund Halley, of comet fame, and other members of the Royal Society to convince Newton to publish his results.

When he did publish his *Mathematical Principles of Natural Philosophy (Principia)* in 1687, he followed Galileo's lead in couching his arguments in the language of mathematics.

> Since the ancients esteemed the science of mechanics of the greatest importance in the investigation of natural things, and the moderns, rejecting substantial forms and occult quantities, have endeavoured to subject the phenomena of nature to the laws of mathematics, I have in this treatise cultivated mathematics as far as it relates to philosophy ... and therefore I offer this work as the mathematical principles of philosophy.

Principia was written in a style that was almost totally opaque to his contemporaries. The book is filled with propositions, lemmas, philosophical scholia, and demonstrations using an inconsistent mix of Euclidean geometry and the new calculus. Unlike his popular book, *Opticks,* Newton did not write *Principia* so that it could be easily read by the uninitiated. As Newton later wrote: "To avoid being baited by little smatterers in mathematics, I designedly made the *Principia* abstract; but yet so as to be understood by able mathematicians who, I imagine, by comprehending my demonstration would concur with my theory."

The theologian John Bentley wrote Newton asking for help in deciphering the text. Newton wrote back: "... it's enough if you understand the Propositions with some of the Demonstrations which are easier than the rest." The philosopher John Locke, a strong supporter of Newton, was fairly certain that much of the mathematics was a cover, and after getting reassurance from Christian Huygens in Amsterdam, proceeded to master the physics by ignoring the detailed mathematical arguments. A friend of Newton's, the Reverend Jean T. Desaguliers, described how Locke had decoded *Principia:*

> But to return to the Newtonian Philosophy. Tho' its Truth is supported by Mathematicks, yet its Physical Discoveries may be communicated without. The great Mr. Locke was the first who became a Newtonian Philosopher without the help of Geometry. For having asked Mr. Huygens whether all the mathematical propositions in Sir Isaac's *Principia* were true and being told he might depend on their certainty, he took them for granted and carefully examined the reasonings and corollaries drawn from them and became Master of all the Physics and was fully convinced of the great Discoveries contained in that Book.

We can follow Locke and decode some of the main features of Principia in the same way.

The proper manipulation of infinitesimally small quantities is the subject of the differential calculus. A network of workers in the 1640s and 1650s—Isaac Barrow, Blaise Pascal, René Descartes, Christian Huygens, Henry Oldenburg, and John Wallis—building on the work of Galileo and Cavalieri, brought the subject to the point where the final decisive steps could be taken by Leibniz and Newton, each working independently. Among the many results discovered during this period that still have the power to charm we may mention just one—a pretty expression for the number π, the ratio of the circumference of a circle to its diameter.

$$\pi/4 = 1 - 1/3 + 1/5 - 1/7 + 1/9 - \ldots$$

What had been discovered was that the new infinitesimal arithmetic could be used to express geometrical relationships numerically. A bridge had been found between geometry (shape) and arithmetic (counting).

Not everyone was happy about the new mathematics. Thomas Hobbes attacked "the whole herd of them who apply their algebra to geometry" and referred to John Wallis's book *Arithmetica Infinitorium* (1655) as "a scab of symbols."

But Newton had his language. What did he want to say with it?

The central feature of Newton's physics is his framing of physical influences in the language of force. The idea is that physical influences—gravity, springs, pushes, pulls—produce accelerations. One measures the acceleration of a body. The magnitude of the force acting is then *defined* to be equal to the product of the mass of the body and its acceleration.

Thus one can use the observed acceleration of the planet Mercury in its orbit about the sun to define the gravitational force. One then assumes that this form of the force is the same between any gravitationally interacting bodies. As Newton put it: "... I offer this work as the mathematical principles of philosophy, for the whole burden in philosophy seems to consist in this—from the phenomena of motions to investigate the forces of nature, and then from these forces to demonstrate other phenomena."

The scheme would be of limited value if the gravitational interaction between the sun and Mercury were different in kind from the gravitational interaction between the sun and the earth or between the earth and the proverbial apple. But it is not. As far as we know, gravitational influence does not depend on the composition of the interacting bodies: it depends only on their masses and the distance between them.

The jewel in the crown of *Principia* is Newton's solution of the so-called two-body problem—the motion of a planet around the sun. Boretti, Halley, Hooke, Huygens, and Wren had already shown that Kepler's third law—the relationship showing that the periods of the planets varied as the three-halves power of their distance from the sun—implied that the acceleration of the planets varied as the inverse square of their distance from the sun. Newton provided the computational scheme (calculus) that permitted one to compute the position of a planet at any time and the shape of its orbit (an ellipse) from a knowledge of the acceleration. It is a calculation now routinely carried out by second- and third-year undergraduate physics students.

But what is important in Newton's model is not a precise formula for the shape of a planetary orbit. In any case the formula is only an approximation since perturbing effects such as the influence of the other planets, the solar wind, or the oblateness of the sun have been neglected. Not important also are the mathematical techniques that allow one to find solutions to Newton's equations in terms of algebraic formulas. For most cases the advent of cheap high-speed computation has made these techniques obsolete.

What is important in Newton's work is the realization that phenomena that seem disconnected on the surface are in fact interrelated, that there is a common dynamical origin to the motion of the planets, the moon, the comets and the tides, that the gravitational interaction is universal.

Newton's work completed the demystification of the heavenly bodies begun by Galileo. Not only were the astronomical objects not perfect—the sun had spots, Venus had phases (did not have its own light), and the moon had mountains—but the forces that produced earthly motion (the falling apple) were the same forces that produced heavenly motion (the elliptical orbits of the planets). Celestial mechanics had been united with terrestrial mechanics. The earth and its influence was a speck. It was not the center of the universe.

There was a logical price to be paid: the gravitational force had to act instantly across empty space.

The idea of instantaneous action across a vacuum gave Newton trouble. Five years after the publication of *Principia* he wrote to the Reverend Dr. Richard Bentley: "That gravity should be innate, inherent, essential to matter so that one body may act on another at a distance through a *vacuum* without the mediation of anything else ... is to me so great an absurdity that I believe no man who has in philosophical matters a competent faculty of thinking can ever fall into it."

But if one pays the price of an instantaneous gravitational force acting across the void, the motions of the heavens and earth fall into a beautiful consistent whole. With the sun as center we see the earth pulled in an elliptical orbit about the sun with a semi-major axis of 93 million miles, an eccentricity of .0167, and a period of one year. At the same time the moon revolves about the earth in its elliptical orbit with a semi-major axis of 237,000 miles, an eccentricity of .055 and a period 27.3 days. The gravitational pull of the moon on the oceans produces the tides. And from Simon Stevin's compilations of the heights of the tides Newton was able to estimate the mass of the moon to be one-eightieth that of the earth.

The earth itself spins on its axis once every twenty-four hours. The tilt of the axis produces the seasons. At the summer solstice in London the sun is high in the sky, rising to an elevation of sixty-two degrees at midday. At the winter solstice in London the sun rises to only fifteen degrees above the horizon at midday. A fairly simple calculation then gives an estimate of the tilt of the earth's axis to the plane of its orbit to be $(62° - 15°)/2 = 23.5$ degrees.

The earth's spin flattens the poles and causes the equator to bulge. By calculating the centrifugal forces on the earth at the equator, Newton estimated the size of the bulge. And, in the best calculation of all, Newton calculated that there would be a torque, a twisting force, exerted on the bulge by the combined gravitational influence of the sun and the moon. The torque would cause the earth's axis to rotate slowly—to precess—with a period of 26,000 years. And thus Newton provided a dynamical explanation of the so-called precession of the equinoxes, a slow periodic change in the time of the autumn and spring equinoxes, an effect observed eighteen hundred years earlier by the Greek physicist Hipparchus (190 B.C.–120 B.C.).

The power of the scheme lies in its ability to account for the actual details of experience. Not for Newton were vague metaphors. Experience was concrete; so too would be its understanding.

Descartes had proposed a vortex model of planetary motion. The idea was that the planets were in a whirlpool and were being sucked in toward the sun. The inward sucking was balanced to varying degrees by a planet's spin, thus giving different orbits for the different planets.

Descartes's vortex model was a plausible mechanism for planetary motion. So Newton calculated in detail the hydrodynamics of vortex motion. In the second edition of *Principia,* he showed that Descartes's model implied that the periods of the planets should be proportional to the square of the distance from the sun instead of the observed dependence of the three-halves power of the distance. The vortex model was out. It was not good enough to describe the detailed texture of real experience. As Newton wrote: "Let philosophers then see how that phenomenon of the 3/2 power can be accounted for by vortices."

Principia was the text that consolidated the advances in the understanding of motion made in the sixteenth and seventeenth centuries. Within its framework are numerous beautiful calculations: Newton's calculation of the precession of the equinoxes; Stevin's analysis showing how large the sails of a windmill have to be to pump water to a certain height, given the size of the gears and the prevailing wind velocities; Galileo's calculation showing that a catenary curve distributes the stress equally in an arch; Galileo's calculation of the breaking point of flexible beams showing that the breaking point is proportional to the area times the thickness of the beam and inversely proportional to its length; and Vincenzio Galilei's analysis of the vibrations of stretched strings showing that the frequency was proportional to the square root of the tension and inversely proportional to the length.

The list can be made longer. And each item can bring pleasure to the receptive mind. What had been accomplished was the creation of a coherent framework for analyzing mechanical phenomena within a certain range of experience.

Impressed by the revelation that planetary and terrestrial motion could be understood in concrete detail where they had not been understood before, members of succeeding generations, including our own, have believed that at bottom the entire world can be understood in terms of matter in motion.

Taken uncritically, the Newtonian program implies that if we knew the positions and velocities of all the particles in the universe at some time and all the forces acting, we could, in principle, predict every detail of the future. Gone in the Newtonian framework is human history and the autonomy of human action. The Newtonian vision is a vision of the world as mechanism. This vision still dominates Western scientific thought.

Early attempts to implement this program failed. Even an apparently straightforward problem such as the motion of three bodies under their own mutual gravitational influence proved too difficult to calculate. The dynamics of the earth-sun interaction—a two-body problem—were relatively easy but not at all easy once one included the moon as a third interacting body. For two hundred years the three-body problem was the most celebrated unsolved problem in Western science.

In 1908 Henri Poincaré showed that the three-body problem was insoluble. Insoluble for the early twentieth century meant that, in general, a formula could not be written down for the shapes of the orbits or for the position of the three bodies as a function of time.

But by 1908 the question of exact formulas was no longer of much interest. The three-body problem may have been insoluble but that did not necessarily mean Newton's equations were incomplete. The idea was that one could use the equations to follow the motion numerically. Knowing how far apart the three bodies were initially, one could calculate the forces from the law of universal gravitation. From the forces one could calculate the accelerations—the way the velocities of the three bodies would change in the next instant of time. From the new velocities, one could calculate the new positions. And then from the new positions one could calculate the new forces and begin the cycle again. Thus in an iterative way the motion could be followed with as great an accuracy as one's patience, or later, as one's computer, permitted.

But it can happen in the three-body problem that two of the bodies can periodically undergo a strong mutual attraction. In the case of the sun, Jupiter, and Saturn, such a periodic attraction occurs between Jupiter and Saturn once every 548 years. Their close approach causes the two planets to wobble in their orbits. Such a phenomenon is called resonance. If the resonance is strong enough it can destabilize the orbits, causing the two bodies to resume their motion in a completely different way.

The existence of resonance was the basis of several important theorems proved in the 1970s to the effect that there can be a fundamental instability in physical systems such that the tiniest, minutest change in the specification of how the motion began produces wildly different trajectories. Subsequent development of these ideas caught the attention of journalists and we now have an increasing number of accounts about the discovery of chaos, as it is now called, in physical systems.

Chaos theory is an analysis of dynamical instabilities. Although hyped beyond measure by most media treatments, chaos theory does represent a positive advance. For the first time we now have consciously recognized that there are limits to the validity of Newtonian mechanics. There is more to heaven and earth than forces and initial conditions.

The foundation of the theory of chaos can be understood by repressing the three-body problem as a problem in geometry, the technique adopted by Poincaré.

For a single particle, one considers points in a so-called phase space specified by the three coordinates of position and the three components of velocity. A knowledge of these six numbers defines the motion: once the motion starts in a particular place with a particular velocity, the forces take over and guide the motion ever after. In Poincaré's geometric picture, the action of the forces defines a unique path between an initial point in phase space and a final point in phase space at a later time.

Analysis of Poincaré's geometric formulation of the three-body problem shows that because of possibilities such as resonance, the final point in phase space can be so sensitively dependent on the specification of the initial point that the motion cannot be reliably calculated.

Thus in numerical work, one can approximate the initial position of one of the three bodies by a decimal number of 137 places. One calculates the subsequent motion with a computing machine and arrives at a final position through a well-defined path. However, if one now approximates the initial velocity with a slightly different decimal by altering the 137th place by a single unit, say, and runs the program again, the subsequent path can be radically different from the first. In technical language, one says the path is unstable with respect to small changes in the initial conditions.

The investigations of the 1970s showed that other equations had similar instabilities. The famous butterfly effect was one of them. A relatively simple mathematical model of convective fluid flow intended to model the weather proved to be remarkably unstable with respect to a choice of initial values. With a fine sense of showmanship, the investigators presented this result to the media using an arresting aphorism: a butterfly flaps its wings in Sumatra and there is a hurricane in England.

Such a framing of the technical problem of dynamical instability has great appeal. There is comfort to be had in the thought that the tiny butterfly can influence a vast weather system. By implication, we too can exert an influence on the vast uncontrolled movements of world affairs. But it is silly. A Sumatran butterfly cannot cause the English hurricane. The flutter of the butterfly is a metaphor that stands for the alteration of the 137th place in the number that specifies the initial conditions in the equations of convective flow. This alteration has nothing to do with the dynamics of real weather systems.

Recent studies have shown that the incidence of intense hurricanes on the Atlantic coast of the United States is strongly correlated with the level of rainfall in the West African Sahel. The Sahel, a semiarid region south of the Sahara encompassing Senegal, southern Mauritania, the western part of Mali, and the Gambia and Guinea Bissau, is subject to cycles of dry and wet weather lasting decades. In the years 1947–69, when the Sahel was wet, the number of intense hurricane days (wind velocities greater than 110 mph) was four times the number of intense hurricane days in the drought years of 1970–87. And during the ten wettest years of the forty-three-year period 1947–89, there was an average of 12.4 intense hurricane days per year compared to an average of 1.2 in the ten dryest years, a ratio of ten to one. The heavy rainfall affects large-scale circulation patterns over the tropical Atlantic, leading to conditions conducive to the development of hurricanes.

Wet conditions in the Sahel tend to lower the temperature gradient in the lower troposphere north of the Equator. The reduced temperature gradient reduces the strength of the jet stream over the Sahel. As a result, convective atmospheric currents move more slowly. The slowly moving air mass then has more time to form highly concentrated weather systems that can become transformed into cyclonic motion. In contrast, in the dry season, a strong jet stream moves the weather disturbance along faster, producing a line of quickly dissipating squalls.

Wet conditions in the Sahel are also associated with several other factors known to be favorable for the generation of hurricanes. These include a reduction of vertical winds that disrupt cyclone formation, a strengthening of westward moving upper atmospheric winds that propel the weather system out into the Atlantic, and a weakening of the eastward upper atmospheric winds from the Caribbean known to block the formation of tropical storms.

The connection between heavy Sahel rainfall and hurricane conditions on the East Coast of the United States is an expression of the complicated global dynamics of ocean-atmospheric circulation. But the connection between the Sumatran butterfly and the English hurricane is a figment of the mathematical imagination. Causality is contained entirely in the complex real forces that produce the weather, forces that do not include the flapping of a butterfly's wings. The true meaning of the butterfly metaphor is that weather systems, while comprehensible, are so complex that they are essentially unmodelable over longish time scales.

We may ask how an analysis of dynamical instabilities in physical systems received the compelling name of chaos theory. Jim Yorke, an applied mathematician at the University of Maryland, published the first paper in 1975 using the word "chaos" ("Period 3 Implies Chaos"). "I was trained the abstract, terminology bound traditions of pure mathematics and I very much wanted to get get away from that. So I chose something a bit more glamorous." But why chaos? Was he influenced by René Thom's superhyped catastrophe theory circulating at the time? A pause. "No. Not a bit."

The psychological reasons underlying the choice of a name cannot be explored in a single telephone interview. But it is clear that whatever may have been going on for Jim Yorke in his choice of chaos as a name for dynamical instability, the phrase has struck a deep social chord. Chaos theory? Now *that* sounds interesting. Perhaps—so we think—we can learn something from the scientists about our present condition.

The danger in trying to extract meaning for social relationships from an analysis of our experience of nature is that we tend to project our experience of society onto our experience of nature in the first place. "Survival of the fittest" was a phrase coined by the philosopher Herbert Spencer to describe social relationships in mid-Victorian Britain. Taken over by Charles Darwin as a metaphor to describe a mechanism for the evolution of biological species, it was then taken back by social theorists as a confirmation in natural history of processes occurring in human history. The value of chaos theory as a framework for understanding human social relationships is minimal. The origin of chaos in human relationships as we commonly understand it usually arises from the failure of social structures to meet basic human needs.

The real lesson of the three-body problem and its elaboration into chaos theory is that there are strict theoretical limitations to the applicability of the Newtonian program. In many situations of interest, we cannot calculate how a physical system will evolve in time. The possibilities of resonance or of wet conditions in the

Sahel rear their heads, and we actually have to wait and see which path a real physical system may take. What has been conceived as a global success of philosophical proportions is really quite less than that. Newtonian mechanics is useful and beautiful. It is even worth celebrating. But it is an understanding applicable to only a small part of our experience of the physical world.

In the last few years chaos theory has transformed Newton's mechanics from its isolation in the pantheon of Western accomplishment into a more workaday tool with well-defined strengths and limitations. But we are still left in our intellectual culture with the toxic residues of mathematical obscurantism. Even experienced specialists have difficulty deciphering arguments from neighboring disciplines. As mathematician John Franks has written: "It is difficult for the professional scientist much less the general public to distinguish excessive hype from solid scientific achievement. Chaos has given us both." Or as Einstein once said: "Ever since the mathematicians have gotten hold of relativity I myself no longer understand it."

Students of politics will have had their appetites for their subject considerably dulled by the presence of so-called quantitative methods in the syllabus. Historians will have been equally oppressed by the rise of "scientific" history in which the autonomy of human action is replaced by presumed quantitative laws of historical motion. Economics has labored for years in the conceptual desert of econometrics, forsaking serious analyses of ownership and control in favor of the dubious pleasures of manipulating mathematical models. We have journals of mathematical sociology, mathematical psychology, and mathematical biology.

Our academic pecking order reflects the continuation of the elitist attitudes toward mathematics that made it a safe house for the physics of the seventeenth century. At the very top of the heap are the kings of abstract thought, the pure mathematicians. Following them but several levels down are the applied mathematicians and the theoretical physicists. After theoretical physicists come the theoretical chemists. After them come the experimental physicists and the physical chemists. Decidedly inferior are the organic chemists, their laboriously accumulated repertoire of recipes barely qualifying them for membership in the club of the so-called hard sciences.

After the hard sciences come the so-called softer sciences, notably geology and biology, only now just beginning to fight back against the invidious claim of their inferiority. Psychology barely qualifies as a science and, along with anthropology, history, sociology, and the other so-called human sciences, occupies the bottom levels of academic status. Medicine lies somewhere above psychology and somewhere below biology. Taken in its entirety, the hard sciences lord it over the soft sciences, the whole dreary hierarchy inhibiting the development of a coherent understanding of the multifaceted, complex aspects of human experience.

It would be false to claim that mathematics does not have a central role to play in physics. It does. But its limitations have been underemphasized and poorly understood.

What is important about the mathematical expression of Newton's physics is that the mathematics expresses real relationships. The relationships are the physics. The mathematics is the language in which the relationships are expressed. Why is it that these relationships can be expressed mathematically?

The relationships of physics are relationships between measurable quantities—force, mass, distance; pressure, volume, temperature; frequency, tension, density. The reason that mathematics is the language used to express them is that number is the language of measurement. The mathematical structures of number—arithmetic, symbolic arithmetic (algebra), and infinitesimal arithmetic (calculus)—are relevant to physics because the relationships of physics are relationships between measurable quantities of the physical world.

So number is central to physics. Nevertheless, it is still true that the importance of number has been exaggerated. This is so because even though number is central to measurement, it is still the relationship between measured quantities that is the important thing.

What has happened is that number has become irrationally reverenced: the form in which understanding in physics is expressed has been mistaken for the understanding itself. Forgotten is the fact that mathematics is only a language, a rich language with a structure and internal relationships worth exploring, but nevertheless only a language.

Whether a mathematical sentence says something is by no means obvious. In some historical periods there is a great deal to say and physics advances, the clarity of mathematical expression lending itself to an elucidation of relationships between measurable quantities. In other periods, physics stagnates and winds back on itself in a mystical fascination with mathematics for its own sake. The two sides of mathematics are ever present and it takes a critical approach to find out whether the impressive looking formulae of a mathematical argument are in fact saying anything worth listening to.

To illustrate the limitations of mathematical discourse we have only to look at the recent successes in geology and biology. In geology we now have, in the theory of plate tectonics, a fairly complete picture of the history of the earth's crust. This theory is expressed in words, not equations. It is nonmathematical because the subject under investigation, the floating of the earth's continents on their bed of magma and their spreading apart from the ancient single continent Gondwanaland through the mechanism of sea floor spreading, is a subject with a complex developmental history.

In molecular genetics it is also clear that mathematics has little to offer. Our understanding of genetics has been advanced, not because we can write down a relationship between the positions of the atoms in the DNA molecule but because we know the specific structural and functional details of that molecule, knowledge which is expressed in words not mathematical formulae.

Nowhere in the achievement of molecular genetics, an achievement equal in historical importance to the Newtonian synthesis, is there a formula. Nor can there be one. What wants understanding is not a relationship between measurable quantities but process: how is it that a virus can enter a bacterial cell and within half an hour produce about one hundred copies of itself? Since we now have a reasonably detailed step-by-step understanding of the process of viral replication in bacteria, it can be said that we now understand the secret of life. This understanding is not mathematical in form.

The fact that a result as significant as a solution to the mystery of life is not expressed mathmatically leads us to an important general conclusion: the domain of validity of mathematical discourse is limited.

In other words, we cannot make mathematical models say anything we want them to say. We must accept the fact that their usefulness is restricted to the well-defined areas for which they were invented.

In fact, mathematical models have limited usefulness in physics as well. Newton's solution of the two-body problem tells us only that the orbit of the earth can be an ellipse, a hyperbola, or a parabola. Indeed, if it is an ellipse, Newton's equations can only tell us that the period of revolution is proportional to the three-halves power of the size of the ellipse. They cannot tell us that the semimajor axis of the earth's orbit is 93 million miles or that its eccentricity is .0167. To understand the origin of these things we must know the energy and angular momentum with which the earth began its motion around the sun.

The Newtonian program divides a physical system in two. There is the part of the motion that is accounted for by the forces. And there is the part of the motion that is accounted for by the so-called initial conditions. The Newtonian program does not deal with the initial conditions.

Thus while it could be said that we have a rather good understanding of motion under the influence of gravity as evidenced by our ability to launch orbiting spacecraft, our knowledge of the origin of the solar system has not significantly advanced in the three hundred years since the publication of *Principia.*

We do not know why planets lie in the same plane, why they all spin in the same direction as their orbital motion, why their axes of rotation are all perpendicular to the plane of their orbits, why the arrangement of moons around the planets is so similar to the arrangement of planets around the sun, and we do not know why the solar system divides into small rocky inner planets and large gaseous outer planets. Until recently these problems have been considered intractable. And indeed they are if one insists on working entirely within the framework of Newton's equations of motion.

* * *

With the Restoration in England in 1660, physics gave up its revolutionary edge. In return for the space to work, physics cut itself off from its roots in the productive activities of the society that nourished its growth. The progressive social forces of northern Europe were stronger than those of northern Italy, but they were not strong enough to create a physics of broad popular appeal. In its place came a new God in the form of obscurantist mathematization, a return to social hierarchy in the form of the exclusion of "rude mechanicks" and a new conservatism in the form of a renunciation of politics of any kind. The final resulting compromise has given us the legacy of the elitist mathematized physics we know today.

Our physics appears to be incomprehensible because it continues to be written obscurely. As a result we have been deprived of an appreciation of the clarity that is a genuine part of the Newtonian synthesis. The great variety of physical situations that can be understood simply in terms of matter in motion has been a source of delight for three centuries. But this positive development in human history has been obscured by the mathematization that accompanied the institutionalization of physics in the seventeenth century. For three hundred years commentators have been deceived into thinking that the central feature of the success of physics is its mathematical form.

Nothing could be further from the truth. And the fact that obscurantist mathematical argument continues to find resonant responses in our culture signals that we have not yet completed the project of liberation begun four centuries ago.

CHAPTER 2

Paris 1824/Berlin 1916

As is well known, the Romantic poets of the early nineteenth century did not like the industrial revolution. Blake's famous phrase "these dark Satanic mills" still evokes the horrors associated with the machines of mass production. Blake and the Romantic poets were appalled by the industrialization of Europe.

In 1809 Blake had just finished the poem "Milton," his long, angry, metaphorical attack on industrializing England informed in part by his knowledge of conditions in the Albion cotton mills in London where Watt's steam engines had been installed in 1784. At age fifty-two, he was the grand old man of English romanticism.

In 1809, when Blake was fifty-two, Goethe was sixty, Goya was sixty-three. Schiller had died four years earlier at the age of forty-six. William Godwin, who was no romantic but was Shelley's model, was fifty-three. Haydn, the inventor of the symphonic form, was seventy-seven. Beethoven was thirty-nine. Jane Austen was thirty-four; Walter Scott, thirty-eight; William Wordsworth, thirty-nine.

The younger generation in 1809 included Stendhal, twenty-six; Hazlitt, twenty-one; Coleridge, twenty-seven; and Byron, who had been the younger Peel's classmate at Harrow, twenty-one. Advancing toward center stage were Percy Shelley, age seventeen, soon to be expelled from Oxford for atheistic pamphleteering;

John Keats, age fifteen, then apprenticed to a surgeon; and Mary Wollstonecraft, later Shelley, a twelve-year-old girl whose Gothic novel *Frankenstein,* published nine years later, still speaks to our fears about science.

Not only did the Romantics not like machine and factory, they did not like science either. In "Milton" Blake attacked Bacon, Locke, and Newton. Keats, in "Lamia," wrote "Do not all charms fly/At the mere touch of cold philosophy." Wordsworth hated what he saw as an unfeeling intellectualized science.

A fingering slave,
One that would peep and botanize
Upon his mother's grave?

A reasoning self-sufficing thing,
An intellectual All-in-all!
Sweet is the love which Nature brings;
Our meddling intellect
Misshapes the beauteous forms of things:
We murder to dissect.

And Mary Shelley, in *Frankenstein, or The Modern Prometheus,* capped the Romantic distrust of science and scientists with a powerful Gothic tragedy in which the scientist, Victor Frankenstein, after discovering how to breathe life into inanimate matter, creates a horribly disfigured human monster. He then flees his creation, leaving the giant in his rage and isolation to murder Victor's little brother William, his best friend Cherval, and his wife, Elizabeth. Even with the transmogrifications of Hollywood, Shelley's metaphor is still powerful today. In *Fathering the Unthinkable,* Brian Easlea reads the novel as a fable of the scientists who gave birth to the atomic bomb, a monster that can destroy all life on earth.

The Romantic poets responded to the coming of the machine by opposing both the machine and the natural philosophers involved in advancing the new scientific culture. But the natural philosophers were not dissimilar to the poets in their response to the coming of the machine. The natural philosophers were subject to the same pressures in the new commercial and manufacturing societies as were the poets. They saw the same injustices, they were just as hard-pressed to pay their bills, and they complained about the insensitivity of the rich to what they had to offer. The natural philosophers, too, were part of the Romantic movement.

The entire trajectory of the science of the industrial revolution is a Romantic trajectory, a celebration of the human spirit. But it is a celebration of the human spirit, not in opposition to the machine but in sympathy with the machine. For the Romantic scientists the machine was a beautiful piece of humanized nature. As art and artists moved to the margins of the new societies to become the Romantic movement of the bourgeois opposition, science and scientists moved to the center to become the Romantic movement of the bourgeois establishment.

Here is Sadi Carnot, the author of the second law of thermodynamics, writing in 1824 on the magic of the steam engine:

> The study of [steam] engines is of the greatest interest, their importance is enormous, their use is continually increasing, and they seem destined to produce a great revolution in the civilized world.
>
> Already the steam engine works our mines, impels our ships, excavates our ports and our rivers, forges iron, fashions wood, grinds grains and weaves our cloths, transports the heaviest burdens etc. It appears that it must some day serve as a universal motor, and be substituted for animal power, waterfalls and air currents....
>
> The safe and rapid navigation by steamships may be regarded as an entirely new art due to the steam-engine. Already this art has permitted the establishment of prompt and regular communications across the arms of the sea, and on the great rivers of the old and new continents. It has made it possible to traverse savage regions where before we could scarcely penetrate. It has enabled us to carry the fruits of civilization over portions of the globe where they would else have been wanting for years. Steam navigation brings nearer together the most distant nations. It tends to unite the earth as inhabitants of one country.

We are familiar with this kind of writing. The Romantic vision of science lives on today in our science journalism where it is known in the trade as gee-whizzery. Articles on genetic engineering—"destined to transform our agriculture"; articles on microprocessors—"destined to transform the world of work"; articles on chaos—"destined to transform the way we think about the physical world" are commonplace in the science pages of the major newspapers throughout Western Europe and the United States. Their style is derivative Romantic.

Similarly derivative in our science writing is the other pole of the Romantic tradition exemplified by Mary Shelley's *Frankenstein*. The shock-horror story—"New Hazard Found in Genetically Engineered Microorganisms"; "Radioactive Release Threatens North Sea"; "Mystery Virus Fells Hospital Patients"—this is Dr. Frankenstein brought up to date. The shock-horror story routinely exploits Mary Shelley's archetypal image of the monster unleashed by reckless out-of-control scientists.

Both Romantic traditions maintain the supremacy of the human spirit. For the Romantic scientists, each bolt and joint of the steam engine expresses a deep human responsiveness to the requirements of nature. For the Romantic poets each bolt and joint of the steam engine chains the human spirit into abominable relationships of production.

We suffer this polarization of views to this day. Only a few perceptive commentators have seen that both Romantic sensibilities are sides of the same coin and that a resolution of the contradiction between artistic and scientific Romanticism requires a resolution of the very deepest contradictions in the way we have constructed our productive life.

In the meantime we are missing out. The mathematization of physics has been one factor contributing to the inaccessibility of science. Another has been the Romantic tradition. The persistence of shock horror/gee-whizzery in our science writing has prevented us from making informed judgments about our scientific culture. Our lives are diminished by our lack of critical appreciation of the second law of thermodynamics, the origin of the blue of the sky, and the special and general theories of relativity.

We have lost our connection to the great classics of human understanding of Western civilization. The scientific literature of nineteenth-century Europe is a unique record of human accomplishment. For it is not simply that nineteenth-century Europe gave the world the steam engine, the telegraph, the dynamo, and the Palm House at Kew Gardens. Nineteenth-century Europe gave the world a set of stylish understandings of these devices at the highest cultural level. This literature can be engaged once one has critically reconstructed events to show what the workers in the field wanted to understand. In this way, even a postmodern sensibility can assimilate the understandings created as part of the process by which the human race learned to transform the materials of the physical world into the artifacts of modern industrial civilization.

A major technical problem facing European societies in the sixteenth and seventeenth centuries was how to get rid of the ground water that drained into a mining chamber, a typical excavation producing ten pounds of water for each pound of ore or coal. In England 15 percent of all the patents granted during the reigns of Elizabeth I, James I, and Charles I were for pumping devices of one kind or another. By the late seventeenth century the question had become, Could the energy of fire be used to drain the mines?

The Miner's Friend, designed and built by Captain Thomas Savery of the English Royal Engineers in 1702, was the first successful pump to use fire as the prime mover. Savery built a simple machine that actually did raise water by fire.

He stood a large, four-foot-long, cast-iron egg on end. To the top of the egg he connected a pipe running to a boiler. To the bottom of the egg, he connected a very long vertical pipe. One end of the pipe extended downward into the water on the mine floor. The other end extended upwards to the surface of the mine.

To start the pump the operator opened a valve on the boiler pipe. Steam then flowed into the cast-iron egg. When the egg was filled with steam the operator closed the valve. The operator then poured cold water over the outside of the cast-iron egg. The steam inside condensed producing a partial vacuum. The operator then opened a valve on the pipe leading to the mine floor and the partial vacuum sucked up water from the bottom of the mine into the cast-iron egg.

The pump now being primed, the operator opened a valve on

the pipe leading to the surface and the boiler valve. Now the pressure of the incoming steam would push on the water in the cast-iron egg and force it up to the surface. Then all the valves would be closed, the cast-iron egg doused with cold water to form the vacuum and the cycle started again.

Savery's cast-iron egg was a neat way to exploit the properties of a vacuum. But it needed to withstand relatively high pressures and the egg needed to be located halfway down the mine shaft.

Thomas Newcomen, an iron dealer who furnished the tin mines of Cornwall with tools, observed the limitations of Savery's machine and in 1712 devised a radically improved version that could operate on the surface without high pressures.

Newcomen's machine consisted of a huge beam twenty-four feet long and a foot and a half square rocking up and down like a seesaw. One end of the beam was attached to an ordinary mechanical pump. The other end was attached to the piston of a steam cylinder. On the up stroke, the rising piston drew steam from the boiler into the steam cylinder. At the top of the stroke, a valve automatically opened, letting cold water into the cylinder. The steam in the steam cylinder condensed, creating a partial vacuum. Atmospheric pressure then pushed down on the steam piston from the outside, producing an upstroke on the pump, which sucked up water.

Newcomen's engine was a great success in areas where coal was cheap and plentiful. In 1722 the first Newcomen engine was sold outside England to J. E. T. von Erlach of Vienna for use in his mines at Konigsberg. By mid-century Newcomen engines had been installed in Belgium, France, Germany, Hungary, and Spain. A typical machine operated at twelve strokes per minute. Each stroke raised eighty pounds of water (ten gallons) to a height of 150 feet for a respectable power rating of 5.5 horsepower but at the low thermal efficiency—the conversion of the heat energy in the coal to mechanical work—of about .5 percent.

Subsequent modifications to the Newcomen engine were able to raise the efficiency first to 1.5 percent and then to 3.5 percent. Among the numerous inventors working on improving the Newcomen engine—Deighton, Leupold, Hulls, Bellido, Payne, Blake, Fitzgerald, Emerson, Black—it fell to James Watt to secure the decisive patent in 1769 with his now celebrated idea of the separate condenser.

Watt's idea was to save energy by keeping the steam cylinder constantly warm. He vented the spent steam to a separate vessel. Only there would it be cooled to create the vacuum. A contemporary observer, Professor John Robinson of the University of Glasgow, where Watt was a scientific instrument maker, recalled his excitement on learning about Watt's innovation.

> At the breakup of the College (I think in 1765) I went to the country. About a fortnight after this I came to town and went to have a chat with Mr. Watt, and to communicate to him some observations I had made on Desaguiliers's and Belidor's account of the steam engine. All the while, Mr. Watt kept looking at the fire. At last he looked at me and said briskly, "You need not fash yourself any more about that man; I have now got an engine that shall not waste a particle of steam. It shall be all boiling hot;—aye, and hot water injected if I please." I was very anxious to learn what Watt had contrived and found Mr. Alexander Brown, a very intimate acquaintance of Mr Watt's, walking with another gentleman. Mr. Brown immediately accosted me with, "Well, have you seen Jamie Watt?"—"Yes."—"He'll be in high spirits now with his engine isn't he?" "Yes," said I, "very fine spirits." "Gad," says Mr. Brown, "the condenser's the thing: keep it but cold enough, and you may have a perfect vacuum, whatever the heat of the cylinder." The instant he said this the whole flashed on my mind at once.

Robinson tried it for himself using a steam vessel, a tea kettle, a condenser vessel, and a glass receiver, and concluded: "In short, I had no doubt that Mr. Watt had really made a perfect steam engine."

Nevertheless steam was still a chancy business. Introduction of the separate condenser helped solve the problem of the loss of energy due to the clumsy cooling system. But there were still to be solved the detailed engineering problems associated with the construction of any real working device. Even with his patent Watt was not happy. Watt wrote to his friend Snell in 1769: "... in life there is nothing more foolish than inventing."

But the demand for power was there—for millstones, saws, bellows, ore-crushers; for grinding flour, for working metal, for pumping water, for grinding glass, for working wood, for making paper, for grinding clay, for grinding pigments, and for powering the expansion of the Lancashire textile industry. The statistics of economic growth of Europe in the early phase of the industrial revolution dramatically illustrate the magnitude of the changes sweeping Europe.

English foreign trade doubled in the first half of the eighteenth century and nearly tripled again in the second half. Manufacture for export quadrupled between 1700 and 1790. In France, foreign trade tripled between between 1716 and 1755 and then doubled again between 1755 and 1789 while French national wealth tripled from 731 million FF in 1715 to 2 billion FF in 1788.

The islands of the Caribbean were turned into French, Dutch, and English plantations producing sugar, coffee, cotton, and cacao. In the British Caribbean 86 percent of the population were slaves, in the French Caribbean 88 percent, in the Dutch Caribbean 83 percent. Sugar imports to France and England from plantations in Barbados, Guadeloupe, Jamaica, Martinique, and Santo Domingo rose from 106,000 tons in 1741 to 160,000 tons twenty years later and then almost doubled to 290,000 tons in 1790. In Britain cotton imports increased tenfold from 5 million pounds of raw cotton in 1770 to 54 million pounds in 1800 and then increased sevenfold again to 360 million pounds in 1836.

The slave trade accounted for one-third the value of European commerce. Between 1680 and 1786, 2.1 million slaves were sold to the British colonies and over a comparable period 7 million to Brazil. In the United States the number of slaves increased more than tenfold from 300,000 in 1701 to more than 4 million in 1790. In 1700 the Virginia and Maryland tobacco plantations produced 20 million pounds of tobacco with 400,000 slave laborers. In 1776 the figures had increased to 220 million pounds of tobacco produced by 2.4 million slave laborers.

The sale of slaves formed the most profitable leg of the so-called Golden Triangle in which guns, refined sugar, and textiles were shipped down the coast of Europe to Africa, African slaves were shipped across the Atlantic to the New World, and cotton and sugar were shipped back across the Atlantic to England. Profits on single voyages could be as much as 500 percent.

Contemporary observers were not oblivious to the origins of European wealth. "All this great increase in our treasure proceeds chiefly from the labour of negroes in the plantations," wrote Jonathon Gee in 1729 about England. In 1773 Richard Pares commented on his shame of the wealth generated by slave labor: "When I think of the colossal banquets of the Barbadoes planters ... of the younger William Beckford's private orchestra and escapades in Lisbon, of Fonthill Abbey or even of the Codrington Library, and remember that the money was got by working African slaves twelve hours a day on such a starvation diet, I can only feel anger and shame."

And in 1838, after the European economies had moved on from slave labor, Sir William Howitt reviewed the realities of what had been the slave trade in the following words: "The barbarities and desperate outrages of the so-called Christian race throughout every region of the world and upon every people they have been able to subdue are not to be paralleled by those of any other race however fierce, however untaught, and however reckless of mercy and of shame in any age of the earth."

Slave labor not withstanding, the prosperity of British commerce was the talk of eighteenth-century Europe. Voltaire, in his *Letters from England,* wrote: "Commerce which has enriched the citizens of England has helped make them free, and that liberty in turn has expanded commerce. This is the foundation of the greatness of the state."

As Europe increased its domination of world trade, pressures were brought to bear on its manufacturing capacity. The equation—produce more to sell more—created opportunities for a new class of inventors to try to get a piece of the action. Potential investors were besieged for money to develop new devices. As financier Nathan Rothschild said in Paris: "There are three ways of losing your money: women, gambling, and engineers. The first two are pleasanter, the last is much the most certain." Rothschild was right. Very few ideas were successful. But the failures formed the humus that nourished the growth of the famous successes.

Matthew Boulton, Watt's business partner, read the market

correctly. In 1776 Boswell noted Boulton's confidence on a trip to the Boulton/Watt factory outside Birmingham: "I wish Johnson had been with us; for it was a scene which I should have been glad to contemplate by his light. The vastness and the contrivance of some of the machinery would have matched his mighty mind. I shall never forget Mr Boulton's expression to me: 'I sell here, Sir, what all the world desires to have,—POWER.'"

Part of the business problem was knowing what to charge. The breweries wanted to know how many horses Watt's engine could replace. By stringing a rope over a pulley and lowering it into a mine, Boulton found that a horse could pull a weight of 150 pounds at the rate of a medium fast walk (about two and a half miles per hour). Boulton's definition of power is with us today: one horsepower equals 150 pounds times 2.5 miles per hour (3.67 feet per second) or 550 ft.-lbs/sec.

By 1779 Watt realized the business was finally a goer. Sales were coming in, demand was holding steady. He wrote to Boulton in an ecstatic mood:

> Hallelujah! Hallelujee!
> We have concluded with Hawkesbury,
> 2171. per annum from Lady-day last;
> 2751.5s for time past; 1571 on account.
> We make them a present of 100 guineas—
> Peace and good fellowship on earth—
> Perrins and Evans to be dismissed—
> 3 more engines wanted in Cornwall—
> Didley repentant and amendant—
> Yours rejoicing
> JAMES WATT

By 1780 Watt and Boulton had installed sixty of their steam engines. In 1781 Watt evaded a previously held patent on the invention of the crankshaft and introduced a gearing system that translated the up-and-down motion of the steam piston into a rotary motion suitable for driving machinery. In 1787 Robert Peel, father of the future prime minister, installed Watt's engines in his textile factories, running them, with the help of child labor, for twenty hours a day. In 1790 the first machine-made nails came on the market.

By 1800, when Watt's patent ran out, there were 496 Watt engines in use in the mines, metal plants, textile factories, and breweries. Of them, 308 were rotating machines, 164 pumping; 24 generated blast air. The average power ratings were fifteen horsepower. By 1835 there were 1,369 engines installed in the Lancashire cotton industry alone. There were steamships and steam locomotives. Europe had entered the age of steam.

Watt and the early steam engine designers were good engineers. The separate condenser was one of many continuous improvements in the development of machines capable of converting the energy of a fire into the energy of a turning wheel. The area of the chimney, the area of the fire grate, the quantity of air to be admitted, the design of the fireplace itself all required thoughtful attention in order to maximize the energy delivered to the boiler. The optimum volume of the boiler, the least diameter of the safety valves, the accurate machining of the steam cylinder, the optimum diameter of the steam passage were required to maximize the energy delivered to the piston. And improvements in metallurgy and the working of iron were needed to maximize the transmission of power from the steam piston to the rotating shafts of the dark Satanic mills.

Rules of thumb developed that expressed what had been learned about the design of the new machines. The volume of the boiler needed to be five to ten times the volume swept out by the piston stroke. The optimum diameter of the steam ways needed to be about one-fifth the diameter of the steam cylinder. One inch of piping needed to be allowed for each horsepower the engine could deliver.

And slowly as the steam engine began to dominate the productive landscape it began to attract theoretical attention. Could the incremental improvements in thermal efficiency be continued indefinitely or was there an upper limit, a maximum efficiency, beyond which one could not go? The question of the maximum possible efficiency of a steam engine was a leading problem for Western savants for fifty years until it was solved by Sadi Carnot in 1824.

* * *

A lasting result of the French Revolution was the creation of the École Polytechnique in 1795. The École Polytechnique offered the best of French science and technology to an elite postrevolutionary generation. Only one hundred young men were admitted each year compared to the two thousand admitted at the University of Paris.

The instructors were trained by Jean Hachette, a "fervent revolutionary," according to contemporary observers. By the second generation, the instructors were the names that now dominate the physics and mathematics textbooks: Cauchy, Poisson, Fresnel, Fourier, Ampère, Arago, Malus, Gay-Lussac.

Political economy, industrial and agricultural techniques, engineering practice, and applied chemistry as well as mathematics and physics were part of the curriculum at L'École. Under the influence of Jean Hachette, the school became a center for study of the problems of industrialization and economic organization. Among the early students who were trained to become the managers, directors, and theorists of French industrial development was Sadi Carnot, author of the second law of thermodynamics, one of the great classics of the scientific literature, the definitive statement about the efficiency of heat engines.

Sadi Carnot was a child of the revolutionary elite. His father was Lazare Carnot, celebrated in French history books as *le grand Carnot* and the *organisateur de la victoire* of the French Revolution.

Trained as a Royal Engineer, Lazare Carnot had early in the Revolution campaigned at the National Assembly for radical army reforms, including promotion by merit, not birth, and for a united engineering and artillery corps governed by an elected council rather than the usual military hierarchy. He was elected to the Legislative Assembly in 1791, to the National Convention in 1792, and to the twelve-member Committee of Public Safety in 1793, where he organized the famous mass mobilization of the entire French population that resulted in the expulsion from France of the 500,000 troops of the Coalition armies of Austria, Prussia, Britain, Holland, and Spain.

Carnot, along with Lindet, was a moderate on the Committee of Public Safety. He opposed the proposals of Robespierre and

Saint-Just to transfer power to the *sans-culottes* on the grounds that the country was not ready for such radical measures. As he later recalled: "I wanted the citizens to be guided in their conduct by institutions—converted in habit—rather than by the menace of law. Finally I thought that it would be better to let prejudices slowly dissipate by the light of reason than to stamp them out by violence."

In 1796, when Lazare was a member of the ruling Directory, Sadi Carnot was born in the Palais du Petit-Luxembourg. A well-known story about his childhood has him berating Napoleon for splashing water on some women on a boating outing. "You beastly first consul, stop teasing those ladies," said the four-year-old child to Europe's man of the hour.

In 1807 Lazare began the education of Sadi and his younger brother Hippolyte. He had much to offer them. He was a central figure in government technical decision-making, serving on fifteen technical commissions annually to evaluate progress in machine technology, mathematics, and military technology. In 1783 he had written a general analysis of machines that he subsequently expanded into a book, *Fundamental Principles of Equilibrium and Movement,* published in 1803. He was concerned with the foundations of calculus and wrote a memoir entitled *Reflections on the Metaphysics of the Infinitesimal Calculus,* published in 1797. In 1806 he took up the problem of heat engines in a short report written with C. L. Berthollet about a machine called the Pyreolophore, an early internal combustion engine proposed by the Niepce brothers, who went on to invent the tintype and then later, with Daguerre, the photograph.

In 1812, at age sixteen, Sadi entered L'École Polytechnique. He studied analysis (calculus), mechanics, descriptive geometry, and, with Nicholas Clement, applied chemistry. Clement was a friend of the family, an experienced business manager, and a man of wide experience of French industrial problems. He had worked on alum production, the production of sulphuric acid, refining sugar beets, alcohol distillation from potatoes, on the problems of receptacles for grain storage, and on the relative merits of oil or coal gas for domestic lighting. He was in charge of higher technical education in France. Through Clement, Carnot became interested in the problems associated with industrial development, including the problem of maximizing the thermal efficiency of the steam engine.

In 1815 Lazare was exiled by the Restoration. Sadi became a second lieutenant in an engineering regiment in Metz.

In 1820, after five unhappy years in the army, he was able to retire on half pay to devote himself to serious study of the problems of industrialization. He furthered his education by courses at the Sorbonne, the Collège de France, L'École des Mines, and the Conservatoire des Arts et Métiers. He made extensive visits to factories in France and the rest of Europe. He visited his father in exile in Magdeburg for several weeks in 1821, where they discussed the applications of scientific principles to industrial management.

In 1823 Lazare died. The taciturn Sadi, possibly liberated by the death of his famous father, took a small apartment with his brother Hippolyte in the Fifth Arrondissement in Paris and began to write. Using Hippolyte as a sounding board, Carnot refined the thinking of his father and of Clement, Hachette, Navier, Petit, and Combes into his classic, *Reflections on the Motive Power of Fire and on the Machines Proper to the Development of That Power,* published in 1824.

Carnot's extensive experience observing the operation of steam engines in France—at the famous Chaillot works, at Oberkampf's advanced machine tool factory in Jouy, at the Littry Collieries—coupled to his close study of fifty years of improvements in English steam engines, made him realize that the condenser indeed was the crucial thing, as James Watt had guessed a half century earlier.

Carnot wanted to solve the presenting problem in the theory of steam engines: was there a maximum possible efficiency?

> The question has often been raised whether the motive power of heat is unbounded, whether the possible improvements in steam engines have an assignable limit—a limit which the nature of things will not allow to be passed by any means whatever; or whether, on the contrary, these improvements may be carried on indefinitely. We have long sought, and are seeking today, to ascertain whether there are in existence agents preferable to the

vapor of water for developing the motive power of heat; whether atmospheric air, for example, would not present in this respect great advantages. We propose now to submit these questions to a deliberate examination.

Following his father, Carnot sought a general principle common to all heat engines no matter what their design and mode of operation: "In order to consider in the most general way the principle of the production of motion by heat, it must be considered independently of any mechanism or any particular agent. It is necessary to establish principles applicable not only to steam engines but to all imaginable heat engines, whatever the working substance and whatever method by which it is operated."

Such a general principle could be found only from the study of the actual operation of existing steam engines. It was Carnot's contribution to realize that the condensing phase was the fundamental common factor in all heat engines: every heat engine *had* to have a condensing phase.

Carnot elevated a fact of experience to the level of natural law. He absorbed the experience of the builders of steam engines and listened to what nature was telling us through the way we were required to construct our machines. We can divert some, *but not all,* of the heat flowing from hot to cold into work. There always must be heat deposited into the environment. And this is the second law of thermodynamics: one cannot construct a heat engine without having a net flow of heat from a high temperature to a low temperature.

Carnot's arguments about engine efficiency based on the required existence of the condenser are, like the arguments of most of our best physics, simple but subtle.

One first hypothesizes a theoretical engine. The theoretical engine takes in heat at a high temperature. It performs work. And then it expels heat at a low temperature. The theoretical engine is also reversible. It can work as a refrigerator, taking in work, extracting heat from a low temperature, and then expelling heat at a higher temperature.

In Carnot's argument, one then couples the refrigerator and the engine together. When the refrigerator and engine work in tandem, the work produced by the engine is used to drive the refrigerator. The refrigerator extracts the heat deposited by the engine at the low temperature and returns it to the high temerature. The net result is that at the end of each cycle the combined engine/refrigerator system remains exactly the same as when it began.

Now, as if from thin air, comes the startling conclusion. One supposes that there exists an engine that is more efficient than the reversible engine. We couple this more efficient engine to the refrigerator, diverting the portion of extra work to the outside. Everything else stays the same. The refrigerator still extracts the heat deposited at the low temperature and returns it to the high temperature. But the result now is a machine that converts heat into work without any net flow of heat to a lower temperature.

Carnot's postulate says that such a machine is impossible. There must always be heat deposited in the condenser. Thus if one believes that the condenser is essential, one *must* conclude that no heat engine can have greater efficiency than a reversible engine operating between the same two temperature limits. In Carnot's words, "The motive power of heat is independent of the agents employed to realize it; its quantity is fixed solely by the temperatures of the bodies between which is effected the transfer of [heat]."

Detailed study of the second law requires attention to the subtlety of the idea of reversibility. But that is a fine point. Once one really accepts that the condenser is a fact of life, or, if you like, a law of nature, it follows that heat engines have a maximum thermal efficiency determined only by the temperature difference between boiler and condenser.

Carnot's analysis lets us see that steam engines in all their variety are works of art, that boiler, chimney and fireplace, steam ways and valves, cylinder and piston—the intricate, detailed works of a steam engine—are materializations of a single great theme, the process of extracting heat at a high temperature, performing work, and expelling heat at a lower temperature. The second law of thermodynamics expresses the unity in the diversity of steam engine design.

* * *

An extension of Carnot's original argument, now given in undergraduate textbooks, gives a simple formula for the maximum efficiency of all heat engines. The formula is $e = 1 - T_1/T_2$, where T_1 is the temperature of the low-temperature heat reservoir—the condenser—and T_2 is the temperature of the high-temperature reservoir—the boiler. (The temperature in question is the so-called absolute temperature in which the zero of temperature is fixed not at the freezing point of water, as in the Centigrade scale, but at the point where all molecular motion ceases. The most frequently used absolute-temperature scale is the Kelvin scale. On the Kelvin scale the freezing point of water is 273° K. while the boiling point of water is 373° K.)

The formula for the maximum efficiency of heat engines is quite handy. Consider for example, the economics of our current electricity supply systems. We generate most of our electricity with steam turbines. High-pressure steam is sprayed through specially designed nozzles onto rotating turbine blades. The steel of the turbine blades can withstand steam pressures of about 1500 lbs./sq. in. at temperatures of about 600° K. This is the maximum temperature T_2. The minimum temperature, T_1, using local water for cooling is about 50°C. (323° K.). With these temperature limits the maximum theoretical efficiency of a steam turbine is

$$e = 1 - 323/600 = .46,$$

or 46 percent.

Thus, given the structural strength of steel and the laws of thermodynamics, the maximum theoretical efficiency of modern steam turbine electricity generators is less than 50 percent. Less than half the energy content of the coal is converted into electricity.

What happens to the other half? It gets discharged into the nearest river as "waste" heat.

Such wastage may be unavoidable when one actually needs electrical energy for lighting or for powering machinery. But can the economics of electric cookers be justified? The heat energy of coal is turned into electricity with an efficiency of less than 50 percent. It is then turned right back into heat. The net result is that half the energy of the coal is wasted at an estimated yearly cost of £300 million, about 3 percent of the annual energy costs of Great Britain.

If the second law of thermodynamics was as much a part of our cultural vocabulary as Beethoven's Ninth Symphony, would the level of our technical decision-making be as poor as it is? Would consumers have bought an electric cooker if they had known how wasteful it was? Would producers have built it if they had known how it might have been judged by a technically aware citizenry?

The second law of thermodynamics can be experienced as a law, as a frustration of the human desire to create a perfect heat engine. But it can also be experienced as a liberation, as a release from a fantasy. Instead of vainly pursuing the ideal of the 100 percent-efficient steam engine, one can see clearly that the ideal is a product of human imagination uninformed by the reality of our material existence.

The second law of thermodynamics, paid for, like the rest of the industrial revolution, at great human cost, was the first step taken by the human race toward maturity in its relationship with nature. One emerges from immature omnipotence fantasies into a more conscious relationship with steam. Because we see the nature of steam energy more clearly we are freed to have a real relationship with this substance, a relationship liberated from wild fantasmal yearnings. With the second law of thermodynamics the human race begins a slow painful march toward a conscious mutuality, still to be achieved, in our relationship with nature.

Carnot's analysis of the steam engine was not the only gem produced in the process of industrialization. The physics of the industrial revolution is so rich and definitive that today it constitutes the main part of the education of physicists in thermodynamics, statistical mechanics, electricity and magnetism, and optics. That so little has had to be added attests to the thoroughness with which the physicists of the period completed this phase of human development. Ohm's Law, the Wheatstone bridge, Fraunhofer diffraction, Fresnel diffraction, Young's double-slit experiment, Michelson's interferometer, Brownian motion, the kinetic theory of gases, the Maxwell-Boltzmann distribution, the Gibbs free energy are topics that carry the physics of the nineteenth century forward for each new generation. In the hands of able teachers, this material has brought pleasure to five generations of students who have felt themselves to be enriched by their increased understanding of their physical surroundings.

One can appreciate the overall texture of this body of human experience by looking at one of the nicest results from the mid-nineteenth century: the discovery by Tyndall of the effect that bears his name. The Tyndall effect gives us an understanding of one of our most commonplace experiences—the blue color of the sky.

> One afternoon I was sitting with some children in the grass and they asked me "Why is the sky blue?"
> "Because the sky is blue."
> "I wanta know *why* the sky is blue."
> "The sky is blue because you wanta know why the sky is blue."
> "Blue, blue, you," they said.
>
> JACK KEROUAC, *THE DHARMA BUMS*

John Tyndall (1820–1893) was in many ways the prototype of the mid-Victorian success story. The son of a sergeant in the Irish constabulary who was too poor to send him to university, Tyndall made his way with great effort to become colleague and successor to Faraday as director of the Royal Institution. He began as a surveyor for the ordnance survey in Ireland, at a salary of less than one pound a week. He moved on to Manchester to work around the clock as a surveyor for private railway firms during the hysterical period of rapid expansion of steam locomotion. He got out because he was afraid he was losing his mind in worry over the performance of his shareholdings. He taught mathematics for four years at a small Quaker college where he developed his skills as a lecturer. In 1848 he went to Germany to study physics at Marburg with George Bunsen. He finally established himself as a physicist through Faraday's willingness to recognize his work in magnetism, and through his friendship with Thomas Huxley, whom he met by chance on his way to a meeting at the British Association for the Advancement of Science.

Tyndall loathed the world of business and profit. He was a radical conservative in the manner of Carlisle and Disraeli, both of whom he admired. He was part of the "Young England Movement" of 1842, a political tendency ridiculed by Marx and Engels in the *Communist Manifesto* as a kind of feudal socialism, a rejection of capitalism in the name of the people but a wish for a return to an idealized version of aristocratic-peasant harmony.

In 1851, as part of an investigation of the causes of the layering of slate in slate quarries, Tyndall and Huxley visited Switzerland to investigate a similar layering effect in glaciers. Like many modern physicists Tyndall became fascinated by the mountains and ultimately gained recognition as one of Europe's best mountaineers. He was the first to climb the Weisshorn and nearly the first to climb the Matterhorn. He spent his summers at a cottage he built near Brig, in Switzerland, using his time there to explore the motion and structure of glaciers.

As part of his exploration, he noticed that the quality of sunlight above a glacier was unusually brilliant. He surmised that glaciers created unusual micro-climates because of the lack of evaporation of water immediately above them. This then led him in his winter months in London to study the effect of sunlight on gases in general. He found among other things that a vapor of amyl nitrate would become cloudy when exposed to an intense beam of light and that when it was viewed at right angles to the beam, a brilliant blue could be seen. Tyndall had demonstrated the same processes that occur in the sky. It was to be a popular public lecture of his for a number of years—the blue color of the vapor slowly appearing as the concentration of amyl nitrate was increased. It is the same effect as the bluish tinge one can observe in cigarette smoke.

We understand the Tyndall effect within the framework of light as an electromagnetic phenomenon. In this model, one pictures sunlight arising from the oscillation of electric charges on the sun. These oscillating charges produce an electric field (light) that travels through space and exerts a force on the electric charges in the rhodopsin of our eyes. The rhodopsin responds by converting the energy received into a nerve impulse transmitted to the visual cortex of the brain. We learn during the early phases of infant development how to recognize and respond to this signal.

The process of evolution has given us a visual system that is capable of discriminating oscillations at different frequencies. These are the colors we see. Measurement shows that blue light corresponds to an oscillation of 7.5×10^{14} cycles per second, red light to an oscillation of 4.2×10^{14} cycles per second, with the other colors falling in between.

Sunlight, although it is predominantly yellow-white in color, has the full range of colors as can be seen in a rainbow. The question then is: How does the sky scatter the blue component of light from the sun into our eyes to the exclusion of all the other colors?

The light scattered by the sky depends on two factors. The first is the intensity of the incident sunlight: the brighter the sun, the brighter the sky. The second factor depends on the light-scattering properties of the atmospheric gases.

One imagines the electric charges in the atmosphere to be bound to their atoms with tight, little springs. The incoming electric field generated by the white-hot gases of the sun forces them to oscillate across a range of frequencies. The oscillating charges in the atmosphere then exert a force on the charges in our rhodopsin, and that is how we see the light scattered from the sky.

Detailed measurements show that, at large distances, the electric field produced by an oscillating charge is proportional to its acceleration. Thus the fast oscillations (blue light) exert a stronger force on our rhodopsin than the slower oscillations. A standard calculation based on these ideas shows that the energy scattered is proportional to the fourth power of the frequency. Approximately ten times as much energy from the oscillations in the blue reaches our frequency-sensitive photoreceptors as from the red. Thus we see a blue sky. In effect the sky is a giant prism scattering the blue light in sunlight into our eyes to the exclusion of the other colors.

The Victorians enjoyed this result and we can, too. But it is important to note its limitations. The model does not really explain the origin of the blue of the sky. To put it bluntly, all we really do is infer the light-scattering properties of the atmospheric gases from the fact that the sky is blue. The details of the spring model tell us that since the sky is blue the charges in the atmospheric gases must be very tightly bound to their constituent atoms. The model says nothing about *why* the sky is blue because it says nothing about why the charges are so tightly bound. So what has been gained?

As in the case of the gravitational force, the electric force proves to be ubiquitous. The same force that makes the sky blue, is involved in making the clouds white, glass transparent, gold shine with a yellow lustre, and grass green. What causes the difference in color is the different structure of the materials, the different way the electric charges are bound. So the light-scattering properties of all materials have a commonality in that they are responding to the same force. Their differences are due to the details of their material structure. What the classical model of light does is to give a delightful coherence so to speak to a wide range of optical effects. It is this kind of unity in difference, a connection existing between apparently disparate experience—the blue sky, the green grass—that can make the understandings of physics so satisfying to the Western mind.

Steam was the first of the two great technological innovations that marked the industrial revolution. Electricity was the second. The history of the second half of the industrial revolution can be told as a chronicle of the advent of modern electrical devices. Electric telegraphs in 1837, electroplating in 1840, the transatlantic cable, 1857; electric lighting, 1860; the dynamo, 1867; the incandescent light bulb, 1878; electric power stations, 1880; radio transmission, 1894; the electrocardiogram, 1909.

There was a logic to the sequence of development. The telegraph found its market with the development of the railroads; electroplated gold and silver tableware with the new middle-class market in early Victorian Britain. The transatlantic cable, the Red Sea cable, and the Indo-European cable followed the growth of the British Empire and its imperial investments. Middle-class prosperity in the 1860s in Europe created a market for electric lighting that in turn created a market for the electric dynamo and commercial power stations. With the advent of commercial electric power the electrification of tram, train, and heavy machinery became profitable.

The story that has been written about this development has emphasized the primacy of basic physics for the success of technical developments. First comes the idea; then the device. For the last hundred years, such arrogance has helped the research community to secure funds to carry on so-called pure research and to preserve a status hierarchy that rates pure over applied, theory over practice. Electric generators make use of an aspect of the electromagnetic interaction to be sure, but there is nothing in the equations of electromagnetism that tells one how to make the things actually work.

The builders of real devices understandably resent the elitist attitudes assumed by those who have none of the skills necessary to create working machines from the implacable materials of nature. Here is Théodore du Moncel, a designer of electromagnets, writing in 1886 about electromagnetic theory: "The complaint is general and not without reason that the subject of electromagnetism is so obscurely treated by scientists and the conclusions reached by them of so little practical value, that the inventor can derive no profit from them. It is certain that the mathematical physicists regard such problems of too high an order to permit themselves to be diverted by a consideration of practical applications." In fact, the present antagonistic division of labor between pure and applied work—each with its partisans—keeps us from seeing that neither can advance very far without the other.

The development of electrical technologies led to many classics of the literature of physics, including the explanation of the blue of the sky, Faraday's law of electromagnetic induction, and, summarizing them all, Maxwell's equations of the electromagnetic field. But the culminating achievement was the consolidation of understanding represented by Einstein's special and general theories of relativity. This classic deserves better than the awestruck mystification that has almost always accompanied its presentation.

Albert Einstein was the son of a manufacturer of electrical technology. His father, Hermann, and his uncle Jakob owned the firm Elektro-Technische Fabrik in Munich, with Hermann organizing the business end and Jakob organizing the technical design and manufacture. The firm was a major competitor with Siemens and AEG in the fight for contracts arising from the electrification of southern Germany.

In 1880, a year after Albert was born, the Einstein family moved from Ulm to Munich. Toward the end of the year, Hermann Einstein and Jakob opened a shop selling water and gas installations while at the same time holding a two-thirds interest in a mechanical engineering shop. In 1885 they opened the Elektro-Technische Fabrik. That year they installed the first electric lights for the Oktoberfest in Munich; a year later they had installed electricity supply systems in the Schwabing quarter of Munich and in the two Italian towns of Varese, near Lake Como, and Susa, just west of Turin.

Jakob Einstein was a knowledgeable and skillful inventor. In the period 1886 to 1893 he took out six patents for improvements in arc lamps and for meters to measure current flow for billing purposes. A review of the market in billing meters by the city of Munich electrotechnical research station commented on J. Einstein's device: "The construction itself is very ingenious, the execution of the work perfectly satisfactory." Similarly J. Einstein's design of a dynamo to supply arc lighting systems featured prominently in a Munich-based review of electrotechnology and became the design of choice for over a decade. By 1891 the company was sufficiently established to exhibit at the major exhibition at Frankfurt where they showed their complete line of eight models of dynamos, and the arc lamps and meters based on Jakob's patents.

But the Einstein firm was too undercapitalized to compete with their more established rivals. The brothers were able to raise only about $3 million of the necessary $10 million (1990 dollars) needed to create a successful firm. In 1893 the contract to light the streets of Munich went to Schuckert in Nuremberg and in 1894 the Einsteins' firm went into liquidation. A 1912 review article of the history of the electrification of Munich noted that it was "driven out by branches of more efficient, out-of-town factories." This process was to be repeated throughout the industrial world as the corporation began to dominate the international economic landscape in the run up to World War I.

Much has been written about the effect the failure of the family business had on Einstein. This much is clear: It made him unhappy. And it made him work hard at the university. In 1898 he wrote his sister Maja: "I have always done everything my small powers allowed and ... year after year not once did I amuse or divert myself unless my studies permitted. I remain upright and must often guard myself against despair."

In the event, Einstein chose a career in physics. There he encountered the major remaining problem in nineteenth-century electromagnetic theory, a subject that delighted him as a student.

In 1820 the Danish physicist Hans Oersted, who had been the first to prepare metallic aluminum, discovered that an electric current could cause a magnetic compass to deflect. Oersted's discovery became the basis for modern telegraphy. The idea was that closing a switch at one end of a circuit could cause a current to flow that would deflect a magnetic needle at the other end of the circuit. In 1832 Samuel Morse devised his dot-dash code and numerous workers—Henry, Gauss, Weber, Wheatstone, Siemens—vied to get electrical telegraphs into production to satisfy the national and international communication needs accompanying the growth of the railroads and steamship lines.

At the Royal Institution in London, Michael Faraday grew interested in the electrical interaction. Oersted had shown that moving charges could deflect a stationary magnetic needle. Was the reverse effect possible: could moving magnets deflect stationary charges?

Faraday was then the leading scientist in England. He worked in the areas of chemistry, metallurgy, bacteriology, physics, applied physics, electrical engineering, and civil engineering. His work included analyses of the composition of materials—cocoa nut oil, palm wine, Damascus and Indian steels, and ales of various strengths. In metallurgy he studied the separation of manganese from iron and the purification of copper ores. For seven years he worked on fumigation and the prevention of dry rot in timber at the Fungus Pit of the Woolwich Dock Yards. In the application of electricity he worked on developing materials for electrical insulation and the problems of insulating underground telegraph cables as well as assessing the commercial prospects of electric silk looms, developing lightning rods for lighthouses, and correcting the magnetic compass in iron ships. In civil engineering he worked on tunnels under the Thames and on the problem of ventilation in coal mines.

In 1832, after ten years of work, Faraday realized that a changing magnetism, either in time or in space, could induce charges to flow in a wire loop.

Unlike Carnot, Faraday was not a Romantic. He was to the literature of the physics of the industrial revolution as Dickens and Balzac were to the literature of the same period. Like Dickens and Balzac he was thoroughly integrated into the culture of the industrial revolution. Like Dickens and Balzac who sought to portray the social effects they observed as they were, without reference to romantic visions of the past, Faraday sought to understand the physical effect he had observed as it was, without reference to Newtonian visions of action-at-a-distance and inverse square laws of force.

Faraday visualized the magnet as creating lines of force filling space in the vicinity of the magnet. He found that the voltage induced in a circuit was simply equal to how fast the flux of magnetic force lines through the circuit was changing.

Faraday's conception of magnetic lines of force reopened up the idea that the physical effects might not be instantaneous, that, in particular, the magnetic lines of force might take time to establish themselves in space. As Faraday put it: "Certain of the results which are embodied in the two papers entitled 'Experimental Researches in Electricity' lead me to believe that magnetic action is progressive and requires *time.*" Faraday's law of electromagnetic induction contains the essential element of the theory of relativity—electromagnetic interactions take time to make themselves felt.

Thirty years later, in 1864, James Maxwell made the classical theory of electromagnetism complete. Following Faraday he framed his understanding in terms of electric and magnetic force lines, now called fields. Faraday had found that a time-varying magnetic field could generate a space-varying electric field. Maxwell saw that for certain kinds of circuits, the magnetic field could not be continuous unless the inverse effect also existed:

time-varying electric fields should produce space-varying magnetic fields.

Manipulation of the completed equations showed that the fields should propagate with a definite velocity that turned out to be equal numerically to the velocity of light. And thus—in one of the mythic feats of physics—optics, electricity, and magnetism had been united into a single framework. Magnetic and electric fields were interconvertible and light was simply a propagating electromagnetic field.

Twenty years later, in 1887, after eight years of work, Heinrich Hertz confirmed experimentally that propagating electromagnetic fields did have the same properties as light. The unity of optical, electric, and magnetic phenomena became an established experimental fact. What then remained was two more decades of tortured attempts to understand how the electromagnetic fields got through space.

Einstein saw that what wanted further understanding was not the mechanism by which electromagnetic waves made their way through space. Following Faraday, Einstein saw that the central problematic of nineteenth-century electrodynamics was the fact that electromagnetic interactions took time. This finite time of propagation of physical effects is the most striking fact of experience to emerge from the industrial revolution.

The content of Einstein's special theory of relativity is a generalization of Faraday's original supposition that the magnetic force takes time. Einstein assumed that the electromagnetic interaction was not an exception, that our physical world is such that *all* interactions at a distance take time. And *that* is the special theory of relativity: all interactions at a distance take time.

The rest of the theory was the difficult project of working out the consequences of the finite time of propagation. As Einstein later recalled: "I must confess when the Special Theory of Relativity began to germinate in me ... I used to go away for weeks in a state of confusion as one who at that time had yet to overcome the state of stupefaction in his first encounter with such questions."

The depth of what must be understood can be made clearer by rephrasing the statement. If all interactions at a distance take time, then there are no instantaneous interactions at a distance. But if there are no instantaneous interactions then there must be a maximum possible speed of interaction. Experience shows that the maximum possible speed of interaction is the speed of the electromagnetic interaction (the speed of light). So it follows that nothing can go faster than the speed of light.

And that is where the bone of relativity sticks in the throat of everyday experience. How is it that nothing can go faster than the speed of light?

If we do live in a world in which there are no instantaneous interactions at a distance, what must be understood is what happens when objects approach the maximum speed. Einstein was the one who worked it out, who was able to relax his hold on everyday experience to permit himself to explore the world of experience opened up by the startling realization that there must exist a maximum possible speed.

A basic part of the theory, necessary to make the concept of a maximum speed possible, is that the maximum speed of interaction must be the same for everyone no matter how they are moving themselves. Things must be such that the maximum speed is the same for all observers. How can this be?

Einstein realized that if moving and stationary observers are to experience one and the same velocity for a light signal they must each experience different distances the light travels and, most shockingly, they must experience different elapsed times between the emission and reception of a light signal.

The relativity of elapsed time is the most striking result of the theory of relativity. In a standard example of how it works, one imagines a railroad car moving with a velocity v with respect to the embankment. The front and back doors of the car are designed to open when struck by a pulse of light. In the exact center of the car is an apparatus that can send out simultaneous pulses of light in the forward and backward directions. When the apparatus is triggered, observers riding in the car will see the front and back doors open simultaneously. But observers standing on the embankment will see something rather different. They see the back door of the car moving forward to meet the light pulse. And they see the front door moving away from the light pulse. Thus observers on the embankment see the back door open *before* the front door. In relativity, simultaneity is relative: zero time difference between two separated events in one frame of reference is not zero time difference between the same two events in another.

Also in relativity, the elapsed time between events not separated in space is different when seen from different frames of reference. The time interval between successive beats of a pendulum clock in a moving frame of reference is longer compared to the identical clock watched by an observer in a stationary frame. As all undergraduates in physics learn: moving clocks run slow. Abundantly observed at particle acclerators, where relativity is common engineering knowledge, the relativity of time has also been confirmed in commercial aircraft in 1971 by J. C. Hafele and Richard Keating. Using accurate cesium beam atomic clocks, they observed an actual difference of elapsed time between identical ground-based and aircraft-based clocks of approximately 300 ± 10 nanoseconds over a total flight time of eighty-nine hours. The relativity of elapsed time is an extremely difficult idea to get used to. Physically it is a consequence of the fact that there are no instantaneous interactions in nature.

The relativity of time permits one to understand what happens when a material particle approaches the speed of light. Following Einstein, one imagines a particle being accelerated from rest by giving it a series of pushes as in modern particle accelerators. What happens in relativity is that as the particle approaches the maximum speed, the duration of the push gets shorter and shorter in the rest frame of the particle because moving clocks run slow. Thus the particle picks up less and less speed. In the laboratory one finds that the acceleration, *a*, gets less and less for the same push, *F*, as the particle approaches the speed of light according to the formula $a = F/m\ (1 - v^2/c^2)^{\frac{3}{2}}$. One sees that when the velocity, *v*, equals the maximum speed *c*, the acceleration is zero. The particle stops gaining speed.

Thus, because of the relativity of time, which shrinks the amount of time the force actually acts on the particle as the particle approaches the speed of light, it becomes harder and harder to increase its velocity. One then can say that its inertia—its resistance to a change in velocity—increases. As we continue to push the particle its inertia starts to increase rather than its velocity. But the inertia of a particle is just its mass. Thus one can say that the energy has gone into giving the particle more mass.

This result became the title of a second paper by Einstein in 1905: "Does the inertia of a body depend on its energy content?" The answer was yes. And Einstein proposed a relationship between inertia and energy, the expression $E = mc^2$, where the mass is the relativistic mass *m*, related to its mass at rest, m_0, according to the formula $m = m_0/(1 - v^2/c^2)^{\frac{1}{2}}$. (Again the ubiquitous factors of $1 - v^2/c^2$.)

This famous, beautifully expressed relationship can give great satisfaction once it is understood. Because we live in a world where there are no instantaneous interactions at a distance, nothing can go faster than the maximum speed of interaction. And as one gives more and more energy to an accelerating particle, what happens is that the energy, instead of going to increase the velocity, goes into increasing its inertia. Thus one consequence of the finite speed of interaction is that energy contributes inertia to a particle. And by implication, when a particle gives up energy it loses inertia.

It is worth noting that the relationship $E = mc^2$ is a *general* relationship with no reference to the energy released in nuclear processes. All that relativity says is that energy has inertia and, by implication, inertia has energy.

In the case of the atomic bomb, the energy comes from specific properties of uranium-235 or plutonium-239 nuclei. Relativity makes no statement about the amount of energy that will be released in the fission of these particular isotopes. The large energies released in nuclear reactions were measured by Rutherford and Soddy in 1903, two years before Einstein formulated the special theory of relativity. Relativity cannot, and does not, make a statement about how much energy is produced in a nuclear reaction. That energy must be measured. It cannot be inferred from the fact that there are no instantaneous interactions in nature. $E = mc^2$ was not the foundation of the atomic bomb.

* * *

With the publication of the special theory of relativity in 1905, the classical physics of the nineteenth century was nearly closed. All that remained was to create a new understanding of the gravitational interaction, an understanding that needed to include the supposition that gravity must also take time to make itself felt.

Einstein's reformulation of Newton's theory of gravitation, the general theory of relativity, was published in 1916 in wartime Berlin. Because the rococco symbols of the differential geometry in which the theory was expressed were unfamiliar to the physicists of the time and because the phenomenon of gravity was far from the central concerns of the period, the British physicist Arthur Eddington remarked that the theory was too difficult to understand. By a complex social process, Eddington's remark was turned into the famous apocryphal story that only three people in the world could understand relativity, with Eddington not being sure who the third person was.

But as in the special theory of relativity the physical content of the general theory is simple. Einstein wanted to reexpress Newton's theory of gravitation to take into account two facts of experience not included by Newton. The first was the fact that there are no instantaneous interactions at a distance in nature.

And the second fact was the remarkable but hitherto marginal fact of experience, measured to a high degree of accuracy, that all objects fall at the same rate under the influence of gravity. A lead ball and a wood ball hit the ground at the same time when released from the same height: motion under gravity is independent of properties of the falling body. Thus it then becomes possible to say that the motion is produced by the shape of space in the vicinity of the object. Einstein's theory of gravity is a theory of geometry.

Einstein's program was twofold: first to show how the shape of space can be determined by the distribution of matter; and second, to show how the motion of matter is determined by the shape of space. This is the general theory of relativity. In the words of U.S. physicist John Wheeler: "Matter tells space how to curve and space tells matter how to move." The centerpiece of Einstein's vision was to show how the curvature of space can be related to the distribution of matter.

This he did after many false starts extending over a period of eleven years by a sophisticated argument expressed in the forest of superscripts and subscripts that is the language of differential geometry. But physically the theory is just a generalization of Newton's law of universal gravitation to include the subtle effects of finite times of interaction and the fact that all objects fall at the same rate in a gravitational field.

One then wants to know what Einstein's theory says that Newton's theory does not say. What gravitational effects can be understood within the framework of general relativity that cannot be understood within the Newtonian framework?

The single most important gravitational effect that has been understood with general relativity has been the detailed motion of the planet Mercury.

In 1859 Urbain Jean Joseph Leverrier published results showing that the motion of the planet Mercury was a beautiful so-called precessing ellipse, the elliptical orbit as a whole advancing around the sun at a tiny anomalous rate in excess of Newtonian effects.

Leverrier was the son of an estate manager in northern France. His father scraped everything together for years in order to send him in 1831 to the École Polytechnique, where his future would be assured. After a tour of duty as a student engineer for the state tobacco company, the present-day Gauloise, he resigned to do research under the famous chemist Joseph Gay-Lussac. By 1837 his interest had turned away from tobacco and chemistry, toward the heavens. He began a productive career analyzing the details of planetary motion using sophisticated mathematical methods developed by Lagrange and Laplace.

The presenting problem of the period was a continuation of eighteenth-century concern with the three-body problem and the long-term stability of the solar system. Astronomy was not the most thrilling work to be doing in the mid-nineteenth century, but it had social cachet, appealing to a poor boy from the provinces, as the elite subject of physics.

In 1845 Leverrier found that no amount of fiddling with estimates of the masses of Jupiter and Saturn could account for the detailed motion of the planet Uranus. And, in spite of sharp polemics in the French and English newspapers over priority, Leverrier is now credited with correctly inferring the existence of the planet Neptune from his detailed analysis of the orbit of the planet Uranus.

By 1847 Leverrier had calculated, in a work of four thousand pages, the orbits of all the planets, taking into account their mutual attractions to one another. He knew by then that Newtonian effects did not account for the detailed motion of the planet Mercury.

By 1859 he had refined his techniques to show that there was an anomalous rate of rotation of the orbit of Mercury above Newtonian effects of .011 degree per century. Workers in successive generations have refined this estimate to its modern value of 43.11 ± .45 seconds of arc per century.

Leverrier's measurement remained an anomaly until Einstein published his calculation of the orbit of the planet Mercury using the general theory of relativity. The result was a rotating ellipse with a period of rotation given by the formula $T = 6GM/c^2a(1 - e^2)$ where *T* is the period of rotation, *G* is the gravitational constant, *M* is the mass of the sun, *c* is the velocity of light, and *a* and *e* are the semimajor axis and eccentricity respectively of the orbit of Mercury.

The measured values and uncertainties of the semi-major axis and eccentricity of Mercury's orbit are $a = .38775 \pm .00128$ AU and $e = .2062 \pm .0016$. Inserting these values into the formula along with the values of the other constants gives a value of 43.03 ± .12 seconds of arc per century to be compared with the measured value of 43.11 ± .45 seconds of arc per century. The agreement is quite good.

Once confirmed, the fuss about the general theory of relativity lies not in the rotating orbit of the planet Mercury but in the completely new vision of space, time, and matter that it affords. Our three-dimensional space is curved. And it may be curved in such a way that it is closed—a light ray sent out from earth in a straight line would eventually return to earth after having gone round the universe. Observationally, the question of the closure of space can be resolved by measuring the angles of a triangle formed by the sun and two other sufficiently distant stars. If the angles add up to more than 180 degrees we live in a closed universe. The measurements are not yet accurate enough to discriminate the possibilities. Other effects encompassed by the general theory of relativity include black holes, the bending of light in a gravitational field, and the slowing down of clocks under the influence of gravity.

Finally the general theory of relativity opens the possibility of a geometry depending on time, a possibility confirmed in the observation of the expansion of the universe by Edwin Hubble in 1936. Hubble observed that the galaxies are moving away from each other at a constant rate and we now have a conception of our universe as expanding from an infinitely small, infinitely dense initial state to its present low-density state in a so-called big bang taking place about eighteen billion years ago.

Thus through observation and the conceptual apparatus of general relativity we have been able to estimate the age of the universe as a whole. An age to the universe means that one can construct a grand historical narrative of the evolution of the entire universe. Some marking points of the grand narrative are the beginnings of the expansion of the universe eighteen billion years ago, the formation of the earth 4.5 billion years ago, the appearance of first life about 2.8 billion years ago, the appearance of *Homo erectus* forty million years ago, the appearance of *Homo sapiens sapiens* a mere forty thousand years ago, and the appearance of agriculture ten thousand years ago. As more than one hearer of this tale has commented, it is the greatest story ever told.

The general theory of relativity was a brilliant end to the physics of the nineteenth century. The breathtaking realization that space, previously considered to be a mere backdrop to events, had a structure, that geometry was determined by the distribution of matter, that it could vary in time, was a discovery that was not merely a tribute to Einstein's vision, but was a landmark of social development.

Like the second law of thermodynamics, the theory of relativity brings us into a more mature, less fantasized relationship with nature. With the second law of thermodynamics we must accept that we cannot make a perfect heat engine. With the special theory of relativity we must accept that nothing can go faster than the speed of light. And with the general theory of relativity we must accept geometry as not a matter for abstract contemplation but a measurable property of the universe.

In each case the gap between our imaginative faculties and our material existence, between what we imagine the world to be like and what it is actually like, closes. And each time we close that gap our relationship with nature becomes less omnipotent, less self-centered, more engaged, and more related.

If there is any mystery to relativity at all it lies in the question, Why has it become so mysterious? Why we have distanced ourselves from Einstein so much that relativity has become a conundrum rather than engaging Einstein and appreciating his accomplishment for what it is, a beautiful example of the human capacity to create understandings.

The Einstein legend, the myth of the incomprehensibility of relativity, has become archetypal in our culture. The clarity, simplicity, and beauty of relativity have been turned into their opposites with Einstein's name becoming a synonym for the impossible to understand.

Addressing the conundrum are over three thousand books on relativity. The literature on Einstein's life has similar Brobdingnagian proportions. The Einstein archive has begun to be published. Thirty-five volumes comprising 43,000 documents are contemplated. The first, covering Einstein's first twenty-three years, attracted the attention of reviewers particularly for the publication among its 142 documents of some fifty letters Einstein wrote to his future wife Mileva Maric. Einstein's school records and reports, his French essays from the cantonal school in Aarau have been scrutinized for clues to the source of his genius. And although first-rate scholarship—the work of Lewis Pyenson and Abraham Pais may be particularly mentioned—has produced fascinating accounts of Einstein's life and work, it is all too much. With the exception of Michel Biezunski in Paris, the historians have located the mystery and incomprehensibility of Einstein within the Einstein personality and not within the wider culture where it belongs.

Einstein's enormous world popularity beginning after World War I is well-known. The trips to Japan, to the United States, to the Middle East, to all the European countries. The cheering crowds. Tickertape parades up Broadway. Packed public lectures. Endless newspaper articles on the mysteries of Dr. Einstein. When Einstein visited the home of J. S. Haldane in England in the summer of 1921, Haldane's daughter fainted as Einstein walked through the door.

Today we accept Einstein's popularity as a fact of history. But why, for a brief period of five years, did relativity capture the public imagination? What did it mean? Why should the achievement of an obscure German-Jewish physicist of radical political leanings have so stimulated the world's imagination in the interwar years only then to degenerate into spectacle, a symbol of our collective stupidity?

Like Galileo's discovery of the moons of Jupiter in 1611, the special and general theories of relativity had a deep revolutionary content. And in the years immediately following World War I, revolutionary feelings in Europe were close to the surface. The theory of relativity spoke to a widespread revolutionary consciousness, a receptivity to change, an eagerness for change, a belief in change including change at a fundamental conceptual level.

What do you mean, space is curved? *What do you mean,* nothing can go faster than the speed of light? The simple statements of relativity had the excitement and anxiety associated with the ring of truth. The ideas challenged the world. This was not the raving of a madman. This represented the acquisition of hard-won knowledge, a knowledge that the people of the times passionately desired to share.

Einstein's conclusions spoke directly to the people, without the mediation of governments, educational institutions, or the media. Anyone can begin to grapple with "space is curved." What could it mean? What had been accomplished? And in a Europe as filled with revolution in 1919 as it had been similarly filled four hundred years earlier, established authority grew fearful and appropriated an accomplishment that was common property. And so in England, with the assistance of Pais, we see a Congregation of Rites at the famous joint meeting of the Royal Society and the Royal Astronomical Society on November 6, 1919. With Dyson as Postulator, Crommelin and Eddington as Advocate/Procurators, and Silverstein as Advocatis Diaboli, we see J. J. Thomson pronouncing the canonization, "The result is one of the highest achievements of human thought."

Outside the temple tremendous popular anticipation awaited Einstein's arrival in Paris. The crowds were everywhere, excitement was in the air. New developments in our understanding of the physical world would be exhibited and explained. Cartoons querying the theory appeared in all the newspapers. Celebrations were in order. A new epoch was dawning.

It proved not to be so.

For the second time in modern history, physics failed to establish itself as a physics of broad popular appeal. Its failure was due to the failure of Europe to transform itself in the aftermath of the disaster of World War I, to democratize its productive relationships and bring the rich experience of the physical world gained in the industrial revolution into the currency of common culture.

In its place we suffer the terrible division between our culture of production and our culture of consumption. The Einstein enigma speaks to a deep need in our culture to be mystified, to be in awe of forces which we cannot control, to feel ourselves small and inconsequential in the face of the movements of the world. The goods we purchase in marketplaces throughout the world materialize before us like genies from magic bottles, while those in our culture whose job it is to transform the materials of the physical world into the objects of everyday life are hidden from view. Without understanding in detail the problems faced by manufacturers of radio transmitters can we really expect relativity, a sophisticated narrative expressing the physical reality embedded in the radio transmitter, to become a living part of the wider culture? Nearly one hundred years on we continue to be mystified by relativity because we need to shield our eyes from abominable relationships of production over which we have no control. We have two cultures because we continue to have dark Satanic mills.

CHAPTER 3

Munich 1919/Alamogordo 1945

The making of the world's first atomic bomb was more than the work of a few hundred of Europe and America's most skilled physicists. Even today, the size of the project is difficult to grasp. In a three-year period from 1942 to 1945 the U.S. government created a nuclear weapons industry equal in size to the entire U.S. automobile industry of the time. It was one of the most remarkable industrial episodes in history.

Organized and headed by Brigadier General Leslie Groves, the Manhattan Project consisted of massive industrial plants at Oak Ridge and Hanford to produce the explosive materials for the bomb, a bomb design and assembly facility at Los Alamos, and research staffs at the Universities of California, Chicago, Columbia, and Iowa State. At the peak of their activities, the uranium separation plants at Oak Ridge employed 82,000 people, the plutonium manufacture plant at Hanford employed 24,000, and the design and assembly facility at Los Alamos employed 5,000, including a machine shop of five hundred machinists and toolmakers.

Groves, who had been deputy chief of construction for the U.S. Army Corps of Engineers before being placed in charge of the Manhattan Project, needed to draw upon the full range of U.S. industrial capacity to organize the construction of the bomb.

Among the tens of thousands of industrial firms who received contracts for work on the Manhattan Project were the largest corporations in the United States.

Du Pont was in charge of the engineering, design, construction, and operation at Hanford. Eastman Kodak supervised the operation of the mass spectrometer uranium separation plant at Oak Ridge. Union Carbide supervised the operation of the gaseous diffusion uranium separation plant at Oak Ridge. Allis-Chalmers made the magnets, General Electric made the power supplies, and Westinghouse made allied parts for the mass spectrometer. The Chrysler Corporation manufactured the gaseous diffusion units as well as pioneering the cleaning methods needed to maintain the high vacuums required to achieve the separation of the two uranium isotopes in which gaseous uranium hexafluoride flowed through a succession of specially built filters. The architectural firm of Skidmore, Owings and Merrill designed and supervised the construction of the city of Oak Ridge.

Groves could not have organized a construction project of this magnitude without the powers of planning and resource allocation that the war gave him. In peacetime neither government nor industry would have been inclined to spend the money and time on a project that was no more than a theoretical possibility in the minds of a few university professors. As Groves put it: "Because of the great costs and difficulties involved and the apparently very small chance of success I do not believe the U.S. ever would have undertaken it in time of peace."

But if the pressures of war were a necessary condition for the building of the bomb, they were not a sufficient condition. War or not, industrial cooperation or not, government sponsorship or not, the bomb could not have been built without the dedication of some three hundred physicists from Europe and the United States whose practical research skills enabled them to find out whether the device was possible and if so to find a way to build it. The value of the labor of an estimated 600,000 people who contributed to the project turned on the success or failure of the physicists to build a device that would make the uranium and plutonium produced at Oak Ridge and Hanford explode. The physicists were the indispensable workers on the project.

Groves understood that he needed to pay special attention to his relationship with the physicists. His first move was to be sure he had enough authority to impress them: "I decided at once, and [General] Styer agreed, that I should not take over the project until I could do so as a brigadier. I thought that there might be some problems in dealing with the many academic scientists involved in the project, and I felt that my position would be stronger if they thought of me from the first as a general instead of as a promoted colonel."

Throughout the project Groves made an effort to keep his scientific staff happy. In the search for the suitably isolated site that was to be Los Alamos, Groves made sure that the climate and surroundings were agreeable: "... this installation would be different [from Hanford or Oak Ridge] because here we were faced with the necessity of importing a group of highly talented specialists, some of whom would be prima donnas, and of keeping them satisfied with their living and working conditions."

At Los Alamos, in contrast to the military discipline he imposed at Oak Ridge and Hanford, Groves took the advice of Dr. James B. Conant, chairman of the National Defense Research Committee, and permitted the physicists to serve on advisory committees to military administration: "... these people were accustomed to making their views known to similar committees appointed by their university administrators."

Groves tolerated an advisory community council to the military administrative staff; a laboratory coordinating council consisting of all the scientific group leaders; and, against all his security principles, an open scientific colloquium. Finally, in 1945, as use of the completed weapon drew near, the scientists were permitted to form an ad hoc advisory committee to relay their views on the use of the bomb to the Interim Committee, the governmental advisory committee that reported directly to the Secretary of War.

In each case, however, the committees were advisory only, without statutory power. Groves boasted after the war that he had no objection to committees as long as he appointed them. "Such an approach to committees may appear cynical," he said, "but in my experience it produced excellent results."

Even with these concessions to academic sensibilities, Groves was uniformly disliked by the physicists at Los Alamos. Postwar comments about his leadership read like the comments of Broadway theater critics in full pursuit of a bad play:

"Almost everyone disliked him heartily...." Luis Alvarez

"... really a terror to his subordinates." George Kistiakowsky

"He never understood the scientists and they thoroughly hated him." Joseph Hirschfelder

"... General Groves could have won almost any unpopularity contest in which the scientific community at Los Alamos voted." Edward Teller

"... the kind of man who always wanted to make an intelligent comment when he should have kept his mouth shut." Roger Hildebrand

"... the biggest sonovabitch I've ever met in my life ... I hated his guts and so did everybody else...." Kenneth D. Nichols

Groves for his part had to tolerate attitudes and behavior on the part of the physicists that he would have much preferred to control. He had to put up with Leo Szilard's penchant for bearding the military brass hats and with Szilard's continuous, if unsuccessful, efforts to have the physicists exercise more control over their work. He had to put up with Richard Feynman's practical jokes ridiculing laboratory security measures. He had to put up with Frank Oppenheimer's Communist Party background. He had to sweat out his mistrust of the large number of foreign-born physicists on the project. Groves had to tolerate a lack of discipline, petty insubordination, minor acts of civil disobedience, and deviant political ideas from the physicists because without them the project could not succeed.

The fact that the physicists were indispensable to the project made them feel that they were entering into an equal relationship with the U.S. government. But the real relationships of power on the Manhattan Project were the traditional relationships of power between highly skilled workers and their often put-upon employers. As Groves said about the pesky Leo Szilard after the war: "[He was] the kind of man that any employer would have fired as a troublemaker."

To General Groves, the physicists were a bunch of longhairs who needed to be cajoled, bullied, and kept under surveillance until the job was done. To the physicists, Groves was a necessary evil that had to be tolerated if they were to make what they considered to be their best contribution to the war against the Nazis. The tension between the two parties was relieved by their stated common purpose in defeating Nazi Germany. But as frequently happens in employee-employer relationships, the short-term interest that Groves and the physicists had in common masked fundamental long-term antagonisms.

While the physicists were working day and night to complete the bomb before the Nazis could get it, British and U.S. authorities knew by mid-1943 from detailed scientific intelligence that the Nazis would not be able to build more than a small research reactor. The physicists and the military were fighting different wars. As Groves testified before the U.S. Congress in 1954: "There was never from about two weeks from the time I took charge of the Project any illusion on my part but that Russia was our enemy and the Project was conducted on that basis."

In December 1938 when Lise Meitner and her nephew Otto Frisch realized that the uranium nucleus could be made to fission, Paul Rosbaud was the science adviser to *Naturwissenschaften,* the leading German physics journal. Rosbaud, who had received a Ph.D. in physics at the Technische Hochschule in Berlin, had extensive contacts in the international physics community. As a Catholic hostile to National Socialism, Rosbaud had used his contacts to help many of his German-Jewish colleagues escape from the Nazis, including Meitner herself. He had helped pack her bags on the night she fled Berlin.

On March 10, 1939, two months after the discovery of fission, Rosbaud met with British physicist John Cockcroft in London at the Athenaeum, the scientists' club in St. James, to discuss the possibilities of a German uranium bomb. Two months later Rosbaud met Professor R. S. Hutton of Cambridge in Berlin for two hours and told Hutton the details of German meetings about the uranium bomb. Thereafter Rosbaud became, as R. V. Jones of the British

Secret Intelligence Service describes it, "an active agent."

As a scientific publisher, Rosbaud was able to maintain close contact with the German physicists and at great risk he succeeded in passing information to the British about the slow progress of the German effort. In 1987, Jones, who had seen all of Rosbaud's most important communications, wrote:

> The clearest of Rosbaud's wartime contributions for which I can personally vouch was his letting us know about the doings and movements of the German nuclear physicists headed by Werner Heisenberg.... Rosbaud's wartime reports were particularly valuable because they led us correctly to conclude that work in Germany toward the release of nuclear energy had at no time gone beyond the research stage: his information thus calmed the fears that might have otherwise beset us.

How widely known was the information contained in Rosbaud's reports? "Only a limited number of people were in the picture," said Jones in 1987.

On June 4, 1942, three months before Groves took charge of the Manhattan Project in the United States, Werner Heisenberg, the head of Germany's atomic bomb effort, and his coworker, theoretical physicist Carl von Weizsäcker, met with high-level members of the German government and military in Harnach House in Dahlem outside of Berlin to discuss the uranium project. Present were Albert Speer, Hitler's economic adviser; Navy Admiral Carl Witzell; General Ernst Fromm; and Field Marshal Erhard Milch. Heisenberg asked for 100,000 marks and von Weizsäcker for an additional 10,000 marks. Surprised by the low sums, Speer and the military brass offered Heisenberg one million marks. Heisenberg rejected the offer, saying that he could not use it. With this meeting the possibility of a uranium bomb ceased to be a factor in the German war effort.

Six days later, Rosbaud traveled to Oslo to pass the information on to Eric Welsh and R. V. Jones of British Scientific Intelligence Services. Two months later, on August 18, 1942, British intelligence told the U.S. authorities that the German effort was unlikely to produce anything of military value. A month later, on September 17, Groves was appointed director of the Manhattan Project.

By the following spring, thanks to the information Rosbaud was able to pass on, the U.S. and U.K. authorities knew that there was to be no German bomb. The official postwar British SIS history states: "The spring of 1943 was the date from which the allied authorities began to feel increasingly reassured in relation to Germany's nuclear research programme." Arnold Kramish, who researched and wrote the Rosbaud story, concludes: "Through Rosbaud, the British knew everything they wanted to know about the German atomic programme from its inception and throughout the war except during a year and a half hiatus in his reporting from the end of 1939."

Meanwhile, at Los Alamos the U.S. and European physicists raced to beat their nonexistent opposition. Very slowly the realities began to leak out. In March 1944, General Groves told James Chadwick, leader of the British team at Los Alamos, that the real target of the bomb was the Soviet Union. Joseph Rotblat, a Polish physicist who worked with Chadwick, was present at numerous conversations between Chadwick and Groves. As he recalls: "When visiting Los Alamos [Groves] frequently came to the Chadwicks for dinner and relaxed palaver. During one such conversation Groves said that of course the real purpose in making the bomb was to subdue the Soviets."

Rotblat was shocked: "Until then I had thought that our work was to prevent a Nazi victory and now I was told that the weapon we were preparing was intended for use against the people who were making extreme sacrifices for that very aim."

Groves was not just making dinner-table talk when he stated that the real purpose of making the bomb was to subdue the Soviets. Earlier that year, in January, Groves had made a key technical decision that clearly signaled his postwar intentions.

The gaseous diffusion plant at Oak Ridge had been in trouble. The copper filters that were to segregate the fissionable U-235 from the nonfissionable U-238 were not working properly because of corrosion caused by the highly reactive uranium hexafluoride gas. Harold Urey, the Nobel Prize–winning chemist in charge of the gaseous diffusion research group at Columbia University, began experimenting with compressed nickel powder as a possible filter. The nickel resisted corrosion but the powder was not sufficiently fine to work as a separator barrier. Two workers in Urey's group, Edward Norris and Edward Adler, devised a nickel-plated wire mesh that seemed to offer both corrosion resistance and small-enough pore size to be an effective filter. On April 1, 1943, with Groves's authorization in hand, the Houdaille-Hershey Corporation began a new nickel filter production factory in Decatur, Illinois.

In October 1943 workers at the Kellex Corporation in New York invented a filter that seemed more promising than the nickel-plated mesh invented by Norris and Adler then in production in Decatur. The stage was set for a fight between Urey and Groves over the fastest way to proceed.

Urey argued that stopping production at Decatur in favor of a new method would delay production of U-235 so much that it could not be used to help shorten the war. Groves appointed an advisory committee to discuss the matter. The committee, composed of British scientists, concurred with Urey: changing over to a new process would take many months.

But Groves had already decided. The day before the British committee met in January 1944, he authorized production of the new barriers even though it was clear that the U-235 produced by the new method would not be ready before the war was over.

Urey understood the significance of Groves's decision. The gaseous diffusion plant was not to contribute to the shortening of the war. Instead Groves had committed the United States to the creation of a postwar nuclear weapons facility. That same month in January 1944 Urey resigned his directorship of the project. His biographers state: "... from that time forward his energies were directed to the control of atomic energy, not its applications."

By December 1944 it had become clear to many of the physicists at Los Alamos that there would be no German bomb. George Kistiakowski recalls: "By the end of 1944 it became pretty obvious that the Germans didn't have the bomb and wouldn't have it in time." To Joseph Rotblat, who had been a witness to Groves's confession that the real purpose in building the bomb was to threaten the Soviets, there no longer seemed to be any real reason for continuing with the project. "When it became evident toward the end of 1944 that the Germans had abandoned their bomb project, the whole purpose of my being ceased to be and I asked for permission to leave and return to Britain." Of the five thousand workers at Los Alamos, Rotblat and Volney C. Wilson were the only ones who resigned once it was clear that the Nazis would not get the bomb.

With the Germans out of the picture, the Japanese became the focus for continuing the bomb effort. Kistiakowski recalls: "Then the argument presented to us became that we must end the war with Japan as quickly as possible ... the feeling was conveyed to us that Japan was very far from surrender, that the war would continue for a long time."

The war, however, was not going to last for a long time. The U.S. Strategic Bombing Survey's official report written less than one year after Nagasaki stated: "... certainly prior to 31 December 1945 and in all probability prior to 1 November 1945 Japan would have surrendered even if atomic bombs had not been dropped, even if Russia had not entered the war and even if no invasion had been planned or contemplated."

Truman's Chief of Staff, Admiral William D. Leahy, wrote in 1950: "It is my opinion that the use of this barbarous weapon at Hiroshima and Nagasaki was of no material assistance in our war against Japan. The Japanese were already defeated and ready to surrender because of the effective sea blockade and successful bombing with conventional weapons."

The release of key documents over the last twenty years, including recent publication of Truman's diaries and letters, has given historians further links in the chain of evidence showing that Truman knew that the Japanese were close to surrender and that the much-feared invasion of Japan was not going to be necessary.

By July 1945 the major politicians and their supporters in the military had other fish to fry. The Soviet Union loomed large on the postwar horizon. Earlier in the year, Secretary of War Henry Stimson had summoned Groves to tell Truman about the bomb the day after Truman had had a stormy meeting with Molotov about Poland. Groves's memorandum of the meeting states that "a great deal of emphasis was placed on foreign relations and particularly on the Russian situation."

While the politicians were beginning to think about the postwar implications of the new weapon, Groves was fighting his own private war against the Russians. On D-Day he had dispatched his famous Alsos scientific intelligence mission—*alsos* is Greek for "groves"—headed by arch anti-Communist Colonel Boris T. Pash to Europe to keep as much information as possible about the German bomb effort out of Soviet hands.

On November 25, 1944, the Alsos mission occupied the physics department of the University of Strasbourg where academic paperwork indicated that the Auergesellschaft Works in Oranienburg, fifteen miles north of Berlin and directly in the Soviet line of advance, was refining uranium and thorium. Unable to send his Alsos agents into the area, Groves arranged for the destruction of the plant. On March 15, 1945, 612 Boeing B-29s dropped 1,500 tons of high explosives and 178 tons of incendaries on the plant, completely destroying it.

Mindful of the niceties of the U.S.-Soviet wartime alliance, Groves disguised the real target of the attack by a diversionary attack on the town of Zossen. "Our purpose in attacking Oranienburg was screened from Russians and Germans alike by a simultaneous and equally heavy attack on the town of Zossen, where the German Army's headquarters were situated."

In March 1945, the Alsos mission occupied the physics laboratories at the University of Heidelberg, where Groves learned that Nobel laureates Werner Heisenberg and Max von Laue were constructing a research reactor in the small town of Hechingen, just north of the Swiss border. Hechingen lay in what was to be the French zone of occupation. Groves distrusted the French physicist Frederic Joliot-Curie, France's leading nuclear physicist and an active member of the Resistance: "... my recent experiences with Joliot had convinced me that nothing that might be of interest to the Russians should ever be allowed to fall into French hands." Groves organized Operation Harborage in which Alsos forces would strike diagonally across the line of French advance to "capture the people we wanted, question them, seize and remove their records and obliterate all remaining facilities."

On May 3, Pash captured Heisenberg in the town of Urfeld. Groves was now satisfied. "Heisenberg was one of the world's leading physicists and ... he was worth more to us than ten divisions of Germans. Had he fallen into Russian hands, he would have proven invaluable to them." On May 7 Germany surrendered. Groves instructed Alsos groups to insure that "no information remained that might eventually fall into Russian hands" and turned his attention to preparations for the Trinity test shot scheduled for July 16.

By July, with Japanese surrender close at hand, the Russian situation was foremost in the minds of the Truman administration. Would the bomb turn out to be a decisive bargaining counter with the Soviet Union or not? Truman postponed his meeting at Potsdam with Stalin and Churchill until the day after the test shot.

At 5:30 A.M. in the morning on July 16 the thing went off. The sinister purple glow of the radioactive fireball filled the morning desert air. Kenneth Bainbridge, the director of the shot, called it "a foul and awesome display." The physicists had succeeded in making a piece of plutonium the size of an orange explode with the force of twenty thousand tons of TNT. Groves told Oppenheimer: "I am proud of all of you." Oppenheimer said: "Thank you." Groves telephoned his secretary in Washington using a special code. His secretary then went to the Pentagon where she used a special cable connection to communicate the news to Stimson at Potsdam.

Truman, on receiving the news from Groves, told Edwin Pauley that the bomb "would keep the Russians straight." U.S. policymakers had a weapon that completely altered their postwar diplomatic strategy. From now on, instead of negotiation, there would be confrontation with the Soviet Union. J. R. Parten, Pauley's aide, recalls: "... everyone was pretty high."

General Dwight Eisenhower, Supreme Allied Commander in Europe, tried to convince the newly minted cold war hawks that militarily it was unnecessary to use the new explosives against Japan. On July 17, the day Groves's first cable arrived, he told Stimson that "Japan was already defeated and that dropping the bomb was completely unnecessary and ... that our country should avoid shocking world opinion by the use of a weapon whose employment was, I thought, no longer mandatory as a measure to save American lives." Three days later over lunch with Truman and General Omar Bradley, Eisenhower challenged Truman's desire to use the new explosives on Japan. As Eisenhower later wrote: "... it was not necessary to hit them with that awful thing."

But Eisenhower and Leahy could not prevail against the feeling that the bomb was a trump card to play against the Soviet Union. It was a dream come true. Right out of the comic books. The scientists had produced the ultimate weapon, a single bomb that could destroy an entire city. What more could a politician ask for as he approached the negotiating table with his former ally? The only thing that remained was to convince the Soviets that the United States would use the new weapon.

In the meantime physicists began to wonder what they had done. Stanislaw Ulam had watched the men get out of the buses after the test shot: "You could tell at once they had had a strange experience. You could see it on their faces. I saw that something very grave and strong had happened to their whole outlook on the future." Groves observed a similar reaction. "I started my plane trip back to Washington with Bush, Conant, Lawrence, and Oppenheimer. They were still upset by what they had seen and could talk of little else.... As for me, my thoughts were now completely wrapped up with the preparations for the coming climax in Japan."

Groves had lost interest in the problems of his physicists. He had already decided how to deal with the troublemakers in his midst. At the important May 31 meeting of the Interim Committee held at the Pentagon where Oppenheimer presented the physicists' proposal to use the bomb as a demonstration, Groves took the opportunity to present his timetable for getting rid of the physicists he no longer wanted on the project. The minutes read:

IX. THE HANDLING OF UNDESIRABLE SCIENTISTS

> General Groves stated that the program had been plagued since its inception by the presence of certain scientists of doubtful discretion and uncertain loyalty. It was agreed that nothing could be done about dismissing these men until after the bomb had actual-

> ly been used, or at best until after the test had been made. After some publicity concerning the weapon was out steps should be taken to sever these scientists from the program and to proceed with a general weeding out of personnel no longer needed.

On August 6 a uranium bomb destroyed Hiroshima, killing half of its 400,000 people. Three days later a plutonium bomb destroyed Nagasaki, killing half of its population. No one was quite sure why the Nagasaki bomb had to be dropped.

On August 14, the day before the Soviet Union was to enter the war in the Pacific, the Japanese surrendered. World War II was over. The Cold War had already begun.

The physicists were dismayed at the way things were turning out. Hans Bethe recalls the mood: "In the summer and fall of 1945, U.S. atomic policy left us troubled and perplexed.... Had Truman indeed reversed Roosevelt's policy of conciliation?"

On August 23 a committee of Los Alamos scientists called a staff meeting for August 30 at 7:45 P.M. in Theater 2, the largest meeting hall at Los Alamos, to discuss taking action against the nuclear arms race in the making. On that day five hundred people attended. They formed an Association of Los Alamos Scientists. Membership was limited to laboratory staff with college degrees, although the possibility of admitting the majority of workers at Los Alamos was to be considered at a later date. A ten-person committee consisting of some of the best-known physicists, including Hans Bethe, Frank Oppenheimer, Richard Feynman, and Edward Teller, was elected to draft a public statement arguing that unless nuclear weapons were brought under immediate international control, a number of nations would have them within two to five years.

Agreeing to work within the system, the physicists sent their final document with the signatures of nearly all the civilian staff members to Oppenheimer. Oppenheimer was to submit it to the Interim Committee for its approval, after which it would be released to the press as a group statement.

On September 10 the document was received by the War Department. On September 14, George L. Harrison, president of the New York Life Insurance Company and secretary to the Interim

Committee, showed it to Stimson, who decided against releasing it. Over the next two weeks the Los Alamos physicists badgered Oppenheimer to find out what was happening in Washington.

On September 21, Groves was the guest of honor at a luncheon organized by IBM at the Waldorf-Astoria in New York. In his speech he attacked the estimate that many other countries in the world could have the bomb within two to five years.

The Los Alamos scientists were enraged. John Manley, a moderate among the physicists, was forced to write to Groves that his speech had given fuel to more militant physicists who were pressing for an immediate release without official approval: "A number of us here are trying very hard to keep our more impatient colleagues from doing anything which might embarrass the administration. We are following this policy in spite of strong feelings in many quarters for contrary action. Your statement is readily interpreted as an attempt to discredit statements by scientists and therefore increases manyfold the difficulty of holding to our present course."

On September 22 from Washington, Oppenheimer teletyped Los Alamos that the document could not be released. "Mr. Harrison points out that since this document was presented to the President who has regarded it as an expression of scientists' views, it is not appropriate for anyone other than the the President to release it for publication."

The Los Alamos scientists accepted defeat. They had been too divided to reach past Groves's security arrangments to speak directly to the American people about the dangers of nuclear war. On September 28 an ALAS meeting recommended no further action be taken with the understanding that "the suppression of our document is a matter of political expediency, the reasons for which we are not in a position to know or evaluate."

At the same meeting the ALAS membership requirement, instead of being relaxed to include the majority of those who worked at Los Alamos, was tightened. Membership in the organization would be restricted to those who had a college degree plus two years of postgraduate study. The physicists had decided to try to influence the policymakers at the top by forming an organization of the elite rather than trying to influence policy from the bottom with a mass organization of wide appeal.

They achieved a limited success. Applying themselves to the task of learning how to work through established channels, they spent hard hours convincing U.S. congressmen to vote for civilian control of nuclear power. They learned to use the media to dramatize the campaign, most notably by sending samples of fused sand from the Alamogordo test to the mayors of forty-two U.S. cities, reminding them what would happen to their cities in the event of an atomic attack. The civilian-controlled U.S. Atomic Energy Commission was the result of their efforts. But it was a case of shutting the barn door after the horse had bolted.

The argument that the United States started the Cold War cannot be tolerated in official circles in the United States. In 1986, at a Bellerive Conference, a European think tank similar to the Rand Corporation, then–Vice President George Bush and U.S. Defense Department theorist Richard Perle debated Georgi Arbatov from the Soviet Union about the origins of the Cold War. Joseph Rotblat, in his capacity as chair of the Pugwash Conferences, a high-level scientific meeting place for Soviet and Western scientists concerned with arms control, was in the audience. The debate was acrimonious, with Arbatov arguing that the United States intended to use nuclear weapons to threaten the Soviet Union as early as 1944. Bush and Perle hotly contested Arbatov's argument. At this point Rotblat contributed his account of Groves's discussion with Chadwick in March 1944.

> I spoke from the floor and said that I had dinner with Chadwick and Groves in March 1944 and that Groves had stated very clearly to Chadwick in my presence that of course the real purpose of the bomb was going to be used to subdue the Russians after the war. Both Bush and Perle became furious with me. Perle rushed off the platform and shook his fist in my face, saying, "You have absolutely no right to be saying anything like that." Needless to say I was considerably shaken by Perle's outburst, which was completely consistent with the flak I received when I first published my recollections of Groves's comments the previous year in the Bulletin of the Atomic Scientists.

Today, fifty years after the events, a veil of Cold War propaganda by the politicians and self-justification by the physicists continue to hinder a serious critical appraisal of the Manhattan Project. What did the physicists really accomplish?

Faced with the threat of the Nazis, the physicists volunteered for a project where, by working day and night, they learned how to make nuclear explosives. The Nazis at no time were ever close to making a uranium bomb, a fact known to the British and U.S. authorities as early as mid-1942. The eventual use of the bomb did not win the war nor did it make it shorter. The physicists' main accomplishment was to deliver a bomb to the U.S. authorities that strengthened the hand of the anti-Soviet hawks in the U.S. establishment who, in their attempt to intimidate the Soviet Union, initiated a nuclear arms race that fifty years later has spread across the globe and shows only the most minimal signs of abating. The physicists, motivated by the best of intentions, entered into an employee-employer relationship with the corporate and military power structure of the United States, a relationship over which they had no control. There they were manipulated into creating a technology that gave their employers the power of life and death over the entire planet.

Physicists on the Manhattan Project have a lot to answer for, yet there were very few turning points. If objectively they had the power to stop the project, they had neither the consciousness to conceive of this possibility nor the forms of social organization that could have made such an action practical.

Thus, although there was a sense at Los Alamos that use of the weapons was unnecessary and immoral and would lead to a postwar arms race, the protests by physicists were easily brushed aside by their powerful superiors. For the physicists on the Manhattan project to have achieved their stated objective of simply beating the Nazis to the bomb, they would have had to enter the project with a political awareness of the potential conflict of interest between them and their employers. They would have had to have been able to deal with the right-wingers in their midst who regarded the Soviet Union as a greater enemy than the Nazis. And they would have had to maintain some form of independent organization apart from the organization of the laboratory itself, probably in alliance with other workers at Los Alamos. If these elements had been present then it might have been possible to organize the necessary work stoppage at the end of 1944 when it became clear that there was to be no German bomb.

But the physicists had neither the unity nor the experience to exert any control over how their work was to be used. The instant they finished work on the bomb it was no longer theirs. Although Groves granted their representatives a hearing, and although they made a serious attempt to organize after the bombs were dropped, they had as little real say about how their work was to be used as did the factory workers at Hanford and Oak Ridge. In spite of their high status, the physicists were employees of the U.S. military and had as little control over their labor as any other group of workers on the Manhattan Project.

The social relations of the Manhattan Project were the social relations of the postwar world writ small. The subordination of the Los Alamos physicists to the U.S. military and government, their lack of confidence to use the power they did have, and their lack of unity that could have permitted them to use their power more effectively is the same subordination, the same lack of confidence, and the same lack of unity that we all have in relation to these powerful institutions. The Manhattan Project prefigured the environmentally destructive society in which we all participate.

The reminiscences of the physicists who participated in the Manhattan Project invariably contain passing remarks to the effect that once fission was discovered an atomic bomb was inevitable. Dressed up for academic seminars as the concept of technological determinism, this glib denial of human agency passes for a theory of technological development in some of our most prestigious institutions.

But the concept of technological determinism is no more than a polysyllabic apology for the network of social relationships that constitute the status quo. It is as absurd to argue that the atomic bomb was inevitable as it is to argue that the Cathedral of Notre Dame was inevitable.

The history of the Manhattan Project is the history of how we have lost democratic control over the most powerful institutions in modern life. But although the Manhattan Project itself contained very few turning points, the events leading up to it did. The failure of the physicists on the Manhattan Project to exercise control over their work was the culmination of the political failures of interwar Europe of the 1920s and 1930s. The atomic bomb was the result of those failures. That story begins in Germany in the late nineteenth century.

As is well known, modern Germany was created by an unusual alliance between the neo-feudal Prussian aristocracy who controlled the army, the courts, the land, and the civil service, and the modern class of industrialists and financiers who controlled the manufacturing economy and the financial institutions. As in present-day Japan, the German state strongly supported the growth of Germany industry and trade, created a science- and technology-based education system, helped regulate the financial markets and foreign transactions through the Reichsbank, and effectively subsidized much of industry through military contracts.

The results were impressive. In the period 1870–1914 the German population increased by almost 70 percent from 40 million to 67 million inhabitants. Germany became the second industrial power in the world after the United States, surpassing England, with 45 percent of German income and 42 percent of German employment provided by industrial enterprises.

Along with this growth came, as in every other industrial country, concentration. In 1896 Robert Liefman could list forty combinations that completely controlled the production and sale of the world supply of raw materials. By 1900 Standard Oil controlled 85 percent of U.S. oil refining capacity, bringing an annual return of 20 percent on invested capital. Gustavus Meyer's classic exposé of American millionaires, *The History of the Great American Fortunes,* which ran through four editions between 1907 and 1910, expressed American popular alarm at the processes of concentration.

In Germany, the growth of state-supported cartels—the intraindustry agreements to fix prices and divide markets—signaled the end of nineteenth-century free-competition economies. In 1900 the Rhenish Westphalian Coal Syndicate, the Steel Union,

I.G. Farben, Krupp, and AEG were among the best-known of these forerunners of the multinational corporation. The leading chemical and electrical industries went through consolidation and monopolization, squeezing out among others the innovative but undercapitalized Electro-Technische Fabrik, owned by Hermann and Jakob Einstein.

In twelve years eight giant electrical firms contracted to four, and then by 1912 to two. AEG, started by Emil Rathenau and headed by his son Walter, and the Siemens-Halske/Schuckert combine both cooperated in attending to Germany's internal and external electrical markets. By 1913 they and the U.S. firm of General Electric controlled 84 percent of the world's electrical products. The small family firm, owner working alongside "his" workers, was an institution of the past. In the aftermath of the depression of 1873–1890, the corporation had emerged as the leading institution in capitalist societies.

At the same time that Germany advanced economically it retained a political backwardness that was the despair of its democratically minded friends. The alliance of industrialists, merchants, and bankers with the Prussian landed aristocracy resulted in the retention of political power by the aristocracy and the disenfranchisement of the working- and middle-class majorities. The German Empire was ruled by an emperor, four kings, six grand dukes, four dukes, and eight princes.

The Drei Klassen Wohlrecht, the three-class franchise, whereby each class elected the same number of delegates, ensured the domination of the aristocratic ruling minority. In the 1893 Prussian elections, class one with 3.5 percent of the vote and class two with 12 percent of the vote had equal representation in the Prussian Diet with class three, which had 84 percent of the vote. In the 1908 Prussian Diet elections, the Social Democrats for the first time won six seats with 600,000 votes, while the Conservatives won 212 seats with 418,000 votes.

Such a political structure could not possibly resolve the labor problems that were produced by the rapid industrialization and financial concentration over the forty-year period preceding the 1914–18 war. With the Prussian leadership adopting a policy of repression instead of cooptation toward working-class organizations, there emerged a powerful revolutionary social democratic party that was the model for working-class organizations throughout Europe. The German SDP was imitated by the French, Italian, and Belgian social democratic parties. The Dutch, Scandinavian, Swiss, and U.S. labor movements followed the lead of the German labor movement. Speakers from Germany were headlined affairs at trade union meetings throughout Western Europe and the United States. The Russian and the Slavic working-class movements looked up to the Germans, while the Second International was under the acknowledged leadership of the German party.

German SDP membership was over one million in 1912, while trade union membership was two and a half million. The party owned ninety daily newspapers and operated its own press service in addition to its weekly and monthly publications. And although social democratic and trade union successes had created a powerful reformist current within the party during the prewar years, Germany alone among the great powers was two separate nations. One nation was the new industrial working class, organized around the Social Democratic Party. The other nation, organized around the state, was the landed aristocracy, big business, and the middle class, among them the university professors and physicists.

A major consequence of industrialization was the emergence of a new physics of materials accompanying the growth of the chemical and electrical industries. Part of this new experience of materials was consolidated into theory with the invention of quantum mechanics in the 1920s. Another part led to the discovery of nuclear energy. The work of the German chemist Robert Bunsen was central to both developments.

Bunsen was the youngest of four sons of Christian Bunsen, a professor of modern languages at the University of Göttingen. In addition to studying chemistry, physics, mathematics, and mineralogy at the University of Göttingen from 1828 to 1832, Bunsen's training included a government-financed three-year study of European factories, laboratories, and geological sites. Included in his itinerary were trips to K. A. Henschel's factory in Kassel to inspect the design and production of new steam engines, visits to the laboratory of Friedlieb Runge, the discoverer of aniline dyes; Justus Liebig's laboratory in Giessen; and Gay-Lussac's laboratory in Paris, where he worked for nine months. He visited the porcelain works in Sèvres to inspect new methods of ceramic manufacture. And from May to July 1833, he made the rounds of the newest factories in Vienna.

From 1838 to 1846, in collaboration with Lyon Playfair, Bunsen developed methods for the identification and recovery of gases emitted in cast-iron production in Germany and in England. His book, *Methods of Gas Analysis,* published in 1857, summarized his twenty years of experience with the measurement and identification of gases emitted in industrial processes.

In 1860 Bunsen developed a special burner to facilitate the further identification of gases emitted from burning materials. Bunsen's burner, familiar today to every beginning student of chemistry, involved introducing plenty of air at the base of the gas burner so that the flame was hot and almost colorless except for a bluish-green cone. The cone temperature was about 1800°C., hot enough to produce light from the chlorides of many metals. Thus sodium chloride—ordinary table salt—was orange in a flame test, strontium chloride was red, thallium chloride green. The flame test is a standard part of the elementary chemistry curriculum today. It can be tried at home with ordinary table salt and the gas flame of the kitchen stove. Salt crystals will flare up with the characteristic bright-orange color of sodium if sprinkled into the flame.

After successes in isolating the metals lithium, barium, calcium, and strontium from their naturally occurring forms as chlorides, Bunsen began to experiment with the possibility of identifying minute amounts of new elements by their appearance in flame tests. With the help of physicist Gustav Kirchoff he soon identified two new elements by their characteristic colors. Cesium, identified from a few drops of mineral water, was named for its sky-blue color. Rubidium was named for its dark red appearance. The method was adopted by other investigators and in the following twenty years other elements—indium (1863), gallium (1875), scandium (1879), and germanium (1886)—were identified by their characteristic colors as shown in flame tests.

The rise of the electric lighting industry with the development of vacuum pumps and evacuated glass tubes facilitated the further exploration of the so-called optical spectra of the elements. Three generations earlier, in 1808, Humphry Davy, using the new powerful battery at the Royal Institution, had generated a brilliant arc of light between two carbon electrodes. By 1836 arc lighting was in use at the Paris Opera. By 1848, Joseph Swan had begun research on filaments that could be suitable for incandescent lighting. In 1858 the first electric lighthouse at South Foreland came on line, and by the early 1880s Swan and Edison were in partnership for the production and installation of electric lighting. A key development was the development of good vacuum pumps in the early 1860s so that the glass bulb could be evacuated.

Instead of using flames to observe the colors of heated gases, subsequent investigators were able to use the gas discharge tube, an evacuated tube filled with the chosen gas and connected to the terminals of a battery. Gas discharge tubes are in wide use today in nighttime urban environments. Shaped into letters, their vivid colors draw attention to establishments such as Joe's Bar and Grill.

Bunsen became an internationally known chemist. In 1860 he was elected a fellow of the Royal Society and awarded the society's Copley Medal; in 1877 he was the first recipient of the Davy Medal. His laboratory in Heidelberg became an international center for work on the chemistry of industrial processes, attracting visitors from all over Europe, among them the young Dmitri Mendeleev from St. Petersburg, who, over a period of ten years, devised a way to group the newly discovered elements according to similarities in their chemical properties. Mendeleev's grouping became the now familiar periodic table of the elements hanging above the blackboard in every school chemistry classroom today.

By the end of the century the gas discharge tube had been used to produce the rich literature on optical spectra that was to be finally understood in terms of quantum theory. And in another mode of operation, the tube led to the observation of new forms of matter.

At extremely low pressures of about one-millionth of an atmosphere, the gas of the tube is no longer luminous. Instead, a thin bluish thread appears from the cathode extending across the tube. These so-called cathode rays were little more than a curiosity until 1895.

In 1895 Konrad Roentgen, a mechanical engineer turned physicist, made the accidental discovery of X-rays during an attempt to settle the dispute about whether cathode rays were waves or particles. Roentgen had been amazed to observe that his discharge tube caused a screen of potassium platinocynanide crystals to phosphoresce even when the tube was covered by black paper. These were new unknown rays that could penetrate black paper. Roentgen called them X-rays.

In a nice series of experiments Roentgen showed that the new rays originated from a dull green phosphorescent area where the blue cathode rays struck the glass wall of the tube. He also found among other things that metals were relatively opaque to the new rays. Since bones contain a much higher percentage of metallic atoms than muscle tissue, the bones of the hand would cast a shadow when exposed to the rays.

Roentgen's observations caused a sensation. Laboratories all over the world raced to make their own X-ray tubes. Within a year X-rays were in widespread use in hospitals. Within two years archeologists were using X-rays to examine mummies in the Egyptian tombs.

In Paris Henri Becquerel, engineer-in-chief of the Department of Bridges and Roads and head of the Museum of Natural History, thought that since the X-rays originated from a green phosphorescent area of the gas discharge tube perhaps they were associated somehow with the phenomenon of phosphorescent crystals, a line of research that had been taken up by his father and grandfather.

In an exceptionally simple experiment Becquerel placed a crystal of potassium uranyl sulphate in front of a photographic plate and found that the crystal caused the plate to blacken. He then dissolved crystals of uranium nitrate in water and found that uranium nitrate in solution also emitted rays. He concluded that the emanations were not a property of the crystal but were a property of uranium ions. Becquerel had observed the naturally occurring radioactivity of uranium.

Hearing of Becquerel's experience with uranium, J. J. Thomson, the discoverer of the electron and director of the Cavendish Laboratory in Cambridge, pulled his student Ernest Rutherford off research in X-rays and set him to work investigating the new radiation from uranium.

Rutherford did a good job. He found that there were two types of rays given off by uranium—an easily absorbed current of rays and a much more penetrating current. One current had its intensity reduced by one half with only four layers of .0005cm thick aluminium foil. The other needed one hundred layers of the foil to reduce its intensity by one half. He called the two types of rays alpha and beta rays. Further experiments over the next ten years showed that the alpha rays were helium nuclei and the beta rays were electrons.

In the meantime back in Paris, Pierre and Marie Curie began the systematic investigation of radioactivity for which they are now famous. They called the new elements radioactive because the rays came out in a straight line from the center—"along a radius." They noticed that uranium ores from mines at Johanngeorgenstadt, Joachimstal, and Priban gave activities between two and three times that of pure uranium metal. Guessing that the increased activity might be due to the presence of other, more radioactive elements in the ore, they did the laborious chemical separation of uranium ores. In 1898 they reported their identification of the radioactive elements radium, polonium, and actinium isolated from uranium ores.

In 1903 Rutherford and Soddy measured the energy released in the decay of thorium to radium by alpha particle emission to be 4.2 million electron volts (MeV) of energy. This was a million times the energy released in chemical reactions, even the most energetic. (The spectacular explosion of hydrogen gas in the dirigible *Hindenburg* in 1937 in New Jersey released only 4.86eV for each burning hydrogen molecule.)

Six years later, in 1909, the basic structural features of matter became clear. Geiger and Marsden, working in Rutherford's laboratory in Manchester, exposed very thin platinum foils .00004cm thick to the naturally occurring alpha particles emanating from radon gas. Using a phosphorescent zinc sulphide screen as a detector, they observed, to their great surprise, about one in eight thousand of the highly energetic alphas being scattered backwards from the foil. In a classic analysis Rutherford showed that the back-scattered alphas were evidence for the existence of a small but massive nucleus within the platinum foil. The picture we have today of matter as consisting of a central nucleus surrounded by electrons was put together from these relatively simple early experiments using phosphorescent screens, platinum foils, and naturally occurring radioactive materials refined from uranium ores.

On the eve of World War I the human race had in its possession knowledge of the basic features of the structure of matter. How this knowledge developed was to depend significantly on the outcome of the war in Europe and on how the physicists related to postwar developments.

World War I was the first worldwide convulsion of industrial capitalism. The Western nations, their internal class conflicts unresolved, set upon each other in an intoxicating glow of newfound national unities. Ecstatic parades preceded marching orders with young middle-class men going off to save civilization, and young working-class men urged by their parties and unions to forget class loyalties in defense of their fatherlands. National chauvinism was the order of the day throughout Europe. As Einstein observed in 1915 from Berlin: "Planck does all he can to keep the chauvinist majority of the Academy in check. I must say that in this respect the hostile nations are well matched."

The war solved nothing. The real problems caused by the transition to concentration and monopoly remained intact, but with sharpened intensity, as the working-class majorities saw how little those in control of their nation-states were capable of representing their interests. The result was powerful reformist and revolutionary upsurges throughout Europe.

In 1916 Ireland rebelled against British occupation. Also in 1916 the Finnish Social Democratic Party won its first electoral majority and two years later declared an independent workers' republic, which was suppressed with German troops. In Britain the Labour Party broke through in the elections of 1918 while extensive strike actions, including Red Clyde (the occupation of the Scottish shipyards) won demands for social security and unemployment benefits. In Scandinavia in 1918, working-class parties, aided by the new universal suffrage, won majorities and installed the social welfare programs that are still the envy of reformers in Western Europe and the United States. In the spring of 1919 in Hungary, the Social Democrats and Communists created a Soviet Republic under Béla Kun that was repressed by an invasion of the Romanian army with French and English backing, which restored the feudal aristocracy to power in the form of the Horthy dictatorship. In France in 1919 a general strike and revolt of the fleet forced the government to adopt the eight-hour day. In Italy in 1920, the working-class parties won major electoral victories in an atmosphere of general strikes and factory occupations but were unable to consolidate their power, thus paving the way for the capture of the Italian state by Mussolini and the Fascists in 1922.

But it was in Germany, the most deeply divided of the European countries, that the pivot point of the terrible failure of Europeans to build politically on the successes of the industrial revolution was located. The failed revolution in Germany led directly to the 33 million deaths in Europe in the Second World War, to the 10 million deaths in the extermination camps, and to the construction of the atomic bomb.

The naïve nationalism that swept through the industrialized countries on the eve of World War I deeply touched the German revolutionary labor movement as well. Tired after years of being on the margins of German society, the reformist wing of the party wanted not power but *Gleichberechtigung*—belonging. Won over by a longed-for acceptance by the Kaiser, who said, "I know no more parties, I know only Germans," the SDP, voted unanimously for war in the famous vote of August 4, 1914.

But as the imperialist character of the war became clearer, German opposition to the war increased. In May 1915, the Appeal of the Thousand, a petition of one thousand SDP members and officials, urged the party to fight for an immediate peace without annexations or indemnities. This was followed by a sensational public appeal for peace by the top leadership of the party. At the end of 1915, twenty party members voted against the fifth war budget. Five months later, on May Day 1916, Karl Liebknecht, despite his parliamentary immunity, was arrested at a demonstration of ten thousand Berlin workers against the war. Two months later, on June 28, fifty thousand Berlin workers struck against Liebknecht's sentence of two and a half years' hard labor.

In November 30,000 workers in Frankfurt demonstrated against the war, calling for immediate peace without annexations. In April 1917, 250,000 workers struck, the first mass strike of the war. Their demands included peace without annexations or indemnities, liberation of all political prisoners, an end to press censorship, an end to the ban on public meetings, and for the first time (following the lead of Russian revolutionaries) a call for the election of factory councils. In July the Reichstag finally voted a resolution calling for peace without annexations or indemnities. Finally, in January 1918, in the greatest political strike of the war, over one million armament workers struck in opposition to the punitive treaty of Brest-Litovsk against the new Soviet Republic. The Great Munitions Workers' Strike was a rehearsal for the November 1918 revolution.

In October 1918, while General Ludendorff was asking France and England for an armistice, the German army ignored its officers and demobilized itself by leaving its positions and going home. On November 3, 1918, sailors of the German fleet mutinied in the northern port of Kiel. A sailors', soldiers', and workers' council took control of the government of Kiel.

Over the next six days, the revolution fanned out through the country. On November 6, a hundred kilometers to the south of Kiel, sailors', soldiers', and workers' councils took control of Bremen, Hamburg, and Lübeck. Two days later, on November 8, the revolution had spread to Cologne, Frankfurt, and Stuttgart in the west of the country; to Leipzig and Dresden in the east; to Braunschweig, Magdeburg, and Nuremburg in the center; and to Munich in the south. The following day, on the ninth of November, Berlin fell to the sailors', soldiers', and workers' councils.

On the day Berlin fell, the Kaiser abdicated. Chancellor Max von Baden resigned. In response to massive demonstrations in Berlin, the new Social Democratic State Secretary Phillip Scheidemann stepped through a window in the Reich's Chancellery and shouted to the crowd, "Long live the German Republic." The monarchy had been abolished by popular upheaval. Thirteen out of sixteen major German cities were in the hands of working-class political organizations.

As in the Paris Commune forty years earlier, military defeat had created the conditions for revolution. And also, as in the Paris Commune, lack of decisive action by the revolutionary movement, this time over a five-year instead of a five-month period, permitted the restoration of the former ruling groups.

The first National Congress of the governing bodies of the towns and cities of revolutionary Germany was held in December in Berlin. There the four hundred delegates voted overwhelmingly, 302 to 98, to create a national assembly. They voted in favor of continuing the municipal power held by sailors', soldiers', and workers' councils. The Congress affirmed its support for previous government decrees for social reforms, including the eight-hour day. It called for socialization of key industries and it passed a tough resolution about the army, calling for removal of all badges of rank, for control of the army by soldiers' councils, for the election of officers by the ranks, and for the abolition of the standing army in favor of a people's militia.

The National Congress rejected force as a means to implement its decisions. Violence was not part of the vocabulary of the German revolutionaries. As Rosa Luxemburg wrote on December 18:

> In all bourgeois revolutions bloodshed, terrorism, and political murder have always been the weapons in the hands of the rising classes, but the proletarian revolution needs no terrorism to attain its ends, and its supporters abominate murder. It needs none of these weapons because it fights against institutions, not against individuals.... The proletarian revolution is not the desperate attempt of a minority to shape the world by violence according to its own ideal. It is the action of the overwhelming

majority of the working people called upon to fulfill a historic mission and to make historical necessity into historical reality.

But the German High Command, led by Generals Groner and von Hindenburg, remained intact. From their base of operations in Kassel in central Germany two hundred miles from Berlin, they refused to recognize the National Congress resolution on military organization. Groner told the Social Democratic leader Ebert that they would resign if it were implemented. Ebert, along with Gustav Noske, immediately gave in and began the now well-known secret collaboration with the high command to abolish the councils and return effective power to the army. As Groner was later to write:

> Every evening between eleven and one we spoke on the phone from the General Staff Headquarters to the Chancellery by means of a secret wire. Our first task was to drive the Berlin workers' and soldiers' councils from power. Ten divisions were to march on Berlin. Ebert assented and agreed that the troops be heavily armed. We worked out a program which included a mop-up of Berlin after the troops marched in. We also discussed that with Ebert to whom I am particularly grateful.

In the months of January, February, and March 1919, street fighting between army troops and revolutionary workers occurred throughout Germany. The army was responsible for the deaths of thousands of workers. On January 15, 1918, Karl Liebknecht and Rosa Luxemburg, two prominent members of the revolutionary left, were arrested at the home of friends in Berlin's Wilinersdorf. They were taken to temporary army headquarters at the Hotel Eden. A Captain Pabst ordered them taken to Moabit Prison where, according to the army statement, they were shot while trying to escape.

In Bavaria, under the leadership of Kurt Eisner, the revolution succeeded in winning peasant support. The Bavarian Republic was run by a workers', soldiers', and peasants' Council with widespread support owning to Eisner's popularity and acknowledged capabilities. On February 21, 1919, Eisner was assassinated by Count von Arco-Valley, a right-wing nationalist student. The Bavarian workers and peasants responded by arming themselves against future attacks. On May 1, with heavy fighting, government troops occupied Munich. A thousand people were killed. After the fighting, the troops murdered between one hundred and two hundred revolutionaries. The leader of the Communist Party, Eugene Levine, was court-martialed and executed. Revolutionary socialism had been beaten back in Bavaria.

Even with the failure to implement the resolutions of the National Congress, the Social Democratic government still had two other chances to make good the revolution. The first was in the aftermath of the Kapp putsch.

On March 13, 1920, the ultra-right-wing Erhardt Brigade stationed in Doberitz, led by Wolfgang Kapp, marched on Berlin to install a military dictatorship. The army, which had so successfully fought the Soviets, did nothing. The government fled south to Dresden and then west to Stuttgart. The government called for a general strike. The country responded. Even high-ranking members of the civil service stopped work. After four days the putsch collapsed. When the Erhardt Brigade withdrew, the general strike committee drew up new demands that the government parties accepted. They included a new government with the trade unions having a decisive voice, severe punishment for the participants of the rebellion, a purge of the army and of the civil service, and socialization of all suitable industries. These demands were never carried out, primarily because of the refusal of the left-wing socialists to join in a coalition with the majority socialists.

After the failure to institute real change in the aftermath of Kapp, the revolution lost its tenuous middle-class support. Inflation, economic hardship, profiteering, insurrection, and scandal remained outside the power of the government to control. On August 11, 1923, the last great general strike brought down the government of Chancellor Wilhelm Cuno. Still no changes could be pushed through. In September 1923 the Bavarian government organized a mutiny against the central government. The government did not act. Instead the coalition chancellor ordered the troops to move against the regional socialist governments of Saxony and Thuringia. Two months later, on October 22, 1923, the

Social Democratic Party left the government in protest. Weimar was over. The initiatives were now completely with the nationalist anti-Semitic forces of the reactionary far right.

Intoxicated with their success in Bavaria, the National Socialists, led by Hitler, Roehm, and Ludendorff, dreamed of seizing total power by imitating Mussolini and organizing a march on Berlin. On the night of November 8, 1923, they staged their unsuccessful Beer Hall Putsch in Munich. But the army was not yet ready for Hitler. In ten years it would be. This was the world that gave birth to the nuclear arms race.

New social initiatives had been beaten back by compromise or force in every country of the industrialized world. The enthusiasm and eagerness with which Einstein was received in France turned to sour disappointment as the failure of the social revolutions in Europe produced middle- and working-class hostility to new cultural developments. The arts and sciences floundered.

In music, Arnold Schoenberg in Vienna was in the forefront of classical composers who had abandoned the harmonic system of Western music as systematized by Vincenzio Galilei and the Florentine Camerata in favor of a new atonal system that introduced far more tension and anxiety into music than had been possible previously.

In 1918, frustrated by his inability to interest audiences in the new music, Schoenberg withdrew from concert life. He founded a society for music lovers who attended private performances from which critics were banned. Audiences were given strict instructions not to applaud the performances as Schoenberg single-handedly attempted to break through the musical barriers of the previous epoch into new expressive forms.

In 1921 Schoenberg and his students Alban Berg and Anton Webern invented the twelve-tone or serial system. With the same naïve nationalism that characterized prewar European sensibilities, Schoenberg wrote to a friend that he thought that his invention could make German music great again. His student Webern looked to a different social grouping for inspiration.

Responding to the environment of the socialist Vienna of the 1920s, Webern founded the Workers' Symphony Concerts. He became the conductor of the Workers' Choral Society and he took the lead in using the new popular medium of radio to give the new music a wide hearing. The music itself is modern and beautiful. Webern's "Five Sacred Songs," shown on archive film footage being performed to an attentive working-class audience, suggests a Europeanized choral version of the music of Thelonious Monk.

But Alban Berg's *Wozzeck* was jeered at its 1924 Berlin performance, with critics calling it "the work of a Chinaman from Vienna." And socialist Vienna itself was under siege from the right-wing Austrian government headed by Chancellor Engelbert Dollfuss. After a decade of street fighting in which Viennese socialists tried to counter provocations from the Nazis and from the central government, Dollfuss ordered the Austrian army to shell the famous working-class housing settlement, the Karl Marx Hof in the nineteenth Bezirk of Vienna. A potential base for the new music was swamped in the sea of reaction and racism that engulfed Europe in the interwar years.

Like the central European physicists of the interwar years who found a home in the United States, the Viennese composers also found a home there. Max Steiner and Erich Korngold, two of Vienna's leading modernists, became leading composers in Hollywood. Steiner's extensive credits include the score for *Gone With the Wind,* while Korngold's include the score for *The Sea Hawk,* an Errol Flynn adventure movie, which reverberates with the tense dissonant key changes so characteristic of serial music. The serial music tradition lives on in the music for *Star Wars* and in the work of Pierre Boulez and Karlheinz Stockhausen. But it is clear that European music has been unable to effect a breakthrough to the modern era. Jazz, with a powerful base of support in the vast worldwide popularity of African-derived rhythm-and-blues, soul music, and rock and roll, is now the primary source of musical innovation.

In art the Cubist movement, which reached its height between 1907 and the start of the war in 1914, followed a similar trajectory. Cubism claimed architects, designers, poets, and sculptors as well as painters. The isms of the postwar artistic movements—Suprematism, Constructivism, Futurism, Vorticism—were all inspired by Cubism. As with Schoenberg's attempt to replace Renaissance traditions with new music, Cubism aimed to replace the pictorial traditions of the Renaissance with a graphic, diagramatic style that attempted to express what the industrial revolution had made seem possible—a unified, totalized expression of human experience.

The multiplicity of viewpoints of the Cubist painting, the angularity and juxtaposition of disparate forms, the combinations of different media, were attempts to make a new language of art that, like the attempts in music, could express the new experience of industrial society. "All is possible, everything is realizable, everywhere and with everything," wrote André Salmon, the Cubist poet.

The Cubist moment failed because a precondition for experiencing the world as a unified whole is the end of social divisions predicated on exploitation. European societies approached but did not achieve this precondition. In the prewar period, the Cubists were the visionaries of the human possibilities contained but not released in industrialized society. When Europe failed to transform itself, the Cubist vision became a sterile Utopianism. As John Berger has written: "In common even with their experienced political contemporaries, [the Cubists] did not imagine and did not foresee the extent, depth and duration of the suffering which would be involved in the political struggle to realize what had so clearly become possible and what since has become imperative." And just as the arts of the European culture of the previous three hundred years were failing to break through to new forms and new audiences, so too was the physics.

In Weimar Germany middle-class audiences were more interested in mysticism and the decline of the West than they were in physics. Social commentators even identified the materialism of physics as a source of the cultural crisis. Max von Laue, the discoverer of X-ray diffraction, wrote in 1922: "[the school of Rudolph Steiner] raises the most serious charges against today's natural sciences. It is represented as bearing the guilt for the world crisis in which we stand at present, and the whole of the intellectual and material misery bound up with that crisis is charged to natural sciences' account."

Germany had come apart—both economically with the

famous German inflation, the mark doubling at first every three months, and then in 1925, every three days, and culturally as the values of nineteenth-century bourgeois prosperity no longer applied. In 1971 Max Born, one of the principal inventors of quantum mechanics, recalled his experience of the economic disintegration:

> The financial matters [then] are practically incomprehensible today. One has to remember that the inflation of the German currency was beginning. A drop of one half in the value of money may have taken about two to three months at that time. Later on it took only as many days.... Officialdom and public corporations did not understand the situation. The courts supported the currency catastrophe by rigid judgments. I myself lost the greater part of my inheritance. A man who owed me money on a mortgage sent me the entire nominal value of the mortgage (50,000M, I believe) in one single note of the inflated currency which was actually worth 1 M at the time. This was held to be legal. The High Court had decided that a *mark is a mark.* After such experiences as these, my faith in the wisdom of financial and legal experts, instilled in me during my upbringing as the son of middle-class parents, was very much weakened.

With the failure of the 1918 revolution, the German middle class started looking backward away from the triumphs of nineteenth-century physics and chemistry to *Lebensphilosophie* and the mystical appeal of German Destiny. The middle classes, who had previously attended popular lectures on the latest advances in physics, chemistry, and biology, were now caught up in the unfamiliar events of world war, revolution, and monopolization. The comforts of nineteenth-century bourgeois life had been replaced by anxiety, fear, and panic caused by a runaway inflation, bankruptcies, and revolutionary working-class political agitation, all symptoms of deep structural changes at work in the world economy.

Physicists, especially the Anglo-Saxon physicists along the English-Danish-Dutch-German axis, were not equipped by training, class background, or personal history to deal with a social crisis of this magnitude. By all accounts, they were idealistic, choosing physics as a way to serve humankind and avoiding what they considered to be the crass materialism of a business career. Many have spoken about being drawn to a monastic life in quiet temples of learning. They were uniformly of solid middle-class origins. With few exceptions they were center-right in their politics. In 1963 the Belgian physicist Leon Rosenfeld recalled a conversation he had with Niels Bohr in the spring of 1933 on the Rostock/Copenhagen ferry after Bohr had just been to see Heisenberg.

BOHR: "Well, these events in Germany may bring peace and tranquillity to Europe."

ROSENFELD: "Peace and tranquillity? By massacring and persecuting people?"

BOHR: "Well, yes, but you must understand that in Germany with those Communists, the situation was untenable."

ROSENFELD: "Who told you that?"

BOHR: "Well, I have just been to see Heisenberg and you should have seen how happy Heisenberg was [that Hitler was in power]. Now we have at least order. An end is put to unrest, and we have a strong hand governing Germany which will be to the good of Europe."

The right-wing pattern was most pronounced in Germany, where 80 percent of physicists supported nationalist right-wing parties while only 20 percent supported the Free Democrats, the nonsocialist liberal party of Siemans and Rathenau; the Social Democrats were regarded as the party of the enemy. As Hans Bethe remembers of his education in the Germany of the 1920s: "I found that nearly all my colleagues, nearly all my professors were terrible chauvinists talking of nothing else than restoring the glory of Germany and of the unfair treatment that Germany received in Versailles. My father was almost alone in his support of the Free Democrats. I couldn't talk politics to anybody."

But the right-wing trend in Germany was not dissimilar to the political alignments of scientists in the United States, Britain, France, and Italy. The exceptions stand out. Einstein in Germany; Joliot-Curie and Langevin in France; the Oppenheimer brothers in the United States; Bernal, Needham, Levy, and Haldane in the United Kingdom. And in spite of the number of leading Jewish physicists, anti-Semitism was endemic within the physics community. When Oppenheimer asked his adviser at Harvard, Nobelist Percy Bridgeman, for a reference to Cambridge, Bridgeman wrote to Rutherford that he need not be overly concerned by Oppenheimer's Jewishness: "As appears from his name, Oppenheimer is a Jew, but entirely without the usual qualifications of his race. He is a tall, well set-up young man, with a rather engaging diffidence of manner, and I think you need have no hesitation whatever for any reason of this sort in considering his application." Throughout the industrialized world, the majority of physicists were conservative in outlook. They voted Republican or they voted Conservative or they voted for one of the right-wing parties in France. They worked hard and tried to keep their jobs in the face of social turmoil.

Western capitalism left nineteenth-century liberal economics behind and moved into our present epoch of the multinational corporation. In this new context the social base that could incorporate new developments in physics into its thinking sharply narrowed to the physicists themselves and their new sponsors in the corporate world of finance and industry.

Physics became dominated by a small band of international travelers whose trips from the United States, Italy, and France along the Göttingen-Copenhagen-Cambridge high road were financed by the Rockefeller Foundation. When the mathematician Richard Courant, who had been, in his own words, "a very class-conscious foot soldier," got Rockefeller money to build new physics and mathematics institutes on the Bunsenstrasse in Göttingen in 1924, physics had been seduced by the only social group in a position to support it. And physicists accepted this support, thinking they still retained control over their work. Men of their background, with only negative attitudes toward the effectiveness of the withdrawal of labor, could not be expected to understand the powerful social dynamics of the new employer/employee relationship into which they had begun to enter. The political turning point had passed. Alamogordo was now very near.

* * *

The occupying government troops had recruited the young sons of the Munich upper middle class to act as their guides through the city. Among them was the son of the professor of Byzantine languages at the University of Munich. Werner Heisenberg later recalled: "Well, I was, you know, a boy of seventeen and I considered that [it was] a kind of adventure.... It was playing robbery and so on. It was nothing serious at all, but still I was there.... It was a nice summer in 1919."

> When I left Copenhagen, I was afraid that the economic and political conditions in Germany would have a paralyzing effect on scientific activity in the institutes. I was therefore delighted to see that this—at least in Hamburg—is not by any means the case.
>
> —WOLFGANG PAULI TO NIELS BOHR, JULY 1923

Werner Heisenberg and Wolfgang Pauli, Jr., were the *Wunderkinder* of the new physics. Upper middle class, competitive, mathematically precocious, they were Gentile and Jew respectively, united in their contempt for the ordinary and commonplace, utterly committed to achieving an understanding of the previous sixty years' experience of the composition of materials. Heisenberg worked by day, Pauli by night. Heisenberg was ascetic, Pauli bohemian. Both were trained in Munich by Arnold Sommerfeld, who challenged them to surpass him. Both became assistants to Max Born in Göttingen. And they both, as precocious and inexperienced youths, shared intellectual leadership of the new physics with the father figure of the quantum legions, Niels Bohr. Pauli's beautiful article on relativity published in 1921 when he was twenty-one drew the highest praise from Einstein, who, in his review of it, admired Pauli's knowledge of the literature, clear presentation, and "sureness of critical approach."

Pauli, at age twenty-three, found his style in Hamburg. The cultural decadence of the city following the suppression of the Hamburg uprising in the fall of 1923 appealed to him. He and Otto Stern, Gregor Wentzl, and Hermann Minkowski hung out in the restaurants and movies, Pauli doing many of his calculations at café tables. He became involved in the low life of Weimar cabaret. He enjoyed alcohol, drugs, and pornography. He married a dancer. He became the main critic of current research in atomic physics, not sparing himself in the process. "That's not even wrong," he would tell Bohr when presented with Bohr's latest ideas. To Alfred Landé he wrote: "It's an abominable piece of work," describing his own efforts to understand the anomalous Zeeman effect.

In November he began to finish an encyclopedia article on the state of atomic theory. In it, he developed a new idea about the anomalous Zeeman effect, proposed by Edmund Stoner working with Rutherford at Cambridge. This effect was a complicated distortion of the optical spectra of elements having a single valence electron, like sodium, potassium, and hydrogen. When the gas discharge tube was placed in a magnetic field, the pure orange light of the sodium vapor split into six distinct components, each with a characteristic polarization. The effect had defied understanding for a quarter of a century.

Pauli conjectured that the effect could be explained if the valence electron could occupy two different energy states when exposed to a magnetic field. He wrote Landé: "In a puzzling non-mechanical way, the valence electron manages to run about with two different energies in a magnetic field."

Sommerfeld was pleased with the idea: "It is very beautiful and no doubt right." Ehrenfest was also pleased. Heisenberg was less impressed, calling it a "*Schimmel*" (a gimmick). He still smarted from a Pauli rebuff of his own model of the anomalous Zeeman effect. "Why do you beat it to death with so thick a stick?" he asked. Pauli, true to form, replied that the proposed gimmicks were about equally wrong except for Heisenberg's, which was worse than all the others.

An intellectual turning point had been reached. As with Schoenberg and serial music, and Braque and Picasso and Cubist painting, physicists needed to find a way to express new experience. Investigations of the physics of materials over the past sixty years had led to the realization that the electron had a complex two-valuedness. What did it mean?

Kronig suggested that perhaps the electron had a spin. Pauli hooted. This was too mechanical. Too classical. And it was. For the electron to spin it had to have extension. A point cannot spin. If the electron had extension, then, given what the spin had to be, the velocity of its surface would be 137 times the velocity of light. The adepts knew this was impossible.

Nevertheless the idea of spin pushed ahead. As Uhlenbeck later recalled, "We could only understand Pauli's two-valuedness if the electron were a small sphere that rotated." No better understanding was to be forthcoming then, and we continue to live with the mystery of spin today.

In June 1925, six months after Pauli's *Schimmel,* Heisenberg came down with an extremely bad attack of hay fever. He left Göttingen for a ten-day stay on the grassless island of Helgoland in the North Sea. One night in an asthmatic daze, he seized on Pauli's idea of trying to reject classical analogies and invented matrix mechanics. A formal calculus for manipulating the states of the atom had been brought into existence. Most physicists were dismayed.

No one wanted to learn about matrices. Schroedinger in disgust developed an alternative, a wave equation.

Physicists were delighted. Instead of unfamiliar matrices, there were the comforting equations of wave motion.

Dispute centered on the meaning of the waves. If a particle was a wave, what was it exactly that was waving? Max Born, stretched to the limit, developed the concept of a probability wave. Heisenberg developed the uncertainty principle. Bohr and Einstein fought dog fights about indeterminacy at scientific conferences. The younger generation sided with Bohr, the older with Einstein.

Schroedinger showed up in Copenhagen with a bad cold, and every day Bohr went up to his room to argue with him about probability waves. At the end of the week, Schroedinger's resistance collapsed. He said: "I never would have written that equation if I had thought I would have to live with probabilities." Bohr, not to be deflected even a little, responded: "But we are so glad you did because now we see that even a wave theory is consistent with matrix mechanics."

The damage was done. The quantum mechanicians slid back from the threshold of understanding into a hodgepodge of old and new ideas—all arms and legs flapping in the wind. Physics, along with the rest of nineteenth-century European high culture, lost its nerve in the 1920s. As Hertha Pauli, Pauli's sister, was to write thirty years later: "It was the heartbreak of our world."

Ehrenfest was in despair over the developments. The young generation of physicists exemplified by Heisenberg and Pauli had a new style. They went to Göttingen to Born to learn to calculate, and if they had the time they went to Copenhagen to Bohr to learn to think. Ehrenfest, always insecure in his computational skills, hated it. "*Dieser Klugscheisser,*" he said, "always so clever and no one understands anything." In 1932 he wrote a desperate passionate paper for the *Zeitschrift für Physik* with the title "A Few Queries Related to Quantum Mechanics." It was the kind of paper that could never be published today. In it he complained that fundamental questions of interpretation were not being answered. "These questions might well be swept aside as 'meaningless' for the sake of convenience. It is even considered proper to do so," he wrote. "But for this reason particularly someone has to take upon himself the odium of asking these questions."

Pauli responded. It was not that good a response. The demands of the time had exceeded the capacities of the participants to shape them. A few months later, on September 25, 1933, Ehrenfest took a revolver to the hospital where his youngest son, a Down's child, was cared for, had shot the child and then himself.

Ehrenfest's lifelong love for physics, for the rich textured experience of mechanics, of electromagnetism, of thermodynamics, was, in the space of five years, destroyed. Compounded by the painful details of personal history, the night thoughts of a classical physicist had become unbearable.

Pauli in the meantime had withdrawn to Zurich where his critical sensibilities had little to work on. He wrote a sarcastic shortsighted review of Born and Jordan's textbook on matrix mechanics, concluding with the sentence "Print and paper are excellent."

On March 31, 1933, the Jewish judges were dismissed in Prussia. The following day Goebbels announced: "The Jews in Germany can thank refugees like Einstein for the fact that they themselves are today—completely legitimately and legally—being called into account." The Jewish physicists began their exodus—Einstein to Princeton, Born to Edinburgh, Franck to Chicago. Those with well-established names found new jobs in the New World. They became participants in the famous outings to the Oppenheimer ranch in New Mexico. The many visitors—Weisskopf, Serber, Lamb, Schiff, Furry, Bohr, Uhlenbeck—made the ranch a required stop on the European/East Coast/West Coast physics pilgrimages. They ate wild strawberries with Cointreau. Elsa Uhlenbeck cooked Indonesian food. Their attention turned from quantum mechanics to the new developments in nuclear physics.

Nuclear physics had taken a backseat to quantum mechanics throughout the 1920s. But in 1932 James Chadwick, working in Rutherford's laboratory in Cambridge, had discovered the neutron. The last component of nuclear matter had been isolated. In 1934 Joliot-Curie and Irene Curie in Paris discovered artificial radioactivity by bombarding aluminum with alpha particles to produce radioactive phosphorus-30.

Immediately Fermi and his colleagues working in Rome began a systematic program to make new radioactive isotopes by using the neutron as a bombarding particle. Using a neutron source prepared by evaporating polonium onto beryllium, by July he had bombarded sixty elements and had induced radioactivity in forty of them. The bombardment of uranium by the new neutron produced a particularly complex pattern of ten different radioactivities. In 1935 Otto Hahn and Lise Meitner in Berlin took up the problem of trying to understand the radioactivity induced in uranium by neutron bombardment. It was only a matter of time before the workers in the field realized that the neutrons had caused the uranium nuclei to fission into lighter radioactive fragments, each with its own characteristic radioactivity.

Heisenberg stayed behind in Germany as professor of physics in Göttingen. The Nazi regime was not entirely to his disliking. In 1934 Max Born, now in temporary quarters in Cambridge, came to Göttingen to collect his personal effects. Born and his wife, Hedwig, went to visit his former student. Heisenberg, filled with the spirit of the New Germany, conducted himself abominably. An associate of Born recalls: "They were met with anti-Jewish sneers and obscenities and in the end Heisenberg spat on the floor at Max Born's feet."

In early 1937, after the dismissals and subsequent emigration of those Jewish physicists, mathematicians, and chemists who could get out, Heisenberg himself was attacked in the *Schwarze Korps,* the SS newspaper, for being "a white Jew" whose graduate students were "still composed of Jews and foreigners, even today." This was serious business in the Nazi Germany of 1937.

Heisenberg, however, had some loose ties to Himmler. Heisenberg's grandfather and Himmler's father had been teachers at the same gymnasium in Munich. Heisenberg's mother went to see Himmler's mother. The tactic worked. A few months later Himmler responded: "I have had your case investigated particularly thoroughly and particularly correctly just because you were recommended by my family. I am happy to tell you now that I do not approve of the attack in the Schwarze Korps article, and I have forbidden any further attack against you."

The event made no change in Heisenberg's consciousness, or rather, the Nazis knew their man. In August, Heisenberg wrote to Sommerfeld: "It really is a shame at a time when physics is making such marvelous progress, and it is such fun to work on that one is time and time again bothered with political matters."

From the safety of Zurich, Pauli grew interested in ESP and the ideas of C. G. Jung. He and Jung wrote a paper together on archetypes in the work of Johannes Kepler. The conscience of physics had become somnolent.

In March 1938, Hertha Pauli came through Zurich on the run from the Nazi Anschluss in Austria. She was an actress with well-known antifascist views, an habitué of Trotsky's old haunt, the Café Central in Vienna. Along with other well-known antifascists, the playright and poet Bertolt Brecht, the Dadaist Walter Mehring, the actor Peter Lorre, and the writer Max Reinhardt, she was looking for asylum from the Gestapo roundup of left-wingers. Her brother Wolfgang was in England at a conference. Hertha found her way by train to Paris. She was met at the Gare de l'Est by Mehring. From the Hotel l'Univers on the rue Monsieur Le Prince in the Fifth Arrondissement she and the other Central European refugees watched France succumb to fascism.

On November 7, 1938, in Paris, a teenager named Herschel Grynszpan assassinated Ernst von Rath, the secretary of the German legation. Three days later, Hitler took his revenge with Kristallnacht. In Germany, according to Nazi figures, 119 synagogues, 815 shops, and 171 homes were burned. Thirty thousand Jewish men were arrested. Children were not exempt. Cornell University physicist E. E. Salpeter relates that only luck kept him from being arrested along with his father on Kristallnacht. Departure was now most urgent.

A year later Warsaw fell to Nazi troops. Hertha Pauli, George Grosz, and Robert Siodmak escaped through the south of France and Marseilles. The breakup of Central European bourgeois culture was complete, including its physics.

On Christmas Day 1938, Austrian physicist Otto Frisch went to visit his aunt Lise Meitner living in exile from the Nazis in the small Swedish town of Kungalv. He found her studying a letter from her colleague Otto Hahn in Berlin. Impatiently Meitner waved aside his salutations and shoved the letter at him. Hahn and Fritz Strassmann had found that the products of neutron bombardment of uranium-238 included three isotopes of the light element barium. Frisch could hardly contain himself. He was reminded of the process by which bacteria divide. The biologists called it fission. He and his aunt quickly worked out the energetics of the nuclear fission process. Everything checked.

Frisch returned to Copenhagen to tell Niels Bohr. Frisch was, as he later recalled, "in a state of considerable excitement." Bohr was on his way to the United States for the Fifth Washington Conference on Theoretical Physics. "What fools we have been," Bohr said. Paul Rosbaud, the adviser to *Naturwissenschaften*, rushed to get Hahn and Strassmann's results into print, their report appearing on January 6, 1939. On docking in New York, Bohr told Wheeler the news. Wheeler told the Princeton experimentalists. The newspapers got hold of it. The past forty years of speculation about the possibilities of liberating nuclear energy had come true.

In Berkeley, while having his hair cut on Telegraph Avenue,

Luis Alvarez read the story on the inside pages of the *San Francisco Chronicle.* He bolted from his chair, ran up to the lab, and set up his own apparatus. Groups all over the country telephoned each other as they observed the fission reaction. The *Physical Review* was flooded with experimental reports.

Kowarski, Joliot-Curie, and Halban in Paris and Szilard and Fermi in New York found extra neutrons associated with the reaction. One month later, in February 1939, Bohr and Wheeler showed that the extra neutrons could cleave the rare isotope uranium-235.

That spring, Szilard and Fermi wrote the U.S. Navy that uranium could be used as an explosive with "a million times as much energy per pound as any known explosive." In France Joliot-Curie's team filed three patents for a nuclear explosive device. In Holland Uhlenbeck told his government about the developments. The Dutch Finance Ministry ordered fifty tons of uranium ore from Union Minière, the Belgium firm that controlled world uranium stocks. In the United Kingdom, Henry Tizard took charge of Britain's uranium bomb research and immediately began negotiations with Edgar Sengier, president of Union Minière, to keep uranium out of German hands. In Germany, Paul Harteck wrote the German War Office that it should investigate nuclear explosives. By May the Germans had stopped all uranium sales from the Czechoslovakian mines now in German control and had two separate groups working on "the uranium problem."

The war drew closer. On Tuesday, August 22, Hitler met with his top generals to finalize plans for the attack on Poland. Brutality was to be the norm. He told the generals: "Close your hearts to pity! Act brutally! Eighty million people must obtain what is their right.... Be hard and remorseless! Be steeled against all signs of compassion!"

On September 1, 1939, Germany invaded Poland. Between January 1940 and August 1941, 70,000 Germans were killed by gas in institutions for euthanasia. Heisenberg was recruited to work on the problem of creating a sustained nuclear chain reaction. He did his best. He recalled after his capture by Boris Pash of the Alsos mission in March 1945 that "It was bitter ... after the defeat of Germany, when the American victors extolled their scientific superiority and characterized the failure of the German uranium project as a miserable washout for German research."

In July 1941 while Paul Rosbaud, R. V. Jones, and the British SIS were unraveling the truth about the German bomb project, Rudolph Peierls and Otto Frisch, now working in Britain, produced a feasibility study for a uranium-235 bomb. On September 3, the Nazis performed the first experiments with the rat poison Cyclon-B, prussic acid in crystal form, murdering six hundred Soviet prisoners of war at Auschwitz Main Camp. On October 3, a copy of the Peierls/Frisch report was passed to Vannevar Bush, director of the U.S. Office of Scientific Research and Development. A week later Bush and Conant discussed it with Roosevelt. On December 6, 1941, the Office of Scientific Research and Development authorized the program to separate the rare fissionable uranium isotope U-235 from the far more abundant isotope U-238.

On January 20, 1942, at the infamous Wannsee Conference, Reinhard Heydrich presented to senior officials, including those from the Ministry of Justice, the Ministry of the Interior, the Chancellery, and the Foreign Office, government plans for the Endlösung, the Final Solution to the existence of the eleven million Jews in Europe. In mid-1942, death camp commanders requested Degesch, a subsidiary of I.G. Farben, to supply Cyclon-B without its usual indicator, a noxious smell added to warn of its presence. Laywers for I.G. Farben agreed, provided the government would guarantee its patent rights. In the afternoon of December 2, 1942, Fermi and his group achieved the first nuclear chain reaction in the squash court of Alonzo Stagg Stadium at the University of Chicago.

In 1943 the Germans invaded Byelorussia, where they incinerated 628 villages and all the inhabitants in them. On March 15, 1943, the physicists moved to the isolation of the Jemez Mountains in New Mexico. The pressure grew greater. Elsie McMillan remembers the tension. "Even before the end of the first year at Los Alamos, the emotional strain was apparent, the feeling that you've *got* to make that bomb, you've *got* to get it done; others are working on it; the Germans are working on it; hurry! hurry! hurry!... Get that damn bomb done."

Night work was *de rigueur.* The problems were being solved.

Money was no object. "Why use lead when gold will do?" they said to each other. On May 7, 1945, ten weeks before the Alamogordo test shot, Germany surrendered. The pace of the work was stepped up. Feverishly they prepared for Trinity. Eighteen- and twenty-hour days became the norm. Caution vanished along with sleep. Oppenheimer's younger brother Frank made little maps of evacuation routes through the desert in the event of a catastrophe. Over meals, members of the team calculated on their napkins the probability that the test could ignite the nitrogen in the atmosphere. The wives looked on in amazement at the frantic activity of their men.

On July 16, at 5:30 A.M., the sky lit up. At 5:32 A.M. came the sharp *craaack!* of the shock wave. "We are all sons of bitches now," said Kenneth Bainbridge. On August 6 and August 10 the bombs were dropped. The physicists started to wonder what they had done. But it was too late.

> "You know, in 1918, there was a revolution in Germany," said Heisenberg.
> "I know," said Kuhn.
>
> —THE KUHN-HEISENBERG INTERVIEWS, 1962

CHAPTER 4

Cold Spring Harbor 1946

When genetic engineering burst upon an unsuspecting public in the mid-1970s, the media transfixed their audiences with a familiar scenario: basic research, this time in molecular biology, had produced a dramatic new technology that would undoubtedly change our lives. The discovery of bacterial conjugation, the discovery of viral transduction, and the discovery of the so-called restriction enzymes, enzymes that chop up DNA into gene-sized fragments—all these had come together to make it possible to transfer selected genes from one organism to another. Genetic engineering had arrived, giving the human race unprecedented control over the workings of biological inheritance.

But to knowledgeable members of the international corporate community, the appearance of genetic engineering was the long-awaited result of a corporate-sponsored research strategy launched in the 1930s. The science of molecular biology was conceived, named, and nurtured in the corporate culture of the Rockefeller Foundation to hasten the transformation of biology from its descriptive, classificatory style of the nineteenth century to more analytical, experimental methods of working in the manner of physics and chemistry.

Founded in 1912, the Rockefeller Foundation was part of a $500 million Rockefeller program that helped shape the rationalization of U.S. society in the aftermath of *laissez-faire* capitalism from 1890 on. Initially the foundation funded programs designed to improve the standards of secondary education and public health. In the immediate post–World War I period it concentrated on raising the level of medical and scientific education. In 1929 the foundation began a campaign to advance basic research in the United States and Europe.

In 1932 the foundation appointed Max Mason, a theoretical physicist from the University of Wisconsin, to be its president. Mason, a specialist in electromagnetic theory, had little interest in the new quantum physics then completing its spectacular development in Europe with the aid of Rockefeller money. Mason's wife had become seriously mentally ill and Mason wanted to shift the resources of the foundation from physics to address problems in biology and medicine.

Mason appointed Warren Weaver, a junior colleague and coauthor of his text on electromagnetic theory, as director of the natural sciences division of the foundation. Mason and Weaver shared a conviction that the great advances of nineteenth-century electrical technology were due to theoretical advances in physics. Together they decided that the achievements of nineteenth-century biology needed to be placed on a more rigorous theoretical basis by an injection of ideas and methods from physics.

Throughout the 1930s and 1940s, the foundation provided travel grants, equipment grants, and salaries for the leading figures in the new molecular biology. William Astbury, Oswald Avery, Max Delbrück, Salvatore Luria, Linus Pauling, and Max Perutz were all helped by Rockefeller money early in their careers. In 1937 Weaver and his European emissary W. E. Tisdale persuaded theoretical physicist Max Delbrück, who was to become the informal leader of the movement, to leave Lise Meitner's group at the Nazified Kaiser Wilhelm-Institut in Berlin-Dahlem in favor of pursuing studies in viral genetics at Cal Tech. Also in 1937 the British physicist William Astbury, with Rockefeller sponsorship, visited over fifty U.S. universities to spread the word about advances in determining the molecular structure of wool fibers. And the foundation supported three important meetings in Europe—in Copenhagen in 1936, in Klampenborg in 1938, and in

Spa in 1938—that brought physicists and geneticists together to discuss the phenomena of X-ray mutagenesis, mutations, chromosome structure, and chromosome division.

By 1938 the foundation's strategy in biological research was sufficiently developed for Weaver to call the new biology by its now accepted name, molecular biology. As Weaver recalled in 1970: "... progress in the program was sufficiently prompt and promising so that when I drafted the 'natural science' section of the Annual Report of the Rockefeller Foundation for 1938 this section began with a sixteen-page portion, pages 203–219, which was headed in large type, MOLECULAR BIOLOGY."

Weaver's strategy worked. French molecular biologist François Jacob recalled the character of the molecular biological community as he and his colleague Elie Wollman experienced it at colloquia they attended in the United States in the mid-1950s.

> At these colloquia we saw developing what was to be molecular biology: that is the study of structures, functions, and biosynthesis of the two great biological polymers, nucleic acids and proteins. This biology was performed by a very small, very exclusive club; a sort of secret society to which belonged perhaps a dozen laboratories throughout the world. Some forty researchers who wrote to each other, telephoned, visited, exchanged [bacterial] strains and information, traveled to each other's labs to do experiments, met periodically here and there to keep abreast of the current state of the field.

Inspired by the powerful personality of Max Delbrück, the select community of molecular biologists was determined to understand biological phenomena on a level deeper than that of classification. Delbrück gambled that a relatively simple, rapidly multiplying organism like a bacterial virus (phage) might be a suitable model system for exploring the detailed mechanisms underlying genetic inheritance, the central common feature of all biological phenomena.

Starting in 1945, Delbrück brought interested researchers to the leafy surroundings of Cold Spring Harbor on the North Shore of Long Island to participate in the famous summer phage course where, in three weeks, they could learn enough laboratory technique to begin experimental work on the genetics of bacteria and their viruses. In 1946, Delbrück described the project to the Harvey Society in New York in his mocking charismatic style.

> You might wonder how such naïve outsiders get to know about the existence of bacterial viruses. Quite by accident, I assure you. Let me illustrate by reference to an imaginary theoretical physicist, who knew little about biology in general, and nothing about bacterial viruses in particular, and who incidentally, was brought into contact with this field. Let us assume that this imaginary physicist was a student of Niels Bohr, a teacher deeply familiar with the fundamental problems of biology, through tradition, as it were, he being the son of a distinguished physiologist, Christian Bohr.
>
> Suppose now that our imaginary physicist, the student of Niels Bohr, is shown an experiment in which a virus particle enters a bacterial cell and twenty minutes later the bacterial cell is lysed and one hundred virus particles are liberated. He will say: "How come, one particle has become one hundred particles of the same kind in twenty minutes? That is very interesting. Let us find out how it happens! How does the particle get into the bacterium? How does it multiply? Does it multiply like a bacterium, growing and dividing, or does it multiply by an entirely different mechanism? Does it have to be inside the bacterium to do this multiplying, or can we squash the bacterium and have the multiplication go on as before? Is this multiplying a trick of organic chemistry which organic chemists have not yet discovered? Let us find out. This is so simple a phenomenon that the answers cannot be hard to find. In a few months we will know. Perhaps we may have to break into the bacteria at intermediate stages between infection and lysis. Anyhow, the experiments only take a few hours each, so the whole problem cannot take long to solve. Perhaps you would like to see this childish young man after eight years, and ask him, just offhand, whether he has solved the riddle of life yet? This will embarrass him, as he has not got anywhere in solving the problem he set out to solve. But being quick to rationalize his failure, this is what he may answer: "Well, I made a slight mistake. I could not do it in a few months. Perhaps it will take a few decades, and perhaps it will take the

> help of a few dozen other people. But listen to what I have found, perhaps you will be interested to join me.

Delbrück's Phage Group, the people he recruited to his banner with the help of Rockefeller money, brought the intellectual ruthlessness and high-powered competitive habits of physics into the still leisurely nineteenth-century traditions of the biology of the 1950s. The invasion was not without bitter repercussions.

James Watson, a precocious member of the Phage Group, galvanized the Cavendish Laboratory into action on the DNA problem when he arrived there in 1951. For his efforts, which included a legendary rudeness to those he considered irrelevant, he and Francis Crick found the structure of DNA, the genetic material, before anyone else. But it also earned him the nickname of Honest Jim, with close observers of the scene subsequently saying that Maurice Wilkins and Rosalind Franklin did the work, Crick did the thinking, and Watson did the public relations. The wanton races for priority, the bitterness of the subsequent exchanges, the slow shaking of heads of the traditionalists signified that Delbrück's Phage Invaders succeeded in transforming not only the content but the practice of biology.

In the following two decades the pressure-cooker atmosphere generated by members of the Phage Group produced revelation after revelation about the detailed workings of the genetic material. We learned, expressed in flamboyant slogan and metaphor, that DNA makes RNA makes protein. We learned that a bacterial cell was a machine, turning carbon, water, and a few mineral salts into proteins, complex sugars, and fats. We learned that Life, no longer a bowl of cherries, was a sack of enzymes controlled by a master molecule.

The outrageous slogans, personality clashes, rivalries, and piracy were reminiscent of the days of the robber barons translated forward in time and shrunk in size to the laboratories of modern biology. With the officials of the Rockefeller Foundation watching discreetly from the sidelines, the protagonists slugged it out to make their fortunes, fortunes consisting, not of wealth and power (those positions were already filled) but of fame and immortality. The 1950s were a period where our knowledge and understanding of biological processes reached a qualitatively new level. As one leading evolutionary biologist described it in 1967: "There is not the slightest question that more progress has been made in our understanding of the fundamental physicochemical mechanisms of life in the last twenty years than in all the previous history of biology."

The achievement of perhaps one hundred select workers, their work underwritten by the resources of the world's most famous multinational corporation, had done for living matter what *Prinicipia* did for nonliving matter three centuries earlier. Just as the diverse forms of matter in motion became conceptually unified through Newton's definition of force and the equations of motion, the diverse forms of biology became conceptually unified through the picture of the double-helical DNA molecule, the genetic material, its precise sequence of thousands of four different nucleotide bases expressing the unique evolutionary history of each organism in the living world.

Max Delbrück left physics for biology with an unusual vision, unique among his contemporaries and unique still today. Unlike Max Mason and Warren Weaver, who ventured into what they saw as the swampy waters of biology with the view that the analytic methods of physics would drain the marshes and reveal the same simple laws that characterized the development of physics, Delbrück had the opposite view. Delbrück immersed himself in the world of living matter with the view that in the phenomena of biology one might discover new paradoxes and new laws of nature.

In the very deepest sense, Delbrück has been proved right. The successes of molecular biology pose a fundamental challenge to the intellectual frameworks derived from physics that have dominated Western culture since *Principia.*

Part of the charm of molecular biology lies in the simplicity of the materials used to establish major facts about how life reproduces itself. The organism of choice, *Esherichia coli (E. coli),* a harmless bacterium isolated from the human intestine, can be grown in a medium containing only glucose and a few essential mineral salts.

Colonies of bacteria are grown on agar plates, a technique

invented in 1882 by Robert Koch, Pasteur's great rival. Agar (shortened from the Malayan word agar-agar) is a naturally occurring jelling compound produced from the cell walls of seaweed known as Japanese or Ceylon moss. It forms a firm gel at 0.5 percent concentrations. Aside from its use in microbiology, agar is used to make jellied confections, cosmetics, and as a laxative. The Chinese swallow regurgitates seaweed of this type to build its nest, which then becomes a prized ingredient in traditional Chinese bird's nest soup.

In bacteriology a sterile agar solution containing the ingredients necessary for bacterial growth is poured into a petri dish, a flat dish about the size of the palm of the hand. When the agar has set, a suitably diluted solution of bacteria is spread on its surface. After overnight incubation, the agar surface is covered with small white dots, each dot being a colony of ten million or more genetically identical bacteria, descendants of the original plated bacterium.

Agar plates are useful for isolating mutants of *E. coli.* A particularly interesting class of bacterial mutants is so-called auxotrophic mutants, bacteria that cannot grow unless their growth medium is supplemented by a particular amino acid. Such mutants can be isolated by the technique of replica plating.

The bacterial culture is spread on an agar plate containing glucose, the essential mineral salts, and the particular amino acid, for example, histidine. When the colonies have grown, a sterile piece of velvet is pressed into the plate. The prickly velvet surface, acting like a thousand little inoculating needles, is then pressed onto a fresh agar plate that does not contain histidine. After overnight incubation an absence of a white dot signals the presence of a bacterium that requires histidine for growth. The required auxotrophic mutant can then be plucked from the original plate. By analyzing auxotrophic mutants, investigators have unraveled the step-by-step processes by which a bacterial cell produces its own amino acids.

Bruce Ames and his colleagues at Berkeley performed such an analysis for the amino acid histidine. They first isolated nine hundred different histidine-requiring mutants. Through established techniques, they then located the positions of 540 of the mutations on the bacterial chromosome, finding that the mutations clustered together into nine distinct groups. Such a grouping indicated that nine distinct genes were involved in the production of histidine.

They then analyzed the nine enzymes produced by the nine genes. In so doing they were able to construct a picture of the complete biochemical sequence by which the nine enzymes successively chisel out a molecule of L-histidine from the available substrate. It was lovely work, typical of the kinds of advances that were made in the 1950s and 1960s.

A by-product of Ames's research was his invention of an exceptionally simple method to test for the presence of mutagenic substances in our everyday environment. A solution of histidine requiring auxotrophs is grown up overnight. A drop of a candidate mutagenic substance is placed in the center of a petri dish containing all the essential nutrients except histidine. The histidine-requiring bacteria are plated out onto the candidate plate. If the substance is a mutagen it will cause reverse mutations, mutations that restore the ability of the bacteria to make its own histidine.

In a typical test a control plate showed a distribution of about twenty-five colonies randomly spread over the entire agar surface. But the candidate plate showed a concentrated growth of hundreds of colonies distributed neatly around the drop of candidate mutagen. The circular growth of colonies showed that the substance in question had the power to change the genetic material of the bacteria. The Ames test has been used to identify mutagens in food additives, hair dyes, cured meats, cigarette smoke, and hundreds of other commonly used products without, unfortunately, producing the legislation that would restrict the entry of these mutagenic substances into our daily lives.

In addition to the elucidation of biosynthetic pathways and the double-helical architecture of the DNA molecule, the first generation of molecular biologists produced a detailed solution to Delbrück's original puzzle—how is it that a virus can enter a bacterial cell and within half an hour make one hundred copies of itself? The solution to the puzzle of viral replication represents a solution to the puzzle of life. Once one sees in full detail how a bacterial virus replicates, one has demystified the most fundamental property of living matter, its ability to reproduce itself. Even more fundamentally, the solution to the puzzle of viral replication challenges the past three centuries of domination of the Western intellectual tradition by the framework of Newtonian physics.

The story of how a bacterial virus replicates in fact concludes the biology of the nineteenth century. The narrative unifies the experience of the imperial botanists in British Columbia, Madras, Bombay, the Cape Coast, Gibraltar, Bengal, Ceylon, Botany Bay, Penang, Guiana, Trinidad, Hong Kong, and Argentina; the isolation of the etiological agents causing tuberculosis, cholera, typhoid, dysentery, typhus, smallpox, diphtheria, and scarlet fever; the identification of the microorganisms responsible for the souring of beer, of vinegar, of wine; the leading work of Pasteur in locating the microbial origins of anthrax in sheep, of cholera in chicken, of the silkworm disease that threatened the French silk industry in the 1850s. It does all this with a beautiful description of the detailed steps by which the life form known as T4 phage reproduces itself.

The T4 bacterial virus, as seen in electromicrographs, has an icosohedral (twenty-sided) head attached to a narrow sheath. At the bottom of the sheath is a flat base plate. Attached to the base plate is a grouping of tail fibers. The DNA of the virus is compacted inside the icosohedral head.

A random collision brings the T4 virus particle into contact with an *E. coli* bacterial cell. The virus particle then drifts about on the cell surface until its tail fibers make an attachment to a specific T4 receptor located on the inner cell wall. The receptor is composed primarily of a sugar known as L-gala-D-mannoheptose.

After attachment, the virus releases an enzyme that dissolves a hole in the cell wall. The dissolved components of the cell wall act to trigger the virus. Its sheath contracts, expelling the viral DNA held in the icosohedral head through the hole into the bacterial cell. The forces that propel a DNA thread 550,000 Å long and 20 Å wide through a narrow viral sheath 1000 Å long and 25 Å wide within a minute are unknown.

Once inside the cell, the viral DNA begins to produce enzymes which break down the bacterial DNA. It also produces enzymes necessary for the replication of its own DNA. The three most important of these are an enzyme called DNA polymerase, which makes copies of the viral DNA; an enzyme that makes a unique variant of cytosine, a DNA nucleotide base needed by T4; and an enzyme that neutralizes the host bacterial cytosine.

After six minutes, a pool of viral DNA begins to form. The DNA polymerase utilizes molecules in the growth medium as well as breakdown products of the host bacterial DNA to make multiple copies of the viral DNA.

About nine minutes after infection, a pool of viral proteins begins to form. The first step in the production of the viral proteins is the binding of the twenty different amino acids to their own special nucleic acid known as transfer RNA.

Each transfer RNA, a short DNA-like molecule in the shape of a clover leaf, binds its amino acid to one leaf of the clover. Another leaf contains a so-called anticodon, a sequence of three DNA bases. The anticodon will subsequently bind to a copy of a viral gene. These charging reactions are catalyzed by twenty different enzymes known as aminoacyl t-RNA synthetases.

In the meantime, another group of reactions produces messenger RNA, a copy of the viral gene. The messenger RNA is the protein template. The messenger RNA binds to an organelle called the bacterial ribosome and the assembly of the protein molecule begins.

With the assistance of the ribosome, the first three bases of the messenger RNA bind the appropriate anticodon on a transfer RNA. A second triplet of bases binds a second anticodon. The two adjacent amino acids on the clover leaves of the transfer RNAs then bind together. The first transfer RNA is then released.

The process continues until the ribosome "reads" the entire "message" of the messenger RNA. Each triplet of bases on the messenger RNA attracts an anticodon on a transfer RNA. The successive amino acids on the transfer RNAs bind to each other to form a long chain of amino acids. This amino acid chain is the genetically coded protein molecule. The process ends when the ribosome encounters a chain-terminating triplet on the messenger RNA which, by an unknown mechanism, releases the ribosome to accept a new messenger RNA. In this way forty viral genes are translated into the forty proteins that make up the viral protein coat.

After twelve minutes the viral DNA pool contains enough DNA for about fifty to eighty phage particles, and the viral protein pool contains thirty to forty phage equivalents. The first assembled viral particles then begin to appear. Assembly into active virus particles continues until the bacterial cell contains up to two hundred complete viruses. The process is completed when an enzyme is produced that breaks down the bacterial cell wall, releasing active virus particles into the environment where they can attach to other bacterial cells.

Even in outline it is a thrilling story. Particularly amusing is the part where the virus makes the enzyme that neutralizes the bacterial cytosine. The realities of evolutionary development are so logical. Having evolved a different form of cytosine in its DNA, the virus also co-evolves a mechanism for protecting its integrity.

Missing, of course, in this highly stylized narrative of viral replication is the presence of the human hand. But figuratively, like an abstract epic poem from a culture whose referents are unfamiliar, the narrative of viral replication is a representation of observations of flasks of yellow liquid; of the gentle sloshing of bacterial cultures in warm-water baths; of endless plating onto agar-filled petri dishes; of the breathless anticipation of each morning's results followed by elation, dejection, anger according to whether one has been successful, unsuccessful, or stupid; of passionate arguments; of subtle and not so subtle hostility; of the seminars with friends and rivals; of Jim Watson rudely reading his newspaper; of Sidney Brenner screaming on a Los Angeles beach, "It's the magnesium, it's the magnesium!"; of Max Delbrück gesticulating "I don't believe a word of it."

The story of the replication of bacteriophage T4 marks the end to the romanticism of nineteenth-century science well expressed by Pasteur in a speech written for the jubilee celebration of the Pasteur Institute in 1892: "[I hold] the invincible belief that Science and Peace will triumph over Ignorance and War, that nations will unite, not to destroy but to build, and that the future will belong to those who have done most for suffering humanity."

The combination of yearning and cynicism with which we now read Pasteur's fine words shows how little the hopes of nineteenth-century romantic scientists have been fulfilled in our corporate era.

There is a lot to digest in the achievements of molecular biology. The rush of information about fundamental life processes, the possibilities we now have to transfer genetic material between species, the possible survival issues raised by our newfound ability to interfere with evolutionary adaptive mechanisms have been the subjects of an extensive popular literature over the past ten years. What has received less attention has been the challenge that molecular biology poses to intellectual frameworks in the West that have stood for three hundred years.

When we read the narrative of how a bacterial virus reproduces, we see immediately that there are significant differences between the language of molecular biology and the language of physics. Unlike Newton's law of universal gravitation, $F = GmM/R^2$ our understanding of the replication of the T4 bacterial virus is not expressed in the form of mathematical models. There are no equations in the detailed delineation of the steps by which the T4 bacterial virus attaches itself to a bacterial cell, injects its DNA into the cell, makes the enzyme DNA polymerase that copies the viral DNA many times over, and initiates reactions that, with the help of the bacterial ribosomes make multiple copies of the forty-odd proteins of its exterior coat. The secret of life, so to speak, is revealed not through the equations of the laws of physics but through the depiction of a finite sequence of events.

But at the same time that we notice that our understanding of viral replication is qualitatively different from our understanding of gravity, we notice that nothing in the way a bacterial virus replicates contradicts any of the laws of physics. There are no new so-called vital principles at work in the reproduction of a T4 viral particle.

And therein lies the paradox. How is it that the same matter as the matter of physics behaves in ways fully in accordance with the laws of physics but which cannot be accounted for by the laws of physics?

We snip, snip, snip away with our research scissors at the processes of life. Down we go from organism to organ, from organ to tissue, from tissue to cell until we arrive at the DNA molecule in its cellular environment. We keep snipping. The DNA is in parts. The environment is in parts. Lo and behold, we have matter but we no longer have life.

The paradox of molecular biology, a paradox Delbrück felt might be present when he began to explore the phenomenon of viral replication strikes deep into the heart of the Western scientific tradition. Western science relies heavily on mechanical metaphors that explain the whole in terms of the working of its parts. Carried to its extreme, the mechanical world becomes a world of interacting elementary particles from which the properties of the rest of matter can, as the physicists like to boast, in principle, be explained. For the physicist, to understand the quark is to understand the world. The rest is just detail.

But the physicists are wrong. Late in life Pauli grew impatient with the inflated claims of postwar theoretical physicists and sent one of them a framed blank rectangle with the message: "See. This proves I can paint like Titian. The rest is just detail."

All the physicists can do is give us a picture of matter as it was early in the evolution of the universe. The deep structural studies now under way at the major accelerators in the United States and Europe reproduce the high-energy regimes that existed in the very early universe. Understood as historical probes, the new accelerators are in a position to tell us about the composition and interactions of the earliest stages of matter. But understood as structural probes the results of accelerator experiments tell us only, to use a clichéd metaphor, what the building blocks are. They cannot tell us how the processes of history have shaped those building blocks into the material structures we see today.

Consider, for example, a protein molecule. Its three-dimensional structure, which gives it its enzymatic properties, is determined by the sequence of its amino acids. The laws of physics permit amino acid chains to be constructed equally well from any combination of the twenty naturally occuring amino acids, giving, for a typical protein chain of one hundred amino acids, 20^{100} different possibilities. Realization of all these possibilities in nature would produce a mass of protein molecules greater than the mass of the universe. It is natural history that has shaped the possibilities known to physics into the biological realities we see today. Phage T4 DNA polymerase is a protein molecule that has been shaped, amino acid by amino acid, by the processes of history.

Historicity is the central feature of living matter. Every biological object is an historical object carrying with it in its DNA the shaping of billions of years of history. In the often quoted words of Max Delbrück: "You cannot hope to explain so wise an old bird in a few simple words."

Although it is threatening to established frameworks, Delbrück's paradox is also exciting. The recognition of the centrality of historical processes, the emancipation of biology from the timeless relational schemes of physics invites a critical examination of a fundamental concept of Western culture. The world is not a machine. It is a complex, historically evolved network of physical, biological, and cultural structures. And the sooner we liberate ourselves from the then liberating, now oppressive mechanical framework of the seventeenth century the better off we will be.

To begin, consider the reputation of physics as a hard, predictive science. Prediction, in addition to mathematical expression, has been one of the twin pillars that have elevated physics above the more historical so-called soft disciplines of geology, paleontology, and evolutionary biology. Leverrier's prediction of the existence of the planet Uranus, Maxwell's prediction of the existence of electromagnetic waves, Yukawa's prediction of the existence of the pi meson are among the legends of physics.

But prediction in the strict sense of prophecy exists only in theology. Prediction in the sense of *de novo* foretelling does not exist in physics. There always must be prior evidence, a trace, a signal, of a novel effect. Prediction, the stuff of the ancient Egyptian priests, is a mystification of the processes of human inference. Let us see whether there is any significant difference between the processes of inference in paleontology and physics.

The detection of a fossil imprint in a stratigraphic layer requires the comparison of the material in the neighborhood of the fossil with the candidate imprint. Deviations from the surroundings are evidence of fossil remains. In many cases, the detection is trivial. The imprint of a fern leaf, or a tribolite skeleton, stands out clearly against the background of smooth shale. The observation of such a clear signal is simply a trivial example of the powers of human perception. In other cases, the angle of orientation of the fossil imprint, its relationship to other imprints in the immediate surroundings, and the general character of the geological site are all required to separate reliably the signal from the background. Harry Whittington's work on the fossils of the Burgess Shale as reported by Stephen Jay Gould in his best-seller *Wonderful Life,* illustrates the skill required to reconstruct a picture of a whole organism from a series of incomplete two-dimensional imprints of various orientations.

The work of Leverrier in bringing to light the present existence of the planet Neptune was similar to the work of Harry Whittington in bringing to light the former existence of the astonishing five-eyed *Opabinia.* Leverrier reconstructed the astronomical terrain in the vicinity of the planet Uranus, a terrain consisting of the gravitational interaction of three major bodies: Saturn, Jupiter, and the Sun; four minor bodies: Mars, Earth, Venus, and Mercury; and the still smaller gravitational attractions of the asteroids.

Under the assumption of universal gravitation, Leverrier was able to create a picture of the expected orbit of Uranus, the background of smooth shale in the astronomical terrain. The observed orbit of Uranus deviated from the calculated background. The deviation of the observed orbit from the expected orbit was the fossil imprint, the track of the previously undetected planet Neptune.

What gave Leverrier's reconstruction a dramatic quality not available to Harry Whittington is the fact that Leverrier could point to Neptune's hiding place in the night sky. To those ignorant of the methods of physics, prophecy was indeed what it was, a dramatic foretelling of a previously undetected planet. To the cognoscenti it was important only because it was additional evidence in favor of the law of universal gravitation—the deviation from an expected orbit was not due to a deviation from the law of gravitation but was due to the presence of another gravitationally attracting body obeying the law of gravitation.

For too long we have been in awe of the accomplishments of

physics simply because of our ignorance of the methods used to produce the results. In place of informed critical appreciation, we have accepted a description of physics as a predictive science with all the connotations of superiority that such a label implies. But in fact physics is an observational science just like all the others. Its presumed superiority is now an anachronism, a historical artifact of social development in the West.

But old ideas die hard. There is a grouping of biologists, similar to the middle-level priests who made life so miserable for Galileo, for whom molecular biology is not a liberation from mechanics but is a confirmation of a mechanical worldview. In this view, Delbrück's paradox, instead of helping us adopt a flexible, appreciative approach to the unique contingencies of historical development, has been turned into its opposite, a mechanical program of genetic determinism.

In the past two decades these biologists have put forth genetic explanations for just about everything: the XYY criminal chromosome syndrome for crime; a manic-depressive gene on the X chromosome for mental illness; polygenic inheritance determination with partial dominance and incomplete penetrance for variation in IQ performance; ditto for variation in human personality; and finally, with E. O. Wilson's *Sociobiology,* a genetic determination for, in alphabetical order, aggression, allegiance, altruism, conformity, ethics, genocide, indoctrinability, love, male dominance, the mother-child bond, military discipline, parent-child conflict, the sexual division of labor, spite, territoriality, tribalism, and xenophobia.

But just as the replication of bacteriophage T4 cannot be understood in terms of the physics of the constituent atoms of its DNA, the functioning of tissues, organisms, and populations cannot be understood in terms of the biochemistry of their constituent molecules. As Ernst Mayr has written about the liver:

> We know that an inventory of all the molecules of the liver is not sufficient to reconstruct a description of the function of the entire liver. Without a knowledge of the mitochondria and other cellular organelles and structures (membranes), without understand-

> ing blood circulation and the structure of capillaries, without knowing what the normal input and output of the liver is, and without a knowledge of many other aspects of the liver and the body as a whole, it would be utterly futile to try to arrive at a correct picture of liver function.

The emancipation offered by the success of molecular biology has been stalled by a confluence of a still-powerful mechanical materialism within biology and a still powerful ideology of predestination in our society at large. Contrary to Delbrück's paradox, which illustrates the central importance of the emergent properties of historically shaped objects, we continue to believe that we can explain everything that we do not understand about ourselves in the few simple words: "Oh, it must be genetic."

Nearly four centuries after the Puritans, we still find it natural to frame our understandings of ourselves in terms of a predestined script. In modern intellectual life, DNA has replaced the Deity. It is time to do better.

The race and IQ debate of the 1970s raised fundamental questions about our understanding of ourselves. But these questions were not addressed because participants on both sides of the debate shared a similar vision of a genetically determined human mental capacity.

The first stage of the race and IQ debate produced an extensive technical literature challenging assertions that variation in performance on IQ tests was substantially inherited. Leon Kamin made a comprehensive analysis of the history of IQ testing. Stephen Jay Gould chased the subject back to its pretesting origins in nineteenth-century craniometry. General methodological critiques were written by F. S. Fehr, D. Layzer, Hilary Putnam, P. A. P. Moran, R. C. Lewontin and R. Feldman, A. Vetta, and D. J. Cohen and his colleagues.

D. Rosenthal showed that high heritabilities could be computed for taking laxatives and using certain kinds of toothpastes. B. Tizard reported low heritabilities of intelligence in animal experiments. M. Schwartz and J. Schwartz showed that the high heritabilities reported by Arthur Jensen and others were consistent with zero heritability if one computed standard errors, used controls, and properly tested alternative hypotheses. M. Ghodsian and K. Richardson reported zero heritability of intelligence in a study on twins. And finally, D. D. Dorfman showed that Sir Cyril Burt had faked a study showing a large genetic component to variation in IQ performance in a presumed sample of thirty thousand father-son pairs by simply copying out the distribution of their supposed test scores from the mathematical tables.

What it all added up to was perhaps best expressed by Kamin: "The prudent conclusion seems clear. There are no data sufficient for us to reject the hypothesis that differences in the way in which people answer the questions asked by testers are determined by their palpably different life experiences."

In the second stage of the debate the studies were pushed to the side. What was at stake was a central organizing principle of Western social life. As British IQ pioneer Lord Alexander of Potterhill trumpeted to *The Times:* "Some of the statistical evidence is open to challenge. I could not care less. I do not need statistical evidence to recognize the validity of inheritance."

The environmental side of the IQ debate quickly acknowledged the validity of inherited differences in intelligence. Noam Chomsky agreed that intelligence was inherited, arguing that it should not matter who was intelligent and who was not. Christopher Jencks argued that the percentage of variation in performance on IQ tests accounted for by genetic variation was not 80 percent as calculated by Jensen but was only 25 percent. And David Layzer published a mathematical theorem showing that the genetic component to variation in intelligence interacted with the environmental component in just such a way that the genetic part could not be measured.

Political scientist Andrew Hacker was one of the few commentators to notice the similarity between the environmental and hereditarian positions. In *The New York Review of Books* he took Christopher Jencks to task for not believing in the real equality of the middle- and working-class populations in the United States: "One suspects the liberal case would be stronger if its proponents genuinely believed in the fundamental principles of human equality on which this nation was founded."

And here was where an opportunity to advance our self-understanding was missed. We had become so habituated to the idea that our future was encoded in our genes that we had lost our capacity to respond to the fundamental question raised by Hacker's critique. How did the concept of a differentially inherited intelligence come to replace the eighteenth-century Enlightenment ideal of human equality, an ideal that was one of the founding doctrines of the United States of America? The answer gives us a chance to liberate ourselves from one of the more oppressive intellectual constructs of Western societies, the idea of inherited differences in human intelligence.

The literature on human capabilities shows that the decisive shift from the ideal of universal human equality alluded to by Andrew Hacker to one of a genetically based inequality took place in the last quarter of the nineteenth century. A bibliography on human intelligence compiled by the U.S. National Institutes of Mental Health consisting of nearly seven thousand entries contains only four entries earlier than 1890. This overwhelming literature is dismissive of earlier Enlightenment ideals of an equally shared human capacity. A 1925 review described the ideas of John Locke (1633–1704), David Hartley (1705–1750), and James Mill (1773–1836) as "primitive views of intelligence as an arbitrary spontaneous force. They overlooked entirely or to a great extent the individual differences between men *[sic]*."

The first modern theory of inherited ability appeared in 1869 with the publication of Francis Galton's *Hereditary Genius*. Galton directly attacked the Enlightenment ideal of natural human equality: "I have no patience with the hypothesis occasionally expressed and often implied, especially in tales written to teach children to be good, that babies are born pretty much alike and that the sole agencies in creating differences between boy and boy and man and man are steady application and moral effort. It is in the most unqualified manner that I object to pretensions of natural equality."

Contemporary reviewers of Galton's book were struck by the novelty of his argument. The *Westminster Review* welcomed Galton's "bold speculations" and the "originality of his thesis." *The Times* said: "Against these maxims, Mr. Galton opens fire with an artillery of figures ... to support his hypothesis of hereditary genius." The *Examiner* and the *London Review* complained that "Mr. Galton attaches an undue importance to breed and ignores education and training." And the *Spectator,* nonplussed by Galton's argument, said: "His book is a very clever one, though it belongs somehow with its shrewdnesses and crochettinesses and acute sense and absurd nonsense to another age than this."

The *Spectator* was right. There is a dotty fussiness to *Hereditary Genius.* On a first reading, Galton seems to be nothing more than a harmless Victorian crank puttering about with statistics. But the ideas in *Hereditary Genius* became the dominant Western view of human ability. The question is, why?

Galton was born into the Quaker family of Samuel Tertius Galton (1783–1844). Galton's grandfather established the family fortune by selling muskets to the British navy during the Napoleonic wars. While not as successful as Robert Peel, who died in 1830 leaving £1.5 million, Galton's grandfather died in 1832 leaving a fortune of £300,000. A miner's annual wage of the period was fifty pounds per year. Factory workers—nail makers, bleachers, bookbinders, saddlers—made between forty and sixty pounds per year. The equivalent fortune today would be approximately £100 million.

Galton's father was unable to effect a transformation of the family countinghouse into an established bank. The Galton Bank of Birmingham was weakened in the bank run of 1825 and finally collapsed in 1831. The Galton fortune was relatively unaffected and the six eldest Galton children settled into the lives of country gentlemen and women.

Francis Galton, the youngest of seven, was the family misfit. He wrote in his autobiography: "I was ignorant of the very ABC of the life of the English country gentleman, such as most of my family had been familiar with from childhood. I was totally unused to hunting and had no proper experience of shooting." Instead of accepting the country life of his elder siblings, he searched for a career.

He apprenticed as a house pupil at Birmingham General Hospital, he spent a year at King's College Medical School in London, and, over the objections of his parents, he enrolled in Trinity College, Cambridge, to study mathematics. In the England of the "hungry forties" Galton was anxious and depressed about his place in the world. One of his poems from the period survives:

> How foolish and how wicked seems the world,
> With all its energies bent to amass
> Wealth, fame or knowledge; scarce a thought
> Of those great voides which this life bridges o'er
> The future and past eternity.

In 1843 he had a nervous breakdown. "A mill seemed to be working in my head; I could not banish obsessing thoughts, at times I could hardly read a book and found it painful even to look at a printed page." Unable to sit the honors examination, he left Cambridge with a lower-level so-called ordinary degree. When his father died the following year, Galton came into his inheritance and had no pressing need to look further for a career.

Twenty-five years later, after extensive travels in the Middle East, Scotland, and Southwest Africa with some associated writing on geography, mapmaking, and weather prediction, he found his calling. Charles Darwin was his first cousin. The publication of *The Origin of Species* in 1859 drew Galton's attention to the accomplishments of those more successful than he in finding a satisfactory place in the Victorian world. He spent the rest of his life celebrating the achievements of English men of science, their superior genetic endowment, and the necessity of the state to preserve their genetic stock through eugenic programs.

In the United States, Francis Amasa Walker, the third president of the Massachusetts Institute of Technology, was the analogue of Francis Galton. Walker formulated a theory of the rent of ability, a key ideological construct for the new technologists being produced by MIT and an important influence on Fabian thinking in Britain. The idea was that the talented rented their ability to those who could afford to pay for it. Although he is little known today, his death in 1897 brought forth obituaries in 150 U.S. newspapers.

Walker, while not independently wealthy like Galton, came from a similar social background. The Walkers were a seventh-generation New England family unable to remain owners in the transition of the United States from agrarian to industrial capitalism. Walker's father was a prominent Boston merchant and shoe manufacturer whose business faltered in the Panic of 1837, finally going under two years later. He then took a post as lecturer in politics without pay at Oberlin College.

Walker grew up in a progressive antislavery family dedicated to the ideal of service to the state. Before becoming president of M.I.T. he held a series of jobs moving in and out of government service, journalism, and university lecturing. He taught at Amherst, Yale, and Johns Hopkins. He was editor of the *Springfield Republican,* First Superintendent of the Ninth Census, and Commissioner of Indian Affairs. In 1871 he became president of M.I.T., saving it from bankruptcy in the depression of 1873 and overseeing its growth into the most prestigious technical university in the United States.

So a picture starts to form. A faith in the equality of men (but not necessarily women), as articulated by John Locke, by the Encyclopedists, by James Mill, and by nineteenth-century Victorian liberal humanists, no longer seemed relevant as the heroic age of *laissez-faire* capitalist development gave way to monopolization. With the bankruptcy of smaller enterprises and the diminishing possibilities of accumulating individual fortunes in trade or manufacture, the sons of the former owners of enterprises sought new careers in science, engineering, journalism, the civil service, and education. This new professional grouping, a *nouvelle couche sociale,* repudiated the ideology of equality of the previous two hundred years in favor of an ideology of inherited inequality.

Intelligence became their coin. Like money, it was countable. Like money, some had more of it than others. And like money it could be passed on to the next generation. The new social democratic state would be captained by those with superior brains. As George Bernard Shaw put it in Fabian Pamphlet No. 146, *Socialism and Superior Brains* (1893): "This haphazard Mobocracy must be replaced by democratic aristocracy: that is by the dictatorship, not of the whole proletariat, but of that five percent of it capable of conceiving the job and pioneering in the drive towards its divine goal."

The Fabians were the left wing of the grouping of the new salaried professional middle class of administrators, technologists, and intellectuals that developed along with imperialism and monopoly capital in the last quarter of the nineteenth century. Walker and Galton represented the right wing. The left wing was patronizing toward the less fortunate, the right wing hostile. Galton was a vile man writing in 1884 that the Jews were "a race of national parasites" and that the achievements of Chinese culture were due to white men: "... it is perhaps certain that Confucius and other renowned names known to the Chinese were white men." He had similar views about the working class: "A mob of slaves, clinging together, incapable of self-government and begging to be led."

The politics of the right wing of the *nouvelle couche sociale* predated the National Socialism of the Nazis. An 1883 pamphlet, *The Moral Basis of Socialism*, by the statistician Karl Pearson, a disciple of Galton, exhibits the fascist sensibility that was to flower fifty years later in the Germany of the 1930s: "To bring again to the fore a feeling of genuine respect for personified society, the State, is obviously a hard but primary necessity of socialistic action. We must aristocratise as we democratise; the ultimate appeal to the many is hopeless unless the many have foresight enough to place power in the hands of the fittest."

Pearson's philosophy included a precursor to the genocidal policies put into practice by the Nazis: "After all, restriction or removal of population may be a more efficient aid to social progress than an endless rivalry with other nations in the monotonous labour of breeching the less civilised races of the earth."

In Britain, the Webbs and other Fabians led the professional middle class away from eugenics, fascism, and genocide toward the state corporate socialism that has dominated the British left for the past century. In the United States, the professional middle class became the right-wing ideologues of the corporate state that emerged out of the Progressive Era. Their activities were instrumental in having twenty-four states pass sterilization laws and thirty states pass miscegenation laws. In 1924 effective lobbying by the architects of intelligence testing resulted in the passage of the notorious Johnson Act creating immigration quotas based on population percentages of the 1890 U.S. census, quotas that ten years later would cut off an escape route for thousands attempting to flee Nazi persecution.

In Germany, with a far more pronounced social division between the professional middle class and the revolutionary German working class, the *nouvelle couche sociale* veered toward fascism and National Socialism. Beginning with the anti-Semitic literature and the antisocialist laws of the 1873–1890 depression and the doctrine of racial hygiene formulated by Alfred Ploetz in 1895, to the intense nationalism accompanying Germany's entry into World War I, to the anti-Semitic, anti-immigration, anti-working class panic of the German middle class in the 1920s following the failure of the German revolution of 1918, the German *nouvelle couche sociale* proved unable to resist being pushed along the path toward 1933 and the gas ovens.

The historical origins of our present views about intelligence are then clear. The doctrine of inherited intelligence developed as part of the ideology of a social grouping formed at the end of the period of *laissez-faire* capitalism from 1873 on. This social grouping was forced to give up careers of capital accumulation to work for the state or to work in corporate hierarchies as hired hands. They protected their social status by arguing that they had special skills and special intelligence.

The men of the *nouvelle couche sociale* were well placed by virtue of their positions as educators, journalists, and civil servants to impose their views of intelligence on the population at large. The testing procedure developed by Stanford professor Lewis Terman illustrates how successful the early testers were in making their views the norm by which the mental abilities of the rest of the United States would be judged. As Leon Kamin has described it:

> The Stanford-Binet asked 14-year-olds to explain the following: "My neighbor has been having queer visitors. First a doctor came to his house, then a lawyer, then a minister. What do you think happened there?" Professor Terman explained that a satis-

> factory answer must normally involve a death: "The doctor came to attend a sick person, the lawyer to make his will, and the minister to preach the funeral." There were however "other ingenious interpretations which pass as satisfactory." For example: "A man got hurt in an accident; the doctor came to make him well, the lawyer to see about damages, and then he died and the preacher came for the funeral." The following answer was failed by Professor Terman. "Somebody was sick; the lawyer wanted his money and the minister came to see how he was." Professor Terman's high quality genes evidently made him better disposed towards the good intentions of lawyers than did the genes of his failing respondent. To Professor Terman, it seems more logical that a minister at the house next door is there to preach a funeral than to inquire about the welfare of a sick parishioner.

In 1912, Henry Goddard, another pioneer of IQ testing in the United States, went to the immigration center on Ellis Island in New York to test "the great mass of average immigrants." He found that 83 percent of the Jews, 80 percent of the Hungarians, 79 percent of the Italians, and 87 percent of the Russians were "feebleminded."

Sixty years later, when Arthur Jensen and the hereditarians of the 1970s wheeled out the same arguments that had been made by Henry Goddard, Lewis Terman, Karl Pearson, Francis Amasa Walker, and Francis Galton, they were beaten back on technical grounds but no real advance was made in our collective thinking about mental ability.

Part of the problem in advancing our understanding of mental function is the ease with which one can construct plausible models for how variation in individual intellectual performance could be inherited.

Consider, for example, the molecular biology of synaptic transmission. A protein molecule called acetylcholine esterase is responsible for the enzymatic breakdown of the neurotransmitter acetylcholine. If acetylcholine is permitted to build up in the synaptic cleft, the nerve impulse cannot be transmitted from one neuron to the next. Differences in the amino acid sequence of the enzyme acetylcholine esterase caused by a nucleotide base change (mutation) could in principle affect the efficiency of the enzyme, thus affecting synaptic function and by implication the rapidity of mental functioning.

Or consider permanent changes in the ease of synaptic transmission called long-term potentiation. Evidence exists indicating that an enzyme called protein kinase is involved in the process by which the presynaptic terminal becomes permanently modified. Once modified, the terminal releases more neurotransmitter when stimulated. Again, an alteration of a nucleotide base in the gene coding for the protein kinase could alter its structure, possibly retarding long-term potentiation and by implication affecting the ease with which long-term memory is stored or retrieved.

In fact, our thinking about human capability is so dominated by genetic determinism that we tend to think that *every* human activity must have a genetic component to its variation. At the center of our being, we believe our human individuality is at least in part genetic in origin. It goes without saying that variation in mental performance must at least be in part genetic.

But it is not true. There is one very important kind of human mental performance that has no genetic component to its variation, and that is the performance of language.

There are between 5,000 and 10,000 human languages. Of this number 49 percent are Indo-European, 24 percent Sino-Tibetan, and the remaining languages are distributed among six language groups: other Asian languages (5.5 percent); Niger-Congo, Sudanic, and Khoin (5.0 percent); Malayo-Polynesian (4.0 percent); Semito-Hamitic (3.8 percent); Dravidian (3.7 percent); and Uralic-Altaic (2.8 percent). There is no genetic component to this variation. Any human infant raised in Tokyo will learn to speak perfect Japanese. Any human infant raised in Budapest will learn to speak perfect Hungarian. Any human infant raised in the Eastern Cape will learn to speak perfect Xhosa. The language one speaks reflects social circumstance, not genetic difference. There is no physiological or genetic explanation for the existence of 10,000 human languages.

In addition to the variation in world languages there is the variation in accents. In English, the accent of the white U.S. South,

"Y'all come back, heah"; the accent of the black U.S. South, "Lawd, have mercy"; the accent of Cockney London, "'ere Guvnor, give us a light"; the Australian accent; the Scottish accent; the Brooklyn accent; the aristocratic English accent all contain information but none of it is genetic.

The properties of human language suggest an alternative approach to understanding human intelligence. We are so accustomed to thinking about ourselves in mechanical terms as a collection of organs, tissues, and cells all controlled by our DNA that it is difficult for us to accept that just as DNA has emergent properties not accounted for by the laws of physics so does whole-organism biology have emergent properties not accounted for by DNA. One of these is the property of human language.

The DNA molecule cannot exist without the interactions of physics to hold it together. But its structure and function are formed by the shaping processes of history, processes that cannot be accounted for by the laws of physics. You cannot predict the shape of the Albert Hall from the knowledge that it is made of bricks.

Similarly, human language cannot exist without biological structures but its structure and function are emergent properties of human social experience. You cannot predict the language a child will speak from knowledge of its DNA.

So instead of taking as received the views of intelligence formulated over a century ago by the men of the *nouvelle couche sociale* that human intelligence is owned by individuals, that some of us have more of it than others, and that we inherit our own unique allocation from our parents, we can see human intelligence as we see human language, as a property of our species. Differences in human intelligence then are like differences in human language. They reflect differences in social circumstances. Like learning language, we learn to be intelligent.

The idea that we learn to be intelligent is an uncomfortable idea. After owning our own intelligence for so long we are reluctant to give it up to our species. But consider. We do not take histological slices of human brain and assay the synaptic connections for variations in the action of acetylcholine esterase when we judge the intelligence of those around us. Our judgments of intelligence are social judgments. They are similar to the judgments we make of a person's speech. The process by which we make them can be brought to critical consciousness.

Try the fascinating experiment of avoiding the use of the word *intelligent,* its synonyms and antonyms for a week. The words *bright, smart, clever,* the words *dim, slow, stupid* are labels. What are we responding to when we use them? What are we responding to when we (painfully) evaluate our own intelligence, the intelligence of our children or the intelligence of our friends? Describe what you observe in detail. Talk it over with friends. Discover that there are more liberated ways of understanding human differences than by colluding with the racist, sexist, and class-biased views of the frightened men of the *nouvelle couche sociale.*

Finally there is the question of Einstein. We all know we are not as intelligent as Einstein. Indeed, Einstein is a symbol of the intelligence we will never attain. And yet relativity is not that difficult to understand. All that it requires is that we understand that we live in a world without instantaneous interactions at a distance. Every disturbance, every interaction, every signal takes time to make its influence felt. From this simple physical fact comes the radical revision of our everyday concepts of space, time, and energy that Einstein was the first to elucidate.

We feel more intelligent once we understand the theory of relativity. And when we have difficulties in understanding the theory of relativity, the problem lies in our expectations of ourselves and the competence of our teachers, not in the sequence nucleotide bases that make up our DNA.

Myths are powerful imaginative reconstructions of social reality that express a culture's most fundamental beliefs about itself. Myths explain the world in satisfying ways and this is precisely what gives them their great strength, timeless quality, and resistance to change. The myth of prediction in physics, the myth of Einstein's genius, and the myth of intelligence all express our fear of understanding and our awe of understanding, a fear and awe produced by our estrangement from central parts of Western culture.

We have forgotten the most important lesson of nineteenth-century science—that the world is comprehensible—because we have so little experience of actually understanding the world. With the failure of Europe to liberate itself in the 1920s, our cognitive apparatus has fallen into disrepair. We have all become stupider. In place of nineteenth-century certainties and the vigor of modernism has come the fragmentation and incoherence of postmodernism. We no longer believe the world is understandable and we have lost confidence in our capacity to understand.

With Delbrück's paradox we have a new opportunity to discard the oppressive myth of genetic determinism with which we have understood our limitations. Are we not meant to understand the theory of relativity? Of course we are! Delbrück's paradox is both freeing and frightening. It is up to us to see what we can do with it.

Delbrück's paradox has implications not only for our conceptions of human mental function, but for research strategies in medicine and biology. When a research framework is limited, the richness of the relationship with the object is lost and critical pieces of experience cannot be made conscious. Over the past two decades, the negative effects of mechanistic research strategies adopted by the majority of our biologists have increasingly become clear. Consider, for example, research into the condition known as autosomal dominant retinitis pigmentosa (ADRP).

Retinitis pigmentosa is an inherited disease of the retina characterized by the progressive degeneration of the photoreceptors or other retinal cells. ADRP is a major human health problem. About one in 4,000 people worldwide is affected. The degeneration of retinal cells is a leading cause of human blindness.

Since retinitis pigmentosa is inherited, researchers have tried to find the mutation(s) associated with the disease. In early 1990, workers at Trinity College in Dublin reported an impressive success in locating a mutation on the short arm of chromosome three in 15 percent to 20 percent of the sufferers of retinitis pigmentosa. The mutation causes the twenty-third amino acid of the opsin protein in the rhodopsin photoreceptor to change from proline to histidine.

But locating the mutution does not lead to treatment. It is not clear whether or not the proline to histidine substitution leads to degeneration of the retinal cells. Nor is it clear what role the proline at position twenty-three plays, since relatively major amino acid changes in the vicinity of position twenty-three have no effect on rod cell functioning. It appears that a knowledge of the genetics of the condition is certainly not sufficient and may not even be necessary for the development of treatment. As one reviewer of the research commented: "Treatment or gene repair are still out of the question, and certainly will not be possible without a better understanding of the cell biology of the retina."

The same is true for sickle cell anemia. In sickle cell anemia an inherited alteration of the hemoglobin molecule changes the shape of the red blood cells, causing them to clump together with ensuing fever, abdominal and joint pains, and damage to bone, lung and brain. A single base change produces a change in the sixth amino acid from glutamic acid to valine in one of the four amino acid chains comprising the hemoglobin molecule. This knowledge has not led to treatment. A reviewer of recent research in the field concluded: "Sickle cell anaemia has always been the paradigm for molecular analysis of genetic disease and the disappointing progress in treating it could be a warning for those studying other diseases."

On a much larger scale, the disappointing War on Cancer in the United States was organized around the premise that the complexities of cancer could be understood by understanding the molecular genetics of certain viruses involved in the transmission of animal tumors. In spite of the fact that epidemiologists in the World Health Organization had shown that as many as 90 percent of all cancers were caused by environmental carcinogens, in 1971 President Richard Nixon made $100 million immediately available to molecular biologists to find a cure for cancer when oncogenes, genes existing in a small class of RNA viruses (retroviruses) whose product helps transform animal cells into tumor cells, were discovered by Peter Duesberg and Peter Vogt.

In the event, the much ballyhooed war yielded little in the way of effective treatment. One-third of Western populations will get cancer. Cancer is still the leading cause of death for people between thirty-five and fifty-four years of age and, after accidents, it is still the leading cause of death for younger people between five years of age and thirty-four years of age. The five-year survival rates for all major cancers have not improved for the past thirty years. The discovery of oncogenes has not provided useful information about the transformation process in common human tumors. Thoughtful researchers are now arguing that a truly effective intervention must concentrate on prevention rather than cure.

And now in the 1990s we may, horribly, be in the midst of an even greater tragic result of a mechanistic approach to medical research. Serious critiques questioning the role of HIV as the causative agent in AIDS have been raised. These critiques are not being heard because we are so very comfortable with a familiar mechanistic explanation of AIDS. Infection by a retrovirus followed by an indeterminate latency of up to ten years leads to a depletion of the T cells of the immune system, opening the way for the onset of a bewildering variety of opportunistic diseases. Three billion dollars have been rushed to the research front to map the genes of the virus and to find a vaccine against it.

The scenario is reassuring, with Louis Pasteur being played not by Paul Muni but by the vast apparatus of the U.S. National Institutes of Health. Find a way to stop the virus and we will have a prevention and cure for AIDS.

But we have not taken the slightest precaution against the possibility that the virus might not cause AIDS. There is a nonzero probability that after the ten years it will take to produce a vaccine, we may find that the vaccine against the virus does not prevent AIDS. (In private, the research community acknowledges that the search for a vaccine is a long shot. The idea is that the human body already produces a powerful antibody response that has no apparent deterrent effect against the later onset of AIDS.) In the meantime, the AIDS research budgets are sewn up tight by committed HIV investigators. A state of affairs has developed where leading researchers at the highest levels of accomplishment cannot get a minority view acted upon because it is much too frightening to acknowledge.

The epidemiological evidence implicating HIV as the causative agent in AIDS is quite convincing. AIDS was recognized as a distinct syndrome in 1981. Two years later HIV was isolated.

The antibody test for HIV showed that HIV was concentrated in the groups most at risk for AIDS, the famous four H's: male homosexuals, heroin users, hemophiliacs, and Haitians. In countries with little HIV there is little AIDS. In countries where HIV is endemic there is a lot of AIDS. The screening of blood banks for HIV reduced the incidence of AIDS in blood-transfusion recipients. And in one anecdotal incident one of a pair of fraternal twins received a unit of HIV-contaminated blood and developed AIDS as did the donor of the blood while its twin and mother did not.

In broad outline, the epidemiological evidence shows reasonably clearly that infection by HIV does accompany AIDS. And if one adds a powerful sociological conjunction—the existence of a community of retroviral researchers left over from the War on Cancer with ample research tools for manipulating retroviruses—it is easy to understand how the HIV hypothesis has become so entrenched in so short a time. As Peter Duesberg, discoverer of the *src* oncogene and a leading member of the community of retrovirologists, describes the construction of the HIV bandwagon:

> The Baltimores, the Weinbergs, the Varmuses, and the Gallos. Temin, even. Essex. Their reputations are based essentially on this view that retroviruses are significant candidates for carcinogenesis. That hasn't panned out. But it explains why there is generally so little criticism of the view that HIV (a retrovirus) causes AIDS. The view pleases all the old veterans of the virus-cancer program. They're all marching again. They used to be, essentially, on reserve. And now all of a sudden, here's a windmill for them again. And they're attacking. So they get their boots, their uniforms, their tanks, and they're all ready to work on retroviruses. That's what they can do. These guys that used to be latent, somewhere in reserve, and now they're marching. The old tune: retroviruses.

The retroviral cause of AIDS has meant big money to the research community. The $3 billion AIDS budget is being spent on basic research in virology, immunology, oncology, neurology, and hemotology as well as clinical studies in pulmonary medicine, dementia, multiple sclerosis, and pharmacology. Just as they did in the War on Cancer, researchers are rejigging their grant applications to get some of the AIDS money now being made available. Indeed, in 1989 the congressional appropriations subcommittee responsible for funding the NIH gave directors of the Institutes the power to shift money slated for AIDS research into other fields at the discretion of the directors. AIDS is helping the research community at the moment far more than the research community is helping the sufferers of the syndrome.

If it were not for the precedent of the War on Cancer where exactly the same device was used to divert cancer research money into basic molecular biological research, the argument might seem forced. But we must realize that the U.S. national budget allocates pittances for science projects in comparison to its support for military projects. So-called mega scientific programs like the Superconducting Supercollider at $8 billion, the Human Genome Project at $3 billion, or the Advanced X-ray Astrophysics Laboratory at $1.6 billion have been justifiably criticized for taking money away from equally interesting smaller projects. But these sums are not large in comparison to the cost of the F-18 fighter at $53 billion, F-16 fighter at $34 billion, or the B-1B bomber at $27.4 billion. The U.S. Department of Defense *Selected Acquisition Reports* for 1989 lists 101 military acquisitions at a total expense of $844 billion, an average of $8.4 billion per acquisition. The average size military project costs more than the Superconducting Supercollider, the most costly scientific instrument ever built.

We have a situation where strong circumstantial epidemiological evidence, a ready and willing research community starved for funds because of overinflated military budgets, and a culture that believes strongly in a mechanistic epistemology have created an overwhelming social consensus that HIV causes AIDS. So massive is this consensus, and so deeply constructed is the social reality on which it rests, that dissenting voices are labeled heretical and dangerous.

Yet the actual evidence in favor of the HIV hypothesis is less secure than the massive consensus would suggest.

By mid-1990 the scientific literature on AIDS had reached 20,000 published technical papers. Of this literature, only five papers were devoted to a serious analysis of the HIV hypothesis. Three were by Peter Duesberg. A fourth paper, a careful thoughtful effort by Yale clinical virologist Alfred S. Evans, addressed the substantial questions raised by Duesberg. The fifth paper was a disappointing analysis by Manfred Eigen, from whom one expects more, containing only a pretentious mathematical analysis of a relatively minor point and an unreflective restatement of the standard view that HIV causes AIDS.

Less scholarly arguments addressing the point were given by William Blattner, Robert Gallo, and Howard Temin, in a debate with Duesberg in the pages of *Science;* by Jonathon Weber in *New Scientist;* by David Baltimore and Mark Feinberg in an editorial in the *New England Journal of Medicine;* and by Robin Weiss and Harold Jaffe in a commentary in *Nature.*

It is not possible after a careful reading of this literature not to have doubts about the certainty with which we have received HIV as the causative factor in AIDS. Basically the argument rests on a conflict between epidemiological and virological evidence. If HIV is the causative agent in AIDS then it has to have peculiar properties, properties that have not been seen in a retrovirus before. In particular, a major mystery in HIV infection is how the virus can cause the loss of billions of T cells when it is latent in less than 1/400 cells, is active in less than 1/10,000 cells, and is present in the relatively low numbers during AIDS of between 10^0 and $10^{4.3}$ per milliliter of blood with an average of $10^{2.3}$ compared to the activity of the virus involved in hepatitis B, for example, where the count reaches 10^{11} to 10^{13}. The pathogenic mechanism of HIV by which HIV is meant to cause T-cell depletion, B-cell elevation, and immobilization of neurons and macrophages is a mystery with no evidence indicating that the virus has the novel properties it must have if it is to do things that it is supposed to do. This is a major problem for research.

What has given the HIV hypothesis its force is the epidemiological evidence, which has been considered to be so strong that mysteries such as the pathogenic mechanism have been regarded as only details. Blattner, Gallo, and Temin cite Duesberg's work on the retroviral *src* oncogene as an example. The expression of the *src* gene in chickens produces sarcomas. However, the mechanism by which the gene product actually causes the sarcoma is unknown.

But it is also increasingly clear that the epidemiological evidence when scrutinized in detail presents a less decisive picture than is frequently drawn. Independent immunosuppressive risk factors coexist with HIV in 95 percent of AIDS cases. These risk factors include infection by other microorganisms, including hepatitis B, herpes, and Epstein-Barr virus; use of recreational drugs such as amyl and butryl nitrites, which have been linked to immunosuppression; chronic use of antibiotics, which causes T-cell depletion through zinc depletion; the presence of semen in the bloodstream, which produces antibodies causing a depletion of T cells by B cells; and the well-documented role of malnutrition in causing immunosuppression.

As yet epidemiological studies have not controlled for these other immunosuppressive risks. For example, there have been no controlled studies of hemophiliacs that follow matched HIV– and HIV+ groups for incidence of the twenty-five diseases that comprise the AIDS syndrome. Similarly the pattern of disease in which male homosexuals get Kaposi's sarcoma, hemophiliacs get pneumonia, and infants get cytomegalovirus has led leading researchers to postulate that cofactors may be necessary to account for the epidemiological patterns.

Once one allows the possibility of other immunosuppressive risks and cofactors, it is possible to reverse the causal chain. One can argue that it is immunosuppression that permits the presence of HIV, not that the presence of HIV produces immunosuppression. Finally, the lack of an adequate animal model for infection by HIV continues to cause doubt in the more prudent-minded.

The point is not that the research into HIV should stop but that alternative approaches have been attacked, ridiculed, marginalized, or ignored to the tune of "Trust us. We know best." As a result funding has been virtually nonexistent for research proposals that do not include HIV in their titles. Little work has been done on the immunosuppressive aspects of infections by other microorganisms. Treatment research has exclusively focused on antiretroviral agents to the exclusion of treatment of the other microorganisms involved in AIDS. And nothing has gone into research into patient care and the development of ways to support both persons with AIDS and their carers.

Peter Duesberg is a classic whistle-blower. As a leading specialist in retroviruses he has gone public with evidence that the case for HIV as the cause of AIDS is not secure. His information is received by a scientifically illiterate public with confusion and distress. It would be best if the government and the scientific establishment were to use the very considerable resources they command from us to investigate Duesberg's argument in a responsible, democratic way. Instead, Duesberg's $500,000 Outstanding Investigator Grant from the U.S. National Institutes of Health has been withdrawn, the producers of a British television documentary airing the Duesberg argument have been brought before the Broadcasting Complaints Commission, and the argument has been forced to the margins of our society.

Coupled to the HIV bandwagon is the disgraceful priority fight between Robert Gallo and Luc Montagnier for identification of the virus. By mid-1991 $20 million in legal fees had been spent, not simply for honor, but for rights to the royalties for the test for the presence of HIV. These royalties could amount to billions of dollars if World Health Organization estimates of forty million infected persons by the year 2000 prove to be accurate.

In the meantime, the pharmaceutical industry is not entirely unhappy with the progress of events. The DNA replication blocker, AZT, costing $2,500 annually, has the property, as Barbara Ehrenreich has pointed out, "of not diminishing the market by actually curing anybody." If the average lifetime of a person on AZT is three years, the potential market for AZT could be a staggering $300 billion.

The only fly in the ointment is the presence of many drug companies wanting to get in on the act. In May 1991, Burroughs-Wellcome Co., which holds exclusive patent rights to AZT, filed a suit in the North Carolina courts to prevent the U.S. Food and Drug Administration from giving Barr Laboratories a license to market a cheaper generic equivalent. To retain its monopoly, Burroughs must refute the argument that federal researchers had played a fundamental part in identifying AZT and as such the patent belongs in the public domain. Such antics on the part of responsible bodies do not inspire confidence that the treatment of AIDS is in the right hands.

Past experience has shown that citizen action is the only way to get the government or the scientific establishment to respond to minority points of view. Occupational health and safety activists learned epidemiology from scratch and went on to create the anti-asbestos campaign that has succeeded in forcing significant changes in the way we handle this exceptionally hazardous material. Activists in the women's liberation movement taught themselves physiology and medicine, wrote a classic of people's science, *Our Bodies, Ourselves,* and went on to challenge successfully standard medical practice on birth, on hysterectomy, and on mastectomy. Gay activists have successfully challenged the psychiatric establishment definition of homosexuality as a disease.

In the case of AIDS, the gay community has responded to the crisis by mobilizing its own resources. The safe-sex campaign, the search for alternative therapies, the psychological support its members have given each other in the face of an appalling disease are models of courageous community organizing. But the gay community is also divided, with many feeling that the scientific establishment has acted in the best progressive traditions of nineteenth-century science in trying to prevent mass panic and the bigoted labeling of the syndrome as a gay disease. This is all to the good. But what of the research strategy itself? In the absence of a unified public campaign led by those most affected by AIDS, all we can do is hope that Duesberg is wrong and the rest of his colleagues are right. Is this good enough?

Recent developments in the field make it appear that hope has not been good enough at all. In September 1991, as this book was going to press, two research groups reported new evidence which, if supported, calls into question the causative role of HIV in AIDS as first questioned by Duesberg. As *Nature* editor John Maddox editorialized: "Professor Peter Duesberg is probably sleeping more easily at night now than for five years, since he first took up the cudgels against the doctrine that AIDS is caused by the retrovirus HIV."

The two studies are complementary. In Hertfordshire in England, researchers led by E. J. Stott were studying vaccines against SIV, the so-called simian immunodeficiency virus, a close analogue of HIV. Their vaccine consisted of inactivated human T-cells that had been infected with SIV. This vaccine seemed promising since it seemed to prevent SIV injected later from entering the cells of macaque monkeys.

In an effort to understand certain anomalies that seemed to accompany the protection, the investigators were led, *for the first time in these vaccine studies,* to use controls. A group of four macaques was inoculated with the inactivated T-cells prepared without SIV. To their astonishment, two of the four animals were subsequently protected against SIV. A vaccine consisting of human T-cells alone was capable of giving protection against the virus. SIV is not necessarily present when SIV^+ antibodies are produced.

In the second study, researchers in British Columbia found a similar result in mouse strains. A preparation of T-cells was taken from one strain of mice and injected into another. This preparation was found to produce antibodies to two proteins found in HIV. Again the presence of HIV was not necessary to produce antibodies against HIV. The investigators conjecture that the viral proteins are structurally similar to proteins associated with T-cells and that AIDS may be an autoimmune disease.

These new results, if verified, would support the arguments of Peter Duesberg and would suggest that the three billion dollar AIDS research program has been at least partially misdirected. Such an outcome should occasion a serious investigation into the conduct of the research community and how we fund it. But even if not confirmed, the present studies illustrate just how rigid our intellectual structures have become.

We have been prepared to be persuaded that AIDS is caused by a microbe because we want to be persuaded. Conditioned by films, by books, by Dr. Marcus Welby, by the celebrated successes of Louis Pasteur, we are reassured by a familiar scenario of microbial cause and effect. Behind the scandal that is the AIDS establishment's inability to engage in a constructive dialogue with a dissident point of view lies Western structures of consciousness, structures which lead us to have stereotyped rather than creative understandings of the world. Our view of physics as a predictive science, our belief in a mythical individually inherited intelligence, and our ready acceptance of a microbial cause of AIDS are stale nineteenth-century views of reality that no longer suit.

Like all great scientific advances, the successes of molecular biology have the potential to be liberating. But the text has to be read carefully. It is not true that molecular biology has reduced life processes to physics and chemistry. Quite the opposite. Molecular biology has shown that the historically formed living objects of biology cannot be understood in the same terms as we understand the nonliving molecules of which they are composed. The fact that this is so is Delbrück's paradox. We now have to absorb this fact of experience into our consciousness so that the next generation will be more liberated from mechanical frameworks of understanding that now serve to impoverish rather than enrich our experience.

CHAPTER 5

Berkeley 1963/Geneva 1984

A student entering physics in the United States in the 1950s would find a field riding high on its wartime achievements of radar and the bomb. Physics was in the public eye. Physicists were asked about their opinions on everything from foreign policy to ESP. Funds were available from Congress for large capital-intensive research projects if one hinted at the wonders of science (the bomb) in one breath and mentioned the Russians in the next. Jobs were easy to get, if not in basic research in the expanding university system or at Bell Laboratories, then in applied work at Hughes Aircraft, U.S. Steel or General Motors or at Livermore and Los Alamos working on thermonuclear weapons. Socially, physics was the glamour subject of the fifties.

Inside the field there was the same heady atmosphere of success. The Einsteins, Ehrenfests, and other doubting Thomases of the quantum theory had been silenced. The maser had been invented. The transistor had revolutionized electronics. Superconductivity was on its way to being understood. Quantum electrodynamics had been made to work. There was new equipment, new techniques, new energy regimes to explore. The possibilities were infinite.

The textbooks through which the new generation was socialized expressed the new triumphalism with an exciting new pedagogy, a pedagogy that turned physics on its head. Postulates and deductions, not observations, were the order of the day. A century of research could be summarized in one equation. The story of the slow, painstaking engagement of the human senses with the structures of the physical world through the construction of ingenious instruments was lost to the deductions of theory. Most students drew the inevitable conclusion: physics comes out of equations. Student laboratories grew tedious, they were too detailed, too canned, not applicable to the same wide variety of situations as was theory. Ideas were the thing, not experiments.

Thus the new generation was taught that special relativity consisted of two postulates: the principle of relativity and the constancy of the velocity of light. Not included in this presentation was the physical content of special relativity—"There are no instantaneous interactions in nature," a far more profound fact to assimilate into human consciousness than two dry postulates. Thus the new generation was taught that the fabulously rich experience of atomic spectra was all contained in the Schroedinger equation. And thus the new generation was taught that spin, Pauli's classically undescribable two-valuedness of the electron, was a consequence of the relativistic Dirac equation. It was all very impressive.

Dirac, perhaps because of his engineering training, was one of the few physicists who remained clear about where things came from. In 1962 Thomas Kuhn, the well-known historian who had gotten a Ph.D. in theoretical physics at the University of Chicago, spoke to Dirac about his life and work. Among other things, Kuhn was interested in how Dirac came to write down his equation for a relativistic electron with spin.

Dirac said: "I was playing around with equations and I found that Pauli's matrices were quite a nice thing to play with. It needed quite an effort to make the further generalization (from 2×2) to 4×4 matrices, but that work did come about from playing about with the three-dimensional scalar product."

Kuhn said: "Was it a surprise that what came out were spin terms?"

Dirac said: "No, I don't think so. Because one had the Pauli matrices in it [to begin with]."

Kuhn had asked the question that had troubled all the graduate students of his era: "Was it a surprise that what came out were spin terms?"

Dirac, a physicist of the previous generation, was taken aback. The spin terms in his equation did not appear like magic. How could they? After all, equations do not wake up one morning, walk into an office, and write themselves down on a piece of paper. The spin terms came out at the end because he himself had put them in at the beginning. ("Pauli's matrices were quite a nice thing to play with.")

What students of the 1950s were not taught was the understanding of James Franck, one of the leading experimentalists of the 1920s: "What one doesn't put into the equation will not finally be given by the mathematics." In its place, students absorbed a theoretical sensibility inspired, not by an attempt to understand, express, and describe, or, in Bohr's word, communicate, real physical experience, but by spectacular deductions from a few well-chosen equations. And if the equations were poorly understood, well, that was the price one paid.

The postwar isolation of physics has produced a distinct new sensibility in physics. In prewar Europe, physics was more than a career. It was a philosophy, an outlook on life, an object of pride and satisfaction, an integral part of the cultural and material achievements of the age. Victor Weisskopf, formerly Pauli's assistant and later director general of CERN, is a physicist of the old school. In a recent birthday celebration volume for a colleague, Weisskopf, instead of contributing the usual scholarly research article, found it amusing to write a piece about why a dinner fork feels cool to the touch while the napkin next to it feels warm.

The basic idea is that even though both are at room temperature the metal fork, a good conductor of heat, conducts heat away from our fingers rapidly giving us a cooling sensation. The paper napkin, a heat insulator, keeps our body heat close to the surface of our fingers, giving us a warming sensation. The question then is, What is it about steel and paper that gives them their widely differing thermal conductivities?

The answer lies in the nature of the heat carriers in the two substances. In metals heat is carried away by quasi-free conduction electrons, the same electrons that conduct the electric current. In insulators heat is carried away by vibrations (phonons) of the atoms in the crystal lattice of the insulator. Electrons carry less heat than phonons. But electrons both travel faster and, on average, fourteen times further than phonons before they make a collision. Thus in general the net effect is that electrons carry away heat much more rapidly than phonons and so metals feel cool while paper feels warm.

An interesting exception is diamond. Diamond, like paper, is a good electrical insulator. But unlike paper it is also a good conductor of heat. Diamonds have a thermal conductivity twice as great as that of copper. Diamonds feel cool to the touch. This fact, coupled with the hardness of diamond, makes it an excellent cutting tool. The heat generated by the cutting process is conducted rapidly away from the cutting site, thus preventing overheating. Diamond has a high heat conductivity because the carbon atoms of diamond are bound exceptionally tightly to each other in its well-known tetrahedral lattice. This tight binding produces the highest atomic density of any substance, making for a large number of heat carriers. And at the same time the tight binding makes it very difficult to displace the carbon atoms from their equilibrium position. Thus the phonon moves right through the crystal in the same way that an electron moves right through the lattice structure of metals. In diamond the long mean free path of the heat carriers makes it a substance with a high thermal conductivity.

This was the physics of the prewar period. The question of a cool fork and a warm napkin became an opportunity for Weisskopf to express his worldview, a view expressing the nineteenth-century sensibility of the wonderful comprehensibility of the world.

Richard Feynman was a physicist of the new school. A whiz kid in the late 1930s, Feynman grew up without having to make the revolutionary changes in consciousness that quantum mechanics required of the physicists of Weisskopf and Pauli's generation. To Feynman, you never understand a new theory; you just get used to it. Here is Feynman lecturing to a popular audience in 1983:

> What I am going to tell you about is what we teach our physics students in the third or fourth year of graduate school—and you think I'm going to explain it to you so you can understand it? No, you're not going to be able to understand it.
>
> Why, then, am I going to bother you with all this? Why are you going to sit here all this time, when you won't be able to understand what I am going to say? It is my task to convince you *not* to turn away because you don't understand it. You see, my physics students don't understand it either. That is because *I* don't understand. Nobody does.

Feynman was referring to the mystery of the quantum mechanical amplitude, which, along with spin and so-called anti-matter, is classically indescribable and still not understood. The physics of the 1950s and of today rests on a foundation whose incomprehensibility has now become an orthodoxy itself. And in fact, the quantum effects in question are very difficult to believe, let alone to understand.

A photomultiplier is a device that is capable of detecting a single photon. Used routinely in experimental physics, the photomultiplier is similar to the light exposure meters in modern cameras. An incident photon strikes an electrode coated with a metal such as cesium that has the property of emitting electrons when exposed to light. In an exposure meter, the brighter the light the greater the number of electrons emitted and the greater the electric current. The electric current is then used to make a needle deflect: the brighter the light, the greater the deflection.

In a photomultiplier, a single photon knocks out a single electron from the photosensitive electrode. The electron is accelerated by a voltage of about one hundred volts and is made to strike a cesium oxide electrode where it knocks out up to ten more electrons. These ten are accelerated and made to strike to another cesium oxide electrode and so on until a multiplying factor of up to 10^9 is obtained. The resulting flow of electrons is then strong enough to be fed into a conventional amplifier and from there to produce an audible click in a loudspeaker.

Single photons are produced whenever a light source is sufficiently faint. The strange effects they produce can be detected with the aid of photomultipliers. The classic experiment is the two-slit interference experiment.

A faint single photon light source is placed about a meter away from an opaque screen ruled with a narrow transparent slit the width of a razor blade edge. About a meter behind the opaque screen is a photomultiplier. The photomultiplier is positioned so that most of the photons that pass through the slit register at the photomultipier a click at a time.

The experimenter then opens a second slit a few millimeters from the first slit. The clicks stop! No photons now reach the photomultipier. Once the photon has two different ways to reach the photomultipier the two ways can in effect cancel each other out. This is the effect known as quantum interference. It is the fundamental mystery of quantum mechanics.

The distance between the slits can be varied. One then finds that the counting rate varies from zero up to four (!) times the rate produced by a single slit. The addition of a second slit can thus reduce the rate to zero, an effect called destructive interference; or it can quadruple the rate, an effect called constructive interference. All particles, not just photons, display exactly the same interference effects. We do not understand how the interference works.

The mystery deepens because the mathematical model describing quantum interference effects is almost identical to the mathematical framework describing the motion of waves. A wave striking two slits emerges on the other side of the screen as two waves, which, like the effect of dropping two pebbles in a pond, can then interfere with each other, giving an intensity of between zero and four times the intensity of a single wave at a given point.

The problem with a wave model of quantum interference is that nothing is waving. The photon or electron or proton or U-238 nucleus is a particle. Particles do not split into two when they reach the slits. They either go through one slit or they go through the other slit. It is very difficult to understand how a particle can interfere with itself. So instead of understanding the effect, one says that the particle has an amplitude for going through one slit and another amplitude for going through the other. Because they have different phases, the two amplitudes can interfere with each other, giving the actually observed distribution of particles on the far side of the screen. But although we can represent the interference mathematically through the use of the quantum amplitude, we do not understand what is interfering with what. In short, we do not understand the phase relationships that are at the heart of our description of the quantum behavior of matter.

Relativity and quantum mechanics are often described in the same breath as being the basis of modern physics. The pairing is mistaken. Relativity was the consolidation of the experience of electricity gained in the nineteenth century. It is thoroughly classical in its epistemology and at bottom not the least bit mysterious. Anyone can understand the statement that there are no instantaneous interactions at a distance in nature, that every physical effect takes time to make itself felt when acting over a distance.

What is difficult in relativity is accepting the *fact* of the existence of this maximum speed. It contradicts, and not without making us feel anxious, our everyday experience of motion. But there is nothing particularly mysterious about the existence of a maximum speed, just as there is nothing particularly mysterious about the existence of the giraffe. Both are strange-but-true features of the physical world. With enough exposure one gets used to them.

The quantum amplitude, however, is a different kettle of fish. Here we genuinely do not know what we are talking about. We have invented a mathematical script, a set of rules that tell us what to do. But we do not understand the text that we ourselves have written. It is not true that you never understand a new theory, you just get used to it. The reverse is true. You only get used to a new theory when you understand it. The initiates have gotten used to relativity—no instantaneous interactions at a distance—precisely because we understand it. But no one has really gotten used to quantum mechanics. In spite of the determined effort to teach students to put aside their doubts and get on with the task of becoming quantum literate, there is an active if marginalized subcommunity in physics still trying to make sense of quantum effects three generations after the invention of the quantum amplitude.

* * *

The students of the 1950s learned that physics comes out of equations because no deeper understanding had been produced. Ehrenfest's desperate request for clarification about the conceptual problems of quantum mechanics, published shortly before his suicide in the autumn of 1933, questioned the fundamental role of the quantum amplitude, questioned its interpretation as a matter wave—what was waving?—and asked for a clarification, "in a form intelligible to us older physicists," of the new spinor calculus used to deal with the spin of the electron. But the *Klugscheisser,* the calculational experts of the new physics, had little time for Ehrenfest. And the lack of understanding that contributed to Ehrenfest's suicide in the autumn of 1933 became a major feature of postwar theoretical physics.

The irreversible ticking of social processes that is the march of time precludes any simple longing for the virtues of the past. Yet it must be recognized that theoretical physics has suffered the loss of a wider cultural perspective since the 1920s. A sensibility of restricted problem-solving has emerged as the dominant motivation in the work. Feynman's recipe for treating antiparticles as particles moving backwards in time leads to wonderfully accurate computational results. But when we see a giant six-foot-long bubble chamber track of an antiproton we cannot say that we understand what such a metaphor means. The ongoing challenge to our understanding offered by our direct experience of real matter has been met by a technocratic approach that seeks the solution to problems rather than the understanding of the world.

In the 1950s, in a context where the triumphs of understanding enjoyed by the physicists of the nineteenth century were viewed as relics of a physics past, physicists and their graduate students turned to the hottest question in physics—how to account for the multitude of elementary particles that were appearing in cosmic rays and the new particle accelerators?

At sufficiently high bombarding energies, families of entirely new short-lived particles—the pi mesons, the sigmas, the lambda, the K particles, the xi particles—emerged from a collision with a single proton. The community was divided on how to proceed.

Procedures devised in 1949 separately by Richard Feynman,

Julian Schwinger, and Shintiro Tomonaga had turned quantum field theory, a so-so model of point-like electrons interacting through the exchange of photons into a theory of impressive calculating power. Inspired by the success of the new procedures, many theorists set about trying to construct a similar theory for nuclear forces.

Other leading physicists argued that quantum field theory was merely a post hoc computational prescription with no hope of being applied successfully to nuclear forces. The main problem lay in the existence of amplitudes for the point electron to emit and reabsorb a photon at the same point. For these amplitudes, the calculational rules gave a result containing a numerator divided by zero. In such cases, one said that the calculation blew up.

The procedure invented by Feynman, Schwinger, and Tomonaga showed that the amplitudes which blew up could be simply *assigned* numerical values. This post hoc procedure was the unacceptable face of quantum field theory to the physicists of the 1950s. Even the inventors did not like it. Feynman called it "nutty." And Schwinger was writing that the problems of quantum field theory would not be resolved "until physical science has met the heroic challenge to comprehend the structure of the submicroscopic world that nuclear exploration has revealed."

For those who regarded quantum field theory as a mere stopgap, the S-matrix or bootstrap approach championed by the schools of Geoffrey Chew in Berkeley and Lev Landau in Moscow offered an attractive alternative. In the Chew/Landau approach there were no point particles. Instead there was the principle of "nuclear democracy." All particles were to be considered as composites of all the others.

One formed a picture of the S-matrix as a surface of infinite extent in which there were certain mathematically well-defined holes, each hole corresponding to a particle. The U-238 nucleus, the proton, the pi meson were then equally fundamental: they were just located on different parts of the S-matrix surface. No one particle or family of particles was more fundamental than any of the others.

There was an appealing raw truth to the S-matrix representation: collision between any initial pair of particles could, at sufficiently high energy, yield any of the remaining particles in the spectrum. In a grain of sand ye shall find the world.

By 1963 the possibility of doing away with the concept of an elementary point particle and replacing it with an interconnected, mutually determining unity was real. Dissatisfaction with field theoretic ideas and the existence of an intriguing alternative drew in many theorists for a look around. Yet while the theoretical community was able to find ingenious little solutions to keep quantum field theory alive, it did not find the time to find similar solutions to the problems posed by the S-matrix. For a complex of reasons the majority of particle theorists did not find it congenial to devote their considerable abilities to creating a new theory. They chose instead the more limited exercise of attempting to apply an existing intellectual framework to the new experience of matter represented by the particle physics zoo.

Today we have as our theory of nuclear matter the quark model proposed by Murray Gell-Mann in 1964. Present orthodoxy holds that all matter can be understood in terms of the interactions between three pairs of quarks and three pairs of so-called leptons (the electron is a lepton). There is an electromagnetic interaction due to the fact that the quarks and three of the leptons carry electric charge. There is a quark-quark interaction responsible for holding the atomic nucleus together. And there is a quark-lepton interaction responsible for the beta ray radioactivity discovered by Rutherford in 1898.

The interactions are meant to occur by the exchange of a further twelve particles: the familiar photon (the electromagnetic field) responsible for the interaction between electric charges; eight so-called gluons responsible for the quark-quark interaction; and the famous W^+, W^-, and Z^0 particles discovered in 1984 in Geneva, held to be responsible for the quark-lepton interaction.

But in spite of the exotic mysterious-sounding language—quarks, leptons, gluons, strangeness, charm—there is not much really new in the quark theory. The present consensus about the structure of nuclear matter is based on ideas originating in the 1920s and 1930s.

* * *

When James Chadwick identified the neutron as a constituent of the atomic nucleus in 1932 it was immediately clear that the nuclear force was different from electromagnetism. Neutrons, which are electrically neutral, must enter into some kind of attractive interaction with other protons and neutrons in the nucleus in order to overcome the electrostatic repulsion of the positively charged protons. The game, still going on after half a century, has been to try to understand the nuclear force.

The physics of actually existing nuclei has long since been abandoned as being too complicated by those seeking a simple explanation of the nuclear force. Nevertheless, nuclear physics consists of a fascinating body of information about the approximately 1,500 stable and unstable nuclei formed by protons and neutrons. Some basic facts from this wealth of experience are useful to know.

The simplest compound nucleus, the deuteron, consists of a neutron and proton bound together with the relatively weak binding energy of 2.2 MeV. A uranium-238 nucleus, the heaviest naturally occurring nuclide, consists of 92 protons and 146 neutrons with an overall binding energy of about 200 MeV.

Nuclei having ninety-two protons but differing numbers of neutrons are called isotopes of uranium. Uranium has fourteen isotopes. All of them are unstable. Their half-lives range from 1.3 minutes for uranium-227 with 135 neutrons up to 4.51 billion years for uranium-238 with 146 neutrons.

Unstable nuclei decay at random: each individual nucleus has a constant probability, λ, of decaying each second. The more frequently quoted number used to describe unstable nuclei is the half-life, $T_{\frac{1}{2}}$. This is the time it takes for half a sample of radioactive atoms to decay. The relationship between the decay probability and the half life is $\lambda = .633/T_{\frac{1}{2}}$.

Radioactive dating is a pretty little application of nuclear physics. A uranium-238 nucleus decays by successive alpha particle emissions to a final stable daughter nucleus, lead-206. After the solidification of uranium deposits in the earth's crust, the lead nuclei from the decays of uranium-238 become trapped among the uranium deposits. Billions of years later, a simultaneous assay of the amount of lead and the amount of uranium in a sample serves as a clock. A rock consisting of half lead-206 and half uranium-238 would be 4.51 billion years old, since it would take that long for half the uranium in the original sample to decay into lead. In 1907 Boltwood published the results of a uranium-lead dating study that gave ages of various minerals of between 0.41 and 2.2 billion years old. Boltwood's study confirmed the important result that the earth had a long history, longer even than suggested by previous evidence from geological formations.

The hazard of radioactivity arises from the disruption of a biological cell by the passage of a high-energy electron, alpha particle, neutron, or gamma ray. Cellular molecules are bound together with energies no greater than 20 electron volts (eV) while a radioactively emitted electron or alpha typically has energies 100,000 times greater. All radioactivity is harmful. A whole-body dose of 10 mSv to a population produces 120 deaths per year per million persons. In Britain, the annual background radiation of 1 mSv from rocks and cosmic rays produces an estimated 700 cancer deaths each year.

The most controversial nuclide is plutonium-239. Uranium-fueled nuclear reactors will produce between two and three kilograms of plutonium-239 during their lifetimes. A uranium-238 nucleus in the fuel rods absorbs a neutron from the intense neutron fluxes produced by fission. The newly formed uranium-239 nucleus ($T_{\frac{1}{2}}$ = 23.5 minutes) then undergoes beta decay to neptunium-239. The neptunium-239 nucleus ($T_{\frac{1}{2}}$ = 2.3 days) undergoes another beta decay to the relatively long-lived plutonium-239 nucleus of half-life 24,400 years.

The plutonium-239 atoms can be recovered by reprocessing the spent fuel rods, an attractive proposition in some quarters since plutonium-239 has a fission cross section 25 percent higher than that of uranium-235, making it an ideal substance for fission bombs or for fuel for future reactors. Plutonium, when it is recovered from spent uranium fuel rods, has a silvery appearance that turns to a yellow tarnish on exposure to air. A large piece is warm to the touch because of its emission of high-energy alphas. A still larger piece releases so much energy that it can boil water. The *Handbook of Chemistry and Physics* advises that precautions must be taken against a piece or pieces of plutonium going critical. World production of plutonium is about 20,000 kilograms per year. In 1985 approximately 300,000 kilograms had been accumulated worldwide. There is an international black market in plutonium.

Plutonium is an exceptionally hazardous alpha emitter. This fact is not always discussed honestly by atomic energy establishments in Europe and in the United States. Industry spokesmen will often tell the public that alpha emitters constitute no great hazard since they cannot even penetrate clothing. This is true. The doubly charged alpha loses its energy very rapidly in its passage through any form of matter. Most alpha radiation can be stopped by a piece of paper. The primary hazard of plutonium is not external but internal. When it is ingested or inhaled into the body the alpha particles emitted by plutonium now deposit their energy into body tissues rather than into paper, giving a strong absorbed dose, a fact often dealt with by official spokesmen by averaging an inhaled dose over the entire body. Such a procedure is not reasonable. In cases of inhaled plutonium-contaminated dust, the radioactivity is confined to small areas of the lungs. A two-microgram fleck of plutonium-239 can cause lung cancer in ten years. To say that the radioactivity is distributed evenly over the whole body underestimates the hazard and misleads the public, a practice that is all too frequent in the United States and Europe.

The nuclear force is now explained by the quark model, whose main physical idea, the idea of particle exchange, was developed in 1935 by Hideki Yukawa in Tokyo. Yukawa proposed that the newly discovered nuclear force might be understood by analogy to the molecular bond. In the simplest molecule (a singly ionized hydrogen molecule), two protons and an electron form a stable configuration. The negatively charged electron is simultaneously attracted to both positively charged protons. The electron serves as a glue, shuttling back and forth between the two protons and in so doing effectively binding the two protons together.

When an additional electron is present so that two electrons shuttle back and forth, one has the famous covalent chemical bond first elucidated by Linus Pauling in 1931. The primary structure of all molecules, from the simple hydrogen molecule to phage T4 DNA of molecular weight 120 million, to human chromosomal

DNA of molecular weight 80 billion, is held together by pairs of electrons shuttling back and forth between positively charged nuclei.

Yukawa's idea was that a proton and neutron could be bound together by the exchange of a previously undiscovered particle. The short range of the nuclear force indicated that the mass of the exchanged particle should be about two hundred times that of the electron. In 1947 the suggested particle, the pi meson, was found in photographic emulsions that had been exposed to cosmic rays by the Bristol group, led by Cecil Powell.

The problems with implementing the idea of particle exchange as the underlying mechanism of the nuclear force were many. Two secondary ideas were needed to develop the quark model. The first was a way to group the many observed particles.

The lack of a creative response to Pauli's challenging "un-understandable" two-valued electron resulted in an acceptance of the electron as having an abstract quantum number called spin. It then followed that if an electron had spin, why could there not be other abstract quantum numbers?

Isotopic spin was proposed by Heisenberg in 1932 shortly after Chadwick's discovery of the neutron. In analogy to ordinary spin in which an electron could occupy two states in a magnetic field, isotopic spin would manifest itself also as a two-valued orientation but this time of an abstract particle, a nucleon, in an abstract isospin space. In this abstract space the nucleon could occupy one of two states. One state was the proton. The other was the neutron. Generalized in the 1960s to include quarks, symmetry in abstract spaces is an established part of the present particle picture. But we do not have a physical interpretation of the abstract spaces that the particle multiplets are meant to occupy. We do not know what isotopic spin space means. One could say that it is a generalization of the concept of electric charge. But such a statement does not increase our comprehension. Isotopic spin is a mathematical device created in analogy to ordinary spin that quite magically has been useful.

Finally, to complete the picture of the basic elements of the quark model there is the role played by so-called gauge invariance, a bit of mathematical hocus-pocus unearthed by Hermann Weyl in 1919.

In 1954, amid the plethora of exotic new particles turning up in cosmic rays and at the accelerators, the young theorist C. N. Yang cast about for some general principle that could describe their interaction. The problem with Yukawa's concept of particle exchange was that with so many particles there were many kinds of possible exchanges: any particle could be exchanged between any pair of other particles. Was there a way that the form of the interaction could be deduced from some general principle? Yang found a possible answer in Weyl's principle of gauge invariance.

In the aftermath of Einstein's success in creating a geometric theory of gravity, Weyl was one of several mathematicians who tried to see if electricity and magnetism could also be given a geometric interpretation. (Einstein, of course, worked hard on this problem of creating a unified geometric theory of electricity and gravity.) A property of the curved space of the general theory of relativity was that the angle between two vectors changed as one vector was displaced parallel to itself through space. Weyl's idea was to see what would happen if not only the angle of the vector changed, but the length of the vector changed as well.

Weyl sought to identify this change of length or gauge as being due to the presence of electromagnetic interactions. The idea did not work. But in the process of developing it, Weyl discovered a remarkable mathematical fact: requiring that the gauge *not* change in the equations of motion of an electron was equivalent to putting in the correct electromagnetic interaction between electrons into the equations "by hand."

Gauge invariance as discovered by Weyl was a complex way to rewrite the well-known electromagnetic interaction. Such complexity has its attractions. Currently, for example, the French sociologist Pierre Bourdieu sends us coded messages about everyday life in a complex language that has a similar appeal.

> It is clear that critical discourses and displays can break the doxio relation to the social world which is the effect of correspondence between objective structures and personally inter-

> nalised structures only insofar as they objectively encounter a critical state able by its own logic to disconcert the pre-perceptual anticipations and expectations which form the basis of ahistorical continuity of the perceptions and actions of common sense.

With the help of David Lodge we translate this "dense undergrowth of lexical abstraction and trailing tendrils of syntactical subordination" as meaning: "Genuinely original critical thinking is possible only in a revolutionary climate such as *les événements* in France in May 1968."

Many find abstract language such as this appealing because it expresses commonplace ideas in a weird poetry that gives them an aura of importance and profundity. The rest of us can admire the linguistic skill necessary to create these effects while at the same time feeling irritated at the incomprehensibility of the result.

The same process was at work in the revival of gauge invariance. As Yang later expressed it: "The idea was beautiful."

Yang was attracted to gauge invariance because it was a principle that expressed the commonplace idea of particle exchange in a language that gave it an aura of great generality. Instead of crassly writing down expressions for the nuclear force that involved the exchange of various particles, Yang postulated instead that the equations of motion of the nucleon should be gauge invariant. It looked good. And it sounded good. There was only one hitch. The exchanged particle of such a theory would have to have zero mass and there was no nuclear particle with zero mass. Nevertheless, many found the idea beautiful, and over the next twenty years those who were attracted to it tried very hard to get the scheme to work. Most workers in the field would say they have been successful.

The route to the present quark theory has been characterized by technical virtuosity, mathematical obscurantism, and a succession of brilliant conceits. Thus when three identical quarks could not be combined as they needed to be to produce the Ω^- particle because of Pauli's well-accepted exclusion principle, the concept of color charge was introduced to make the quarks distinguishable: each of the six quarks now comes in one of three different so-called colors. When as mentioned above gauge invariance seemed to permit only the existence of massless exchanged particles, the Higgs mechanism was invented to give massless gauge particles mass. When a decay of the K^- meson was found to be twenty times less frequent than an analogous decay of the π^- meson the u quark was given a small amplitude to transform into an s quark to account for it. And when this small amplitude permitted too large a rate for a decay of the K^+ meson, a way was found to cancel this unobserved effect by introducing a fourth quark called charm, which subsequently—to the amazement of all—made its presence felt with the observation the J/psi resonance. When it appeared that the quarks did not exist as free particles, sophisticated schemes of quark confinement were introduced to explain why this should be so. And in one of the most astonishing miracles of all, the treatment of the electromagnetic and quark-lepton interaction together in the same gauge invariant formalism produced an amazing cancellation of two infinite amplitudes that had plagued each theory separately. The result is a contrived intellectual structure, more an assembly of successful explanatory tricks and gadgets that its most ardent supporters call miraculous than a coherently expressed understanding of experience.

Many physicists will say this is a churlish appraisal. Look at the reduction in numbers of basic constituents—from over four hundred to twenty-four. Look at the evidence for quarks in deep inelastic scattering. Look at the discovery of the charmed mesons, predicted by the theory on the basis of the analysis of the decay of K^+ into π^+ plus leptons. And finally look at the discovery of the W and Z mesons with exactly the right masses predicted by the theory.

All this is true. But the physics community has become too habituated, too resigned, to its lack of understanding. The quark model is seen as *predicting* the existence of the W's and Z. Forgotten in the postwar transformation of physics from a culture of understanding to a culture of explanation is James Franck's admonition from the 1920s: "What one doesn't put into the equation will not finally be given by the mathematics." Physicists have lost the motivation to work out what they have put into the equations in the beginning that gives whatever results of value that come out at the end. Equations cannot make predictions. They can only express relationships. Maxwell's equations are a case in point.

After suitable manipulation, these give a simple formula for the velocity, *c*, of electromagnetic waves $c^2 = k_e/k_m$ where k_e is the measured strength of the electrostatic force between two charges and k_m is the measured strength of the magnetic force between two wires carrying an electric current. The value of c computed from this formula comes out to be equal to the measured velocity of light.

Frequently one finds this result presented as a prediction of the equations. But the question for physics really is: How do we understand the relationship between the velocity of light and the strength of electric and magnetic forces? How did the velocity of light get into Maxwell's equations in the first place?

The magnetic force between wires carrying electric currents is quite small. Each wire has a current of negatively charged electrons flowing past positively charged atoms. The whole system is very nearly electrically neutral. Hence there is very nearly zero net force. But because the electric force takes time to propagate between the wires, it can be shown that the charge density of the moving electrons as experienced by the stationary atoms in the neighboring wire is increased ever so slightly by factors containing the now familiar expression $(1 - v^2/c^2)^{-\frac{1}{2}}$ where v is the velocity of the electrons. The tiny residual electrical attraction that results is what we call magnetism.

A calculation of the strength of the residual force gives the formula $k_m = c^2/k_e$, exactly the same result derived from Maxwell's equations. The velocity of light got into Maxwell's equations buried in Ampere's Law (1820), the empirical relationship that expressed the force between current-carrying wires. A measurement of the strength of the magnetic force is really a measurement of the velocity of light, the speed of transmission of the electric force.

A similar situation exists with the quark model. The equations of the quark model yield a relationship between the masses of the W and Z, the strength of the electromagnetic force, the decay rate of the neutron, and the rate of certain lepton-proton interactions. The question for physics is how to understand this relationship. At present it is understood entirely within the framework of gauge invariant quantum field theories with all the difficulties of comprehension that these theories entail. Is there another way to understand this relationship? The answer depends entirely on the motivation (extremely low) of the physics community to look for one. Physicists have sold their birthright for a mess of pottage.

Today we have the same unresolved problems in the foundation of quantum mechanics that plagued Ehrenfest in 1933: The meaning of the quantum amplitude, the meaning of matter waves, and the origin of spin. In contrast with the classical physics of Newton, Maxwell, and Einstein we do not understand the physical content of the equations with which we can calculate so glibly.

In addition, we have numerous unresolved difficulties with the quark model itself. We do not understand why there are three different kinds of charged leptons. We do not understand why each charged lepton has its very own neutrino. We do not understand the origin of the abstract quantum numbers that characterize the strange, charmed, top and bottom quarks. And there is the crazy Higgs mechanism still to be checked out.

The response of particle theorists to the shortcomings of the quark model has been to flee to the greener pastures of superstring theory. Superstring, dubbed by its advocates a theory of everything, promises to unite quantum mechanics, gravity, electromagnetism, and nuclear physics into a grand theoretical scheme situated in a ten-dimensional space where the extra dimensions fold up, by a process called spontaneous compactification, on a scale so small that the folding can never be observed. The wealth of experience of matter that has been built up in the postwar period has been steadily excluded from theory until with superstring we have the logical conclusion: a theory that explains everything which cannot be tested by experiment. Max Delbrück has commented on the process with his usual bite: "One might characterize the physical sciences as those for which explicit connection to actual experience constitutes an annoying constraint from which they are trying to liberate themselves more and more."

The tradition in physics of developing new mathematical forms with which to express new understandings—of Newton developing calculus to express accelerated motion, of Einstein realizing that he needed differential geometry to express gravity as a geometric property of space-time, of Heisenberg reinventing matrix multiplication to express transitions between energy levels in the atom—has been lost in the present period. Theorists no longer use mathematics to express what they have understood. And indeed, not much has been understood.

Instead mathematical experimentation sets the tone for theory. The spirit of "assume A and look! B" has been slowly absorbed by the three generations of physicists since the 1920s. Once one believes that spin is a consequence of the Dirac equation, it is only a short step to try to make physics out of the the thin air of mathematical guesswork.

The patterns of thinking that now dominate theoretical physics approach the classic definition of autistic thinking: thought that is determined solely by the subject's wishes and fantasies without reference to the environment or to realistic considerations of space and time.

Why has it come out this way? What is the confluence of factors that has produced a collective autism in that part of our community to whom we have traditionally looked for the most rigorous standards of understanding of the real world?

The rise and dominance of autistic thinking in physics, thinking that is separated from the realities of space-time, has been possible in large part because of an extreme division of labor that has made incompatible specialties out of experimental and theoretical physics. The division of labor in physics between experiment and theory, a division that, of all the sciences, physics alone has developed, is a leading cause and a leading symptom of its intellectual decline.

An outcome of industrialization and the concomitant growth of physics was the emergence of theoretical physics as a separate and dominant specialty. In the years after World War II the domination of theoreticians over experimentalists has become so pronounced that it is difficult to believe that the subject was not always divided in this way.

Max Planck (1858–1947) was our first true theoretical physicist. Planck, the son of the professor of civil law at the University of Kiel, was raised in the tradition of *Bildung*, the nineteenth-century German high culture of music, art, and science. In 1888, at age thirty, Planck was appointed to the directorship of the Institute of Theoretical Physics that was created specially for him. Planck was not a practical man. As Einstein later remarked about Planck's attitude to the Nazis: "You always have to prove to Planck that some acts of Hitler are not in agreement with Kant. If you prove to him this he will say, "All right, that proves it.'"

In the late Victorian period Planck was an unusual physicist. Physics then was like biology today, with theorists being objects of scorn for their lack of contact with experimental realities. Other physicists from the period who today are known for their theoretical work were skilled experimenters. Gustav Kirchoff (1824–1887) is known now for his theoretical contributions to heat radiation and the analysis of electrical circuits and not for his experimental work with George Bunsen on optical spectra. Maxwell, famous today for his partial differential equations of the electromagnetic field, was professor of *experimental* physics at Cambridge. H. A. Lorentz, the first theoretical physicist in Holland, was an active experimentalist doing work in optical spectra. Max Born, one of the leading pioneers of quantum theory, was an expert in experimental physical optics. And Einstein, known as the foremost theoretician of all time, was experienced in laboratory techniques and interested in technology. With the Habicht brothers he patented a precision volt meter in 1914. In the 1920s, in collaboration with aerodynamicist Rudolf Goldschmidt, he invented a hearing aid. With the Dutch firm N.V. Nederlandsche Technische Handelsmaatschappy he held a patent for a gyrocompass. And with Leo Szilard he patented several refrigerating devices designed to reduce the noise levels of existing commercial machines.

But today the physics community is deeply divided between the theorists and the experimenters. The theoreticians, the pencil-and-paper workers, create the ideas. The experimentalists put in the hours in the laboratories and at the accelerators producing the facts. In a maturation of the trends of the 1920s, the experimentalists now serve as adjuncts to test the ideas of the theorists. The two groups are widely separated in training and sensibility, and share few of each other's skills.

Experimentalists work longer hours, are required to be separated from their families in order to gather data at distant accelerators, and develop particular practical skills rather than a general knowledge of the field. Theorists work more conventional academic hours, travel at their leisure to conferences and summer schools, and are the guardians of the intellectual culture of physics. At the universities experimentalists teach the undergraduate courses. Theorists teach the more advanced graduate courses. Experimentalists cannot understand the mathematized jargon of the theoretical papers. Theorists do not need to understand the practical details of the experimental reports. Experimentalists dart out into the corridors of their laboratories to corner the visiting theorist for suggestions for good things to work on. The subtle little analyses of spin and other quantum numbers reported in experimental papers frequently are ghosted by theorists who find this work easier to do.

This two-class system, theorists at the center, experimentalists circling around them on the outside, has its defenders. We have our secrets, they have theirs, says one experimentalist of the old school. But in fact the disproportionate power to shape the field held by the theorists is resented, albeit resignedly, by most experimentalists.

Sensitive theoreticians have been careful to soothe ruffled feathers by making it a point to acknowledge the role played by experimental work. A recent textbook concentrating on theoretical developments is dedicated to the experimentalists, "the men and women who create the accelerators, the detectors and the experiments from which the concepts of particle physics spring."

Although these words are a much-needed acknowledgment of the fundamental source of physics in observation, they nevertheless confirm the existence of inequality. Their unavoidably patronizing connotations are reminiscent of the dedications made by male professionals of all kinds to their wives and secretaries. Within the field it is the theorists who make physics out of the observations while the experimentalists struggle to get sophisticated apparatus to work accurately and reliably.

The potentially explosive tensions caused by the inequality between experimental and theoretical physicists are kept within bounds by an exceptionally strong belief in inherited intelligence.

Experimental physicists accept second-class status because they feel they are not as bright as theorists. Theorists take their superior position for granted as due recognition of superior intelligence. Physics meetings are famous for their stilted, tense atmospheres as each person is afraid of asking a "stupid" question. Even informal contacts can be dominated by a competitive proving of who understands more of the subject under discussion.

In the context of such a sharply defined and highly defended division of labor, it has proved difficult for experimentalists to constitute the informed critical audience for theory that they should. James Chadwick discovered the neutron in 1932 with his own accelerator consisting of a radium solution deposited on a small silver disk. He built his own detector using a vacuum pump, a cheap amplifier, and a moving-pen recorder. He did his own theoretical analysis. The whole experiment could be assembled, calibrated, run, and analyzed in a few weeks.

This is no longer the case. The construction of the UA1 detector at CERN, which provided the evidence for the existence of the W meson in 1984, took four years in planning and design and involved 134 physicists from twelve different institutions. Special plastic had to be designed for the scintillators, a task subcontracted to a Belgian manufacturer of raincoats. The entire detector was built on the largest railway flatbed car in Europe. The participating groups inspected over a million events in order to produce five candidates for the W particle. And this is just the effort it took to construct the detector. Not mentioned is the accelerator, CERN's superproton synchrotron making a major claim on the research budgets of fourteen contributing European nations, and the colliding proton/antiproton beams necessary to reach the energy threshold for W production.

The change in scale of experimental physics as Chadwick's tiny half-inch-long ionization chamber has grown into the giant thirty-foot-high UA1 detector has inevitably been accompanied by a change in consciousness. Experimental physicists can no longer have the thrill of constructing relatively simple apparatuses with which they can make intimate contact with the structures of the physical world. Leon Lederman, a senior figure in experimental high-energy physics, was taught experimental physics in the immediate postwar period at Columbia University. His teacher was Gilberto Bernardini, a leader of the prewar Italian cosmic ray physicists. As Lederman recalls, Bernardini had a passionate response to direct observation. "Gilberto got hysterical when he saw [those] pulses," said Lederman, describing Bernardini's response to the passage of a cosmic ray through a newly constructed scintillation counter.

The key to experimental particle physics today is not a passion for observation but the skill to plan and coordinate the labor of many individuals over the three or more years it takes to construct and assemble the components that make up a modern multimillion-dollar particle detector. Bernardini's romantic sensibility, so characteristic of the excitement of prewar physics, has been forced to give way to a new sensibility, a high-pressure technical proficiency distanced from the final uses of the machine. The 1984 Nobel Prize, given to Carlo Rubbia and Simon van der Meer for organizing the design and construction of the UA1 detector and the proton/antiproton colliding beam that led to the detection of the W and Z particles, is appropriate. As organizers and coordinators of labor of the many essential workers on the detector and the beam, it is they who constituted the leadership for which the prize is given.

But a price has been paid. The increase in the size of the experimental enterprise has accelerated the division of labor within particle physics to the point where the job of interpreting and understanding observational experience has now been entirely taken over by the theorists.

As a result theorists have become an elite within an elite with little or no accountability to an outside audience. There is the occasional theoretical briefing "to the experimentalists," but in the main theoreticians have, not unnaturally, become ingrown in their approach to physics. Experimentalists, their natural critical audience, are too busy with apparatus and data analysis to do more than shake their heads at the latest theoretical constructs.

Theoretical physics, the physics that is charged with creating a human understanding of new physical experience, cannot be creative under such conditions. Postwar theorists have been unable to generate new physical insight about nature because they are much too cut off from direct contact with the physical world. Achievement at the highest levels of science is not possible without a deep relationship to nature that can permit human unconscious processes—the intuition of the artist—to begin to operate.

Here is Fermi, the last physicist to feel at home equally in theory and experiment, describing his process of discovering the single most important property of neutrons, their exceptionally high reactivity when they are moving very slowly.

> I will tell you how I came to make the discovery which I suppose is the most important one I have made. We were working very hard on the neutron-induced radioactivity and the results we were obtaining made no sense. One day, as I came into the laboratory, it occurred to me that I should examine the effect of placing a piece of lead before the incident neutrons. Instead of my usual custom, I took great pains to have the piece of lead precisely machined. I was clearly dissatisfied with something. I tried every excuse to postpone putting the piece of lead in its place. When finally, with some reluctance, I was going to put it in its place, I said to myself: "No, I do not want this piece of lead here; what I want is a piece of paraffin." It was just like that with no advance warning, no conscious prior reasoning. I immediately took some odd piece of paraffin and placed it where the lead was to have been.

Human insight is the process whereby unconscious perceptual experience is consolidated and raised to conscious understanding. Through a series of unconsciously absorbed perceptual cues Fermi knew that he wanted something light, not something heavy, to produce the desired effect. The act of inserting paraffin instead of lead was his conscious realization of this knowledge.

Theorists today are so divorced from real experience of nature they have no unconsciously absorbed perceptual knowledge to draw upon. Everything they know has been learned from books. And the understandings based on this secondhand knowledge have inevitably been derivative and second-rate.

The proposal to build the $8 billion Superconducting Supercollider expresses, not a new adventure, but an escape from the difficulties of understanding present experience. The SSC is the latest manifestation of the flight begun fifty years ago from engagement with real experience of the physical world.

Beginning with quantum mechanics, physicists have left a mass of unsolved problems behind them in pursuit of an *a priori* vision of what a simple world would look like. The unresolved problems of quantum mechanics were left for the excitement of the then new nuclear physics. The unfolding complexities of nuclear physics were left for the excitement of particle physics. When particle physics produced an embarrassingly rich body of experience, the particle zoo was left for the presumed simplicities of quark physics. And now, physicists prepare to leave behind the manifest unresolved problems of the quark model in favor of exploring a brand-new energy regime.

Each step has represented an abandonment of real experience. Rather than trying to understand the world as it presents itself to us through our instruments, physicists have been attempting to find a corner of nature where their prejudices can be confirmed. Rather than engaging new experience body and soul, physicists have let themselves get hemmed in by problematic frameworks of past understandings as being the only possible understandings. What has worked in the past must work in the present. Otherwise we face a void in understanding, a void that the post-war theoreticians have done their very utmost to avoid confronting.

Physics has been in trouble since the 1920s. It has grown, yes, its growth marked by a tenfold increase in the number of practicing physicists, by a hundredfold increase in the budgets that are available to its practice, by large powerful departments in every major university, by the role of physicists as consultants to corporate boards of directors, and by international jet-setting as physicists commute to accelerator centers and conferences in Europe, India, Japan, and North and South America. But it would be a mistake to equate growth and expansion with development. The development of physics could be said to have stopped 70 years ago.

The SSC project itself, to generate an energy regime of 40 trillion eV that duplicates energies found only in the earliest instant after the Big Bang, has attractions. It would be nice to see if in the very earliest stages of the evolution of matter, matter as it was 10^{-16} seconds after the universe began to expand really consisted of only a single force binding together a mass of undifferentiated particles. To create an instrument that can look back so far in time is a cultural project of intrinsic interest that we all could support.

The estimated cost—which even at the earliest stages has doubled from original estimates in 1987 of $4.4 billion to $8.9 billion in late 1990—is a problem. If the price of the SSC is the starving of funds for everything else then it is not worth it. An esoteric knowledge of primeval matter will do absolutely nothing to help us solve the manifold problems we face today.

One would feel a lot better about the SSC if its proponents had made claims on the overinflated military budgets. A 10 percent reduction in the Department of Defense acquisition list for 1989 would have liberated $80 billion for the SSC and other far more interesting projects than building another round of military hardware. We could afford the SSC easily if we could bring military spending under control. In the absence of checks on military budgets the thoughtful citizen would probably vote no on the SSC with regret.

But there are deeper reasons than financial for voting no on the SSC. The SSC is an unimaginative project. Once again the high-energy physics community is trying to buy its way out of its problems without having to face them. Yet again, a new energy regime seems to offer the promise of a place where *a priori* concepts of simplicity can find confirmation. But experience has shown that every energy regime explored so far has a rich complex structure that has precluded understanding in terms of the framework erected in the 1920s. The degradation of the culture of understanding has advanced so far that physicists have forgotten that understanding does not just happen, it must be created by human effort. Things become simple after they are understood, not before.

As long as an open public purse enables physicists to throw away their notebooks whenever they feel the data in them is too complicated to understand, physicists will never solve the formidable intellectual and social problems that have accompanied the growth of their discipline since the 1920s. The SSC is part of the problem of physics, not part of the solution. It is a continuation of the process that has transformed physics from being an exemplar of human understanding into an arcane, esoteric field accessible only to its initiates.

Physics is a human social activity that has succeeded in extending our powers of observation many order of magnitude beyond our immediate perceptions. Through our instruments we bring evidence of very small, very large, very distant, very fast, very slow phenomena into the range of our senses. Our cultural development, however, is such that we cannot at the moment "see" these phenomena in realist terms. In the present period, physics has become as escapist as most Hollywood movies. As one science journalist has written: "I love physics, not for how well it explains the world, but for how it sounds."

The field of elementary particle physics is a textbook case for what we may, for want of a better term, call science criticism. Like all forms of criticism, whether in art, music, film, architecture, or dance, a science criticism seeks to unravel the connections between what we see, what it means, and how it got that way.

What we see with elementary particle physics are extravagant headlines in the science section of the quality dailies about the Superconducting Supercollider and its controversial cost.

> NEW ATOM SMASHER PROMISES TO YIELD
> THE ULTIMATE SECRETS OF MATTER.
>
> But Critics Question the Cost

We see little else.

What does it mean? As we have seen, it means that the particle physics community has succeeded once again in persuading Congress to fund its pursuit of a holy grail. Physicists now seek to interrogate an unexplored region of matter in the hope that nature will cooperate in confirming present prejudices. Rather than seeking to know more, the quest of the physicists is to confirm what they think they already know.

How has this happened? The lack of originality in particle physics dates from the 1920s. It is a reflection of the structural organization of the discipline where an exceptionally sharp division of labor has produced a self-involved elite too isolated from experience and criticism to succeed in producing anything new.

A century ago the physcial sciences were the symbol of our progress in transforming ourselves and our environment. The delights of electricity and magnetism, of optics, of thermodynamics, will continue to attract those who are receptive to their subtlety and simplicity, to the rich texture of experience that can be expressed so beautifully and concisely in a few symbols and a few logical operations. But physics has slowly and painfully come to forfeit its leadership as a cultural vanguard. From being arguably the most inspiring achievement of nineteenth-century bourgeois culture, physics has become its opposite—a spectacle for entertainment and amusement rather than a tribute to the powers of human comprehension. Until physics faces up to the implications of its size and develops new social relationships we will continue to have a self-involved autistic physics resting on its former glory, rather than a physics that has successfully met the heroic challenge to human understanding posed by our experience of matter on a submicroscopic scale.

CHAPTER 6

London 1991

C. P. Snow wrote his theory of Two Cultures in 1958, a time when romantic hopes for science were still widespread in Western culture. Science, in spite of the bomb, was the key to the future. But Snow, as a physicist educated in Rutherford's Cambridge in the 1920s, and then as a perceptive observer of the London scene of the 1930s, saw at first hand the slipping away of science from being considered a central part of mainstream culture to becoming an isolated specialty of little interest to the arts and politics graduates who ran Britain.

At Cambridge, where general relativity had been tested, where quantum mechanics had taken shape, and where the structure of the atomic nucleus had been limned, Snow saw new achievements that were not being assimilated into the general culture. Instead of the well-informed popular science treatises that he had read as a boy in Victorian Leicester, he saw relativity mystified by newspaper editors more interested in the Einstein spectacle than the Einstein achievement. At Cambridge high table, he heard Paul Dirac, a maker of quantum mechanics, impatient at the ignorance of his fellow dons, snap: "Adiabatic invariants. That's what I'm working on. You don't know what that is, do you?" He saw the politicians of the 1930s befuddled by the nuclear physics emerging from Rutherford's laboratory.

Snow was a witness to one consequence of the interwar crisis in Europe. The failure of the German and Hungarian revolutions, the failure of social reforms in Britain, France, and Italy, the capture of state power by the Fascists in Italy, the economic disintegration of the Great Depression, the capture of state power by the Nazis in Germany were events that precluded the continued development of a science of broad general involvement. Connections between science and the public narrowed. Only three people in the world could understand Einstein.

By 1958 the narrowing trend that Snow had witnessed in the interwar years had hardened into a social division. Even though the culture paid lip service to the importance of science, no one knew much about it. There were two cultures in educated Britain: a culture of high science whose members knew how things worked, and a culture of arts and letters whose members looked down on scientists while at the same time holding magical beliefs that science could do anything.

Today the two cultures have developed into a structural feature of the societies of Western Europe and the United States. In place of informed critical appreciation of science and technology, the lay public has only the vaguest of ideas about what goes on in the laboratories and offices of the scientific establishment. Ironically, in a reversal of historical roles, science, the nineteenth-century antithesis to religion and magic, has today become magical and religious. Particle accelerators are cathedrals, men in white coats are priests, the scientific literature is the gospel, and television is the pulpit where scientists promise miracles in one breath and doom in the next.

Advertising copywriters exploit the present religiosity of science with their inspired creation of the concept of a scientific fact. "It is a scientific fact. Bufferin works three times faster than any other leading aspirin."

A scientific fact is more certain than … than … than what? Than a nonscientific fact? What is a nonscientific fact?

Used freely in hundreds of advertising campaigns, in everyday conversation, in social science colloquia, the scientific fact expresses present consciousness about science perfectly. A scientific fact is a fact that is unchallengeable. The advertising copywriters know whereof they speak. A scientific fact is unchallengeable because the ordinary citizen does not have the means to assess the experience on which it is based.

Broadly speaking, of course, there need be little real mystery to the activities of scientists. Scientists are charged with the responsibility of making sense of human interaction with the physical world. They do this in many ways, from initiating new probes of matter at extremes of energy, pressure, and volume, to seeking improvements in manufacturing processes, to making sophisticated classifications of the world's flora and fauna. But the central feature of the enterprise is comprehension. Science is a way of understanding.

Like painting, music, dance, and poetry, ways of seeing, hearing, moving, and telling, science is a well-defined aspect of human culture. It is that part of culture concerned with creating ways of understanding. But today we are estranged from the experiences of those members of the culture who are responsible for producing understandings of the physical world. We are mystified by science because we do not share the experiences of the natural world that the scientists are meant to understand.

At bottom, the problem of the two cultures is a problem of our estrangement from the culture of production, the human activity that transforms the materials of the natural world into the artifacts of industrial civilization. We inhabit a culture in which, until very recently, production and reproduction, the two primary activities on which the existence of culture depends, have been segregated. Playing house and marriage are for girls. Building blocks and jobs are for boys. Women are estranged from the culture of production because the sexual division of labor has to a significant extent defined the world of work outside the home as a privileged male preserve.

On top of the estrangement produced by the sexual division of labor, we are further estranged from the culture of production because the productive activities of our society are now almost entirely hidden from view. As the variety and number of products has become greater and greater, our knowledge about how they are produced has grown less and less. In the production of wheat and rice, barley and soybeans, peanuts and potatoes; in the cultivation of cotton and hemp, rubber, and silk; in the mining of potash and phosphate, coal and oil, iron and copper; in the manufacture of steels, plastics, buildings, and breads; in the distribution systems of shipping, rail, road, and air, we are surrounded by intense human activity. A modern economy is a fascinating interlocking network of the most sophisticated human activity that can be found in industrialized societies. And yet we know very little about it.

Integrated circuit chips, used in all modern electronic devices, from hearing aids to mainframe computers, are encapsulated in a little blob of black plastic. The plastic must flow quickly enough to cover the chip yet not be too hot so that it damages the tiny wires that connect the interior circuit to the exterior leads. A satisfactory process depends on numerous factors, including temperature, pressure, mold design, composition of the plastic, wire size, and viscosity. When one includes the problems of safety in manufacture and safety in the disposal of plastic wastes one has an interesting problem in how to get optimum results among a large number of interacting factors. Raising the temperature of the plastic melt might get better results on one mold model and not another, increasing the pressure might work for one material but might cause unacceptable levels of toxic fumes with another and so on. The problem is a problem in the statistical design of experiments and it has a number of elegant solutions.

But our attention span is limited. Material production, the glory of the industrial revolution, instead of holding its place as an exciting part of the common culture, has become socially marginalized and split off. Today, the productive process is a generator of miraculous products on the one hand and a dirty, unsafe, exploitative business on the other. The techniques and understandings accrued from our interaction with the physical world in the course of producing our daily lives are not part of cultural life as it is currently experienced in Western Europe and the United States.

Our ignorance of science and technology is a leading symptom of what now is a central problem in the West, an estrangement from the culture of material production extending to every level of society. Expressed structurally in many ways—in education, in the media, in the arts—the problem of two cultures even penetrates deeply into the productive apparatus itself. A division of labor between those who do and those who decide has produced relationships in which the decision makers are cut off from the knowledge of the work process accumulated by those closest to it. Today the problem of two cultures is not simply a question of whether arts and science graduates of elite universities can talk to each other but is a central problem of Western culture of increasing urgency.

On May 24, 1988, George Kenyon, age twenty-five, was minced to death in an industrial accident in Britain. Kenyon, an employee at David Holt Plastics in Rossendale, Lancashire, was working on a machine known as the crumber. The crumber ground up plastic off-cuts into crumbs suitable as feedstock for other plastic manufacturing processes. It consisted of a drum about four feet high and two feet in diameter that had a high-speed rotary blade at the bottom revolving at twenty revolutions per second. The blade chopped the plastic off-cuts so fast they melted and the melt was turned into crumbs by dousing the contents with cold water. Kenyon's job was to feed the machine.

As originally designed, the crumber was fed through a small hole in the top of the drum. The operator extracted the crumbed plastic by removing the top. A compressed air system forced the top bolts into place and the system was fitted with interlocks so that the blade could not run while the top was open. Production proved to be too slow with the interlocks in place so the crumber was modified. The compressed air line was cut. The bolts were removed. And the electric interlock system was rewired so that the machine could run continuously with the top open. The modification produced nearly a 100 percent increase in output.

On the day of the accident, Kenyon had been shown by floor manager Norman Holt how to increase output still further by feeding the open top machine with long sheets instead of cutting the sheets into smaller pieces. Holt told Kenyon to be careful not to get entangled in the long sheets. In the event, a neighboring worker watched, horrified, as Kenyon was pulled in. He hit the stop button. But the blade takes a minute to stop and Kenyon was killed.

The Holt brothers were charged with manslaughter. The judge ruled that the cause of the accident was the "criminal irresponsibility of the employers." He fined the company £25,000, Norman Holt £5,000, and gave Norman Holt a suspended sentence for manslaughter.

Such practices and their accompanying accidents are legion throughout the world of small manufacture. But the point is not the criminal irresponsibility of employers. That critique is only snapping at the heels of the problem. Commercial enterprises both large and small face the problem of needing continuously to increase their productivity to remain competitive in their markets. In the absence of cooperative two-way communication between those who work the enterprises and those who run them, the prevailing method of increasing productivity is to push people and machines to their limit. From small cowboy manufacturing units to large, modern production plants, managements take risks that jeopardize the population both inside and outside their workplaces, often against direct warnings from those who understand the equipment best.

The capsizing, in a calm sea, on March 6, 1987, of the Townsend Thoresen ferry *Herald of Free Enterprise,* bound for Dover from Zeebrugge, killing 192 people, exposed at a more complex level the same risky attempts to increase productivity that led to the death of George Kenyon.

The *Herald of Free Enterprise* was one of three modern ferries built for Townsend Thoresen in the late 1970s by the West German firm Schichhau Unterweser. Townsend Thoresen broke with traditional ferry design specifications by requesting a design that would minimize port turnaround time and channel crossing time. When delivered, the new ferries were the biggest and fastest cross-channel ferries, carrying 1,300 passengers, sixty cars, and sixty trailers, and capable of speeds up to twenty-four knots per hour.

Central to the design was the concept of roll-on roll-off car decks, two completely open decks without compartments so that cars can roll on the ferry on one side and roll off on the other. The major hazard in the ro-ro design is in its sacrifice of the standard safety feature of a hull with closed subdivisions which prevents sinking or capsizing in the event of the ship being holed.

In concert with the design principle to minimize turnaround time were the operating practices adopted by the company. In conventional merchant shipping, captains analyze the stability of their vessel in detail before leaving harbor, taking into account the shape of the ship, its construction, the location and weight of cargo, its fuel load, and its ballast. Such procedures were inconsistent with rapid turnaround time and the company adopted quicker approximate methods monitored by shore personnel.

The captains were not told the number of passengers they carried on the number of lorries. The weight of the lorries was determined by oral declaration of the lorry drivers leading to underestimates. Shore personnel, under pressure to increase productivity, tended to load more passengers than the legal limit. In one instance, a spot check conducted by ship's officers found two hundred passengers in excess of the legal limit. In addition, even though the vessels had marks on their sides that would permit readings of how the vessel was lying the water, these draughts were never read. Finally, in the interest of timesaving there was the practice of negative notification of the state of the front and rear doors. Bridge personnel were to assume that the doors were closed unless informed otherwise.

The shipping community knew about the hazards associated with ro-ro design and operation. In the ten years prior to the accident, there had been 5,100 people killed worldwide in 245 accidents involving roll-on/roll-off ferries. In 1982 a Townsend Thoresen vessel, the *European Gateway,* capsized with the loss of six lives. An investigation by the senior captain of the firm produced a detailed report warning about the dangers of overloading, complaining that captains were not told the number of passengers and the cargo weight, protesting the abandonment of passenger counts by crew, protesting the failure to take draught readings, and finally requesting that the problem of the front and rear doors be addressed by installing automatic sensing devices: "It is so important to the safety of the ship that [the doors] are closed, we should have a bridge indication." The company refused: "Do they need an indicator to tell whether the deck storekeeper is asleep or sober?" wrote a company official.

On the night of the accident, the *Herald of Free Enterprise* sailed with only two officers instead of the usual three. In spite of protests from the pilots' union, the company insisted on reducing staff in a further effort to increase productivity on what was a loss-making Zeebrugge-Dover run. There was no officer to check the closing of the doors. That night there had been an exceptionally high tide. Ballast had to be taken into the front tanks to lower the ship in the water so that the vehicles could be loaded. As a result the front of the ship was half a meter lower in the water than the rear. Following usual practice the draughts were not read; the captain did not know his vessel was riding lower at the front end.

As the ship left outer Zeebrugge harbor with its front loading door open, it made its customary left turn toward Dover. The overloaded ship, its front end lowered, shipped water through the open front door. The water sluiced down the left side of the car deck. As the ship came out of its left turn, a correction on the rudder caused the ship to list in the opposite direction. The shipped water surged across the open, undivided car deck, adding its energy and momentum to the list. The prevailing winds on the superstructure increased the list still further. Water now flooded in on the right-hand side of the car deck. The list then increased further, causing unsecured vehicles to slide across the deck, adding their weight to the list. The ship was now critically under water. As the sea flowed into the partially submerged right-hand side of the deck, the capsize was completed. The whole physical process took about ninety seconds, rendering ineffective modern escape chutes designed for a thirty-minute escape time.

As in the George Kenyon accident, the problem at hand was more fundamental than a profit-minded management. What really informed the Zeebrugge accident was a combination of risky design and risky operating procedures in an attempt to increase the productivity of the vessel. A society might conceivably opt to take such risks in an effort to increase its productivity. But at present such risks are not decided democratically nor are the risks and benefits distributed equally. Whether the hazards are confined to the workplace or spill out into the environment—today's occupational health hazard is tomorrow's environmental crisis—the decisions to take a risk are the prerogative of managements who operate in social structures where it is increasingly difficult to make competent, responsible decisions.

The Japanese have addressed the problem of top-down decision-making by importing into their industrial culture the traditional relationships of medieval Japan. Manager and worker in Japanese enterprises communicate through an elaborate system of reciprocal, if unequal, rights and obligations. The Soviet Union prior to its dissolution had approached the problem by instituting workplace elections of managerial personnel. But in the United States and the industrial nations of Western Europe, in spite of scattered social experiments, top-down, one-way management structures are now so entrenched that they adversely affect the outcomes of even showcase projects. Management thinking in the U.S. space program prior to the *Challenger* disaster was identical to management thinking at David Holt Plastics and Townsend Thoresen Ferries.

We would not know the true story of the *Challenger* disaster had it not been for William Graham, then deputy administrator of NASA. Graham, a new Reagan appointee, was a NASA outsider, having had a career in military applications of rocketry. At odds from the beginning with NASA veteran head administrator James Beggs, Graham saw his mandate as opening up NASA procedures to the outside world. Determined to maximize the chance for the truth about the accident to get out—"It was the only way to save NASA"—Graham wanted to nominate someone to the Rogers Commission who was not associated with NASA and who would bring technical competence and complete integrity to the investigation. Nina Graham, Graham's wife, suggested the name of a physicist who had been Graham's teacher at Cal Tech and whom she had heard give lectures at Hughes Malibu when Graham had worked there. The nomination was approved without question. Aside from the fact that he had won a Nobel Prize, none of the politicians had ever heard of Richard Feynman.

Feynman was the wild card on the commission. Through his inimitable style and his exceptional understanding of physical systems, Feynman was able to blow the story of the *Challenger* disaster with his spectacular disruption of a routine press conference, showing the world that the famous O-rings lost their elasticity when cooled in a beaker of ice water.

Feynman also found out that the problematic O-rings were just one aspect of a management policy to attempt to increase the productivity of the shuttle at the expense of safety against the specific recommendations and warning of its own engineers. The failure of the O-rings was not an isolated accident but the outcome of a series of lesser accidents whose implications had consistently been ignored by NASA management in their effort to achieve greater mission frequencies.

The program to build a space shuttle had to be sold to a skeptical U.S. Congress. The politicians were satisfied that U.S. objectives in space had been completely achieved by beating the Soviet Union to the moon. To avoid disbanding the program, top NASA management looked for ways to exploit its demonstrated capabilities in space. A reusable commercial space vehicle was the answer. Congress was promised a vehicle that would be economical, that would fly reliably on frequent schedules, and that would be safe. In addition to research payloads, the shuttle would be able to explore the possibilities of creating new manufacturing capabilities in the weightless environment of an orbiting vehicle.

The engineers who had worked on Apollo knew that, in the interests of making the sale, NASA management had exaggerated the economy, reliability, safety, and applicability of realizable space technology. The ensuing development of the space shuttle was accompanied by constant pressure to meet unrealistic performance criteria, resulting in a steady degradation of safety standards against a background of warnings from the engineers.

The main component of the shuttle is the orbiter, the familiar stocky, winged vehicle that is capable of flying back to earth after its time in space. For the launch, the orbiter rides piggyback on a giant cylindrical fuel tank 50 percent wider and 35 percent longer than the orbiter itself. The fuel tank is packed with liquid oxygen at the top and liquid hydrogen at the bottom. Specially designed turbo-driven fuel pumps deliver the right mix of liquid hydrogen and liquid oxygen to the engine. Flanking the fuel tank are two solid-fueled booster rockets whose joints are sealed by the rubber O-rings. The shuttle sails into space like a whale tied to a three-log raft.

The immediate cause of the accident as shown in NASA photographs was an escaping flame from a booster rocket. This flame caused a sideways thrust on *Challenger,* which was corrected by the gyros, and a drop in fuel pressure, which automatically shut down the booster rockets. But the flame ignited the liquid hydrogen in the giant cylindrical tank, causing the explosion that destroyed the shuttle and its astronauts.

Before Feynman went to Washington he arranged a briefing with engineering colleagues at Cal Tech's Jet Propulsion Laboratory. The engineers at JPL knew the history of problems with the seals on the booster rockets. Feynman was told that the O-rings had shown signs of scorching. Hot gas from inside the booster rocket had occasionally flowed past the O-ring seals. The engineers told Feynman that if the gas had actually burned a hole in an O-ring, then a tiny hole would in the space of milliseconds burn into a large hole, leading to a catastrophic release of flame—which is just what had shown up in the film of the launch.

In Washington, Feynman, with the help of Bill Graham, got a special Saturday briefing from Michael Weeks, the resident NASA seals expert. Weeks filled in the picture that the JPL engineers had sketched for Feynman back in Pasadena. The booster rockets were made in sections. The separate sections were held together by sealed joints. These so-called field joints were the joints sealed with the O-rings. They were sealed in the field, i.e., just before the launch. The field joints were a complex bit of hardware with leak-testing ports, insulation, pins, and retaining clips all housed in a so-called tang-and-clevis (male-female) coupling structure that girdled the booster rocket. To make the seal, there were two rubber O-rings each a quarter of an inch thick and thirty-seven feet in circumference inside the field joint preventing hot gases leaking out through the tang-and-clevis coupling.

The seals had never worked properly. As designed by the Morton Thiokol Company in Utah, pressure inside the rocket was to have compressed the O-rings tight within each field joint, assuring a perfect seal. But because the rocket casing was much thinner than the bulky field joints, pressure from the hot gases caused the rocket casing to bow outward like a barrel. The outward bowing bent the field joint, causing a gap where there should have been a seal. Called "joint rotation" by the engineers, the gap problem had been discovered early in the project before the shuttle ever flew.

As gas pressure built up, the bowing caused the gap to expand. To maintain the seal the rubber needed to expand as well. The Parker Seal Company, the manufacturers of the O-rings, told Thiokol that the rubber would not perform as was now specified. The O-rings could not be used as expansible seals. Thiokol then tried a number of remedial steps but the joints still leaked. Michael Weeks showed Feynman pictures of "blowby," hot gases flowing out through the gap, and pictures of "erosion" where the rubber had burned.

NASA response to the situation had been to issue two contradictory recommendations. The first recommended immediate action. "The lack of a good secondary field joint is most critical and ways to reduce joint rotation should be incorporated as soon as possible to reduce criticality." The second recommended that since nothing serious had happened in previous flights it was safe to continue using the joints as long as they were tested for leaks before the flight.

On Sunday, the day after his briefing with Weeks, Feynman got a cryptic phone call from General Kutyna, who asked him what the effect low temperature would have on the O-rings. Feynman set to work on it. Kutyna, as it turned out, had been tipped off secretly by an astronaut who had to remain silent.

The following day, at a closed meeting, it was revealed that NASA had investigated the cost of replacing the seals and had decided that it was too expensive. And in a final surprise, a Thiokol engineer showed up uninvited and testified that Thiokol had recommended the night before the flight that to preserve the elasticity of the seals, the shuttle should not fly at temperatures lower than 53°F. The temperatures that night had fallen below freezing to 28°F.

At the close of the meeting, Rogers decided to hold a public meeting the next day to answer questions about the seals problem. Feynman guessed that the public meeting would evade the issue. He had already received evasive answers to his query to NASA about the effect of temperature on the rubber O-rings. Determined to find out what happened, he obtained, with the help of Bill Graham, a sample of the O-ring rubber. With a C-clamp to compress the rubber and a beaker of ice water to chill it, he found that the rubber did not expand at freezing temperatures.

At the public meeting on Tuesday, with General Kutyna helping to judge the best timing, Feynman made his now famous intervention. Using a glass of ice water, a C-clamp, and a piece of O-ring rubber extracted from the demonstration model of the field joint circulating through the audience, he repeated his experiment of the day before. Always a superb showman, Feynman had found a way to show the entire world how the shuttle had blown up.

Having understood the immediate cause of the shuttle failure, Feynman wanted further to understand how systematic was the disagreement between management and engineers over safety. In the space shuttle main engine, he found a history of faults requiring frequent replacement of the turbopumps, bearings, and sheet-metal housings. Because of what is called top-down design, in which components were assembled all together without first being individually tested, the engines had been saddled with serious hard-to-correct difficulties.

The oxygen high-pressure turbo-fuel pump had had to be replaced every five or six mission equivalents and the hydrogen pump every three or four mission equivalents. The top-down design made it impossible to isolate the factors that were causing the pumps to fail. Also not known was how fast the cracks that had appeared in the pump turbine blades would expand to failure and whether the time from crack initiation to failure depended on power level or other operating factors. Overall the pumps were operating at 10 percent of their design specification. In seventy hours of shuttle engine operation the engines had failed sixteen times.

The response of NASA management to this operating history was to claim that the probability of engine failure was one in 100,000 missions. Feynman pointed out that such a figure meant that the shuttle could fly every day for three hundred years without a failure (300 × 365 ≈ 100,000). Management insisted that its "engineering judgment" of the figure of 1/100,000 was a more reliable estimate of shuttle engine safety than past operating history. Feynman, by using the actual operating history of the shuttle, estimated shuttle reliability as being about 1/100, a figure in agreement with estimates of 1/300 made by working engineers at NASA. Feynman concluded: "The management of NASA exaggerates the reliability of its product to the point of fantasy."

In the avionics sector, Feynman found a different story. Because of the inherent flexibility of software where changes can be made with a keyboard, the software engineers were able to hold to a high standard of reliability in spite of management pressures to increase productivity. The computer programs were checked from the bottom up instead of from the top down. Each new line of code was checked and verified. Adversary procedures ruled the final verification: a team of hostile inspectors tested every aspect of the complex computer code of 250,000 lines, looking for errors. (A typical personal computer spreadsheet code has 250 lines.) If an error was found the system was judged to have failed with consequent loss of life and damage to the careers of the software engineers responsible.

These stringent procedures produced only six errors in the tests and none in the actual flights. Feynman concluded: "... the computer software checking system is of highest quality. There appears to be no process of gradually fooling oneself while degrading standards, the process so characteristic of the solid rocket booster and space shuttle main engine safety systems." The avionics sector had been able to resist pressures from management to degrade their safety procedures. But as one software engineer complained: "They keep saying we always pass the tests so what's the use of having so many?"

* * *

The problem of two cultures, a problem of our estrangement from the culture of material production, cripples our productive capacities and deprives us of the experience we need to gain access to the beautiful understandings of nature expressed in our science. The special theory of relativity seems inaccessible because we share little of the human experience of nature that Einstein worked so hard to understand. We are not engaged with the problems encountered in the development of telecommunication by satellite in the development of remote-control video devices, in the development of high-definition television, all of which make use of the wireless transmission of electric signals with finite velocity. A presentation of the implications of that finite velocity falls on stony ground. Einstein's justly celebrated achievement in making sense of the existence of an ultimate speed is difficult to absorb because few of us have conscious experience of electric effects traveling at the speed of light. The special theory of relativity is a brother from another planet—we recognize the kinship but we know nothing of the circumstances.

Our alienation from the theory of relativity is no more and no less than the alienation that is the fundamental condition of modern life. Modernity, the epoch of the profound division between subject and object, returns relativity to us, not as a sublime creation of human being in the world but as a spectacle inciting anxiety, awe, fear, and incomprehension. The giving away of ourselves that is the central feature of modern existence beats against the contradictory reality that recognizes the possibility of self-realization, authenticity, and a totality of access to human experience. With relativity, with modernism, we are at once stimulated and frustrated, together and alone, developing and stagnant, racing through life and stuck in the muck. We experience a world saturated with possibility, unable to materialize lives shimmering in the distance.

We are told that the modernist project is now in grave danger. Freeway and high-rise make a mess of modern architecture, serial music erases memory and continuity, jazz splinters into a thousand self-referent musicians, popular music becomes the visual World Tour, painting the exultant roar of a crowd at Sotheby's, while the mere mention of relativity, nearly one hundred years after its creation, makes every intellectual in Europe and the United States start to stammer. We are of course talking about postmodernism—defeat raised to the level of high culture, a renunciation of the vision of universal emancipation in favor of resigned celebration of the individual enjoyment of goods and services by those who can afford to buy them. With the failure of the European revolutions of the 1920s and with the last outpost of that vision now shattered by the apparent desire of a large fraction of the exhausted peoples of Eastern Europe to share in the culture of commodity capitalism, who is to say no?

But the human subject has never been more present, more overwhelming than it is today. The challenges of modernism have never been more pressing than they are today. The resignation of the postmodernists is the despair and cynicism of those who have pinned their hopes on art as the one avenue that can counteract the giving away of our productive lives to forces over which we have no control. The phenomenon of postmodernism is a symptom of our present difficulty in seeing how to begin to contest a terrain long ago conceded as lost.

For the past century, a conceit of the industrial societies has been that the problems of scarcity have been solved. Those concerned with social justice have focused their attention on the very real inequities in distribution. In 1989 the top 1 percent of income earners in the United States took home thirty-six times the average pay of the bottom 40 percent. In 1989, 20 percent of children in the United States lived below the poverty line. But the problem lies deeper than the question of distributive inequity. Income leveling at our present levels of production is no solution. Nor is it a question of turning up the knobs on the present productive apparatus. Even at full tilt we cannot produce enough to go around. Taken as a whole, the world system is not equal to the task of providing an adequate standard of living for the world's peoples. One quarter of the population of the earth does not live within a fifteen-minute walk of potable water.

The industrial revolution raised the possibility of creating a world of plenty. But a century after the heroic period of Japanese,

European, and U.S. industrialization we are no closer to realizing the dream of the industrial revolution, the dream of modernism, the dream of progress. Our productive economy is riddled with inefficient management structures in which the people who know most about the work tend to have little to say about how it can be improved, and are generally not permitted to talk to us directly about their experience. If they take the risk to do so, we are in no position to act on what they tell us.

Our cultural life is diminished by our lack of engagement with the problems that arise in productive lives. Our writers and filmmakers do not find promising themes on the factory floor. Our poets do not tell of the intricacies of microminiature electronic circuitry. Our songwriters do not sing of the accomplishments of a day's work. Our novelists are attracted to the language of science but still have yet to explore properly the human experience of those who created that language. Our physicists have become autistic, divorced from the realities of space-time, wrapped up in the convolutions of imaginary manifolds, staring vacantly at mathematical expressions of their own creation. Our biologists poke about with sterile mechanical paradigms unable to use their own profound creation of molecular biology to liberate themselves from the dead hand of the past. We look back at the socialist realist sculpture, those monumental hymns to production of the Soviet Union of the 1930s, with condescending smiles at the childishness of the hopes they were meant to represent—Heroes of Socialist Labor? My word—while we shudder at the thought of what happened to the marvelously sophisticated futurists of the decade before.

There are counter examples. Primo Levi has shown that one can create world-class literature from the unpromising materials of industrial chemistry. The films *Blue Collar* and *Nine to Five* are classic Hollywood entertainments in a factory and office setting, respectively. Mark DiSuvero's public sculptures, powerfully arranged iron, steel, and timber constructions, evoke the strengths of industrial materials and *ipso facto* the strengths of industrialization.

In politics the Green movement has succeeded in placing the

environment so firmly on the world political agenda that at the 1990 World Climate Conference in Geneva, King Hussein was able to argue against a Gulf War on environmental grounds. A 1990 Roper Poll in the United States showed that over 50 percent of those polled rated as "very serious" the problems of hazardous waste dumps, water pollution from industrial and agricultural waste, occupational exposure to toxic chemicals, pesticide exposure of farm workers, contamination of coastal waters, and pesticide residues in foods. The Green movement challenges the culture of material production as it currently operates, inviting us to consider whether we can continue to afford to grant prerogatives of private ownership and management's right to manage.

In education, a unique bachelor of science course in new technology begun in 1989 at the Polytechnic of East London avoids the exclusive emphasis on the acquisition of technical skills, beginning instead with a history of past technical innovations including an account of current developments in microelectronics; an analysis of software and hardware manufacture including a history of the economic developments that have led to present machine capabilities; and a microcomputer skills unit. A core curriculum examines the effects of new technology on manufacturing industry, employment patterns, and consumption patterns while at the same time providing state-of-the-art instruction in technological developments. It is a curriculum illustrating that what has not been tried in education has been a systematic attempt to integrate the two cultures at the highest level of specialist training.

These are beginnings.

What now urgently needs to be placed back on the human agenda after a hiatus of one hundred years is the question of alienation from our culture of production. We need to begin to come to terms with our complex feelings of rejection, interest, awe, confusion, and gratitude that accompany our estranged, split-off relationship to work. We need to reintegrate our productive relationships into our lives as a legitimate object of desire. What are we doing all the livelong day? The spectacle of the commodity and the uncomprehending gaze. Are we crazy?

Meanwhile, back in the city, we face our daily lives. Feeling the loss of relationship with the natural world, we go to the zoo. There human and animal no longer interact as free and equal members of a shared habitat. Instead, the human subject observes the animal object as a barren symbol of a once mutual relationship. Or, if we reject the *tristesse* of the zoo environment, we can organize a more active contemplation of nature by going backpacking in the wilderness where the animals are not caged, the vistas are breathtaking, but where we have no real reason for being.

In the streets, a few youths are tinkering with the machines of daily life. If one has grown up male in or near the working class communities of the United States and Europe, one may have emerged with the knowledge of how to repair automobiles or motorbikes. Other male youths have emerged from childhood environments with an uncommon knowledge of practical electronics or, in today's world, with a highly developed knowledge of modern computers. But unless a very particular combination of social circumstances and developmental psychology is at work, this knowledge soon falls by the wayside because there is little in our adult lives that requires us to use any kind of knowledge of nature actively.

And so consumerism becomes another outlet for our longings. We attempt to keep up with our productive culture the only way we can. We purchase the latest high-tech commodity. Beautiful cameras, now equipped with automatic infrared focusing devices, stereos with intricate instrument panels evoking the mystery of industrial control rooms, or, for the truly advanced, dish antennas, offering access to the totality of world satellite broadcasting, are some of the satisfactions the market can offer the engaged consumer. But the purchase of commodities contains an irony not lost to nineteenth-century commentators: we are trying to buy back in the marketplace what we have given up in the organization of our workplaces.

Meanwhile, within science, superconductivity and chaos have been the big stories of the past decade. What is delightful about the existence of high-temperature superconductors is that matter has surprises for us not at the expensive frontiers of high-energy physics but right here in our own backyard. Previously we had thought that the pairing between electrons necessary for the conduction electrons to move together, locked into the lowest energy state of the conducting lattice, could only be achieved at extremely low temperatures. But the copper oxide materials of high temperature superconductors form a planar rather than three-dimensional lattice with a very different array of possible electron states. Although still imperfectly understood, it now appears that in these planar structures the electrons can all lock into the same state at much higher temperatures.

Chaos theory, that spectacularly named development of the century-old theory of dynamical instabilities, represents a genuine intellectual advance in its escape from the confines of Newtonian mechanical determinism. But it is still not clear whether chaos theory is simply a fad with a flashy name or a genuinely new conceptual framework. When one recalls the hype that accompanied the entrance of catastrophe theory into the media in the 1970s, one realizes how much can be attached to a name. Catastrophe theory has vanished without a trace. Chaos theory, as a theory, has an uncertain future.

A more interesting development than chaos is the development of parallel processing computers that will increase current speeds of computation by many orders of magnitude. The fast computer makes possible realistic simulations of natural processes that could only be crudely approximated in the past. High-speed computation is the new mathematical language of science, replacing an algebra and calculus that are both computationally and conceptually becoming obsolete. The computer program is an algorithmic mathematics—a series of instructions rather than a declarative sentence—that permits the dissection of complex processes such as the weather and chess playing.

But as one might expect, advances in this area have already been stood on their heads. The media has celebrated the wonders of a machine that can play chess. Imagine! A machine that can play chess! The point is exactly the opposite. The chess-playing computer represents, not the power of a machine, but the power of the human analysts who have been able to replicate the human decision-making processes in chess in terms of a series of step-by-step instructions to a dumb machine.

We carry on. By the year 2000, of the twenty largest cities on earth, seventeen will be in the Third World. All of them will have more than ten million people, with Mexico City and São Paulo each exceeding twenty-five million people. Finally we will have to address the central problem of our species, the central problem of the modern condition. We are addicted to methods of production that cannot mobilize the full human capacities of its participants. We are still at the beginning of time. The creative moment is yet to come.

Notes and Sources

CHAPTER 1: Florence 1623/Cambridge 1687

NOTES

Bertolt Brecht, the German playwright and poet, dramatized the social transformation that swept Europe in the sixteenth and seventeenth centuries in his play *The Life of Galileo.* As usually performed, the play is a powerful account of events leading up to the trial of Galileo by the Holy Office in 1632. Galileo is grand, a modern hero. His recantation under the threat of torture is a tragic setback for scientific progress and a reminder of the difficult task individuals face when confronted by repressive authority. We ask ourselves: what would I have done in Galileo's place? The play has brought pleasure to thousands of theater audiences since its first performance in 1947, both speaking to and subtly criticizing our need to have heroes.

But is it Brecht? What is missing from Brecht's *Galileo* as it has been performed is the Brecht that saw Galileo not as hero but as fool. Part of the problem is the ambivalence expressed in the play itself. *Galileo* was written in two stages. The first drafts intending the trial of Galileo to be a metaphor for political repression were completed in 1939 when Brecht was in exile from the Nazis. In this early version the play clearly shows the influence of classical Marxist thinking in Brecht's framing of science: science is progressive and the struggle of Galileo is a metaphor for the struggle of the new science, Marxism, the science of the transformation of society, to stay alive against the forces of Nazi Germany.

The war intervenes. Brecht revised the play in 1947, after atomic bombs had fallen on Hiroshima and Nagasaki. All of a sudden, science had taken on a new meaning. Instead of being a positive accomplishment agreed by all, science had now become sinister.

A play that had been a powerful metaphor for political persecution now became a critique of science. Galileo is no hero. In his political naïveté he has left the safety of Venice where he has the support of the Republic and plunged himself into the depths of the Inquisition by accepting an appointment at the Medici court in Florence. Galileo believes that his physics serves no master but the truth. And, in his belief, Galileo chooses the wrong side and places the achievements of physics itself in jeopardy.

In Brecht's postwar writing of *Galileo*, Galileo's recantation is a metaphor for the atomic physicists' recantation of their humanity, their renunciation of a physics in service to humanity as a whole in favor of a physics in service to the interests of the modern state. After the atomic bomb, Brecht saw that the modern implications of the Galileo affair lay, not in the suppression of the truth by the Church, but in the question of whom science was to serve. As Brecht later wrote: "[The atom bomb] was the classical end product of [Galileo's] contribution to science and his failure to society."

SOURCES

Abraham, Ralph, and Marsden, Jerrold E. (1978). *Foundations of Mechanics*, 2nd ed., Benjamin/Cummings, Reading, Mass.

Albury, David, and Schwartz, Joseph (1982). *Partial Progress: The Politics of Science and Technology*, Pluto, London.

Berger, John; Blomberg, Sven; Fox, Chris; Dibb, Michael; and Hollis, Richard (1972). *Ways of Seeing*, Penguin, London.

Brewster, David (1835). "Galileo," in *Lardner's Cyclopedia, Literary and Scientific Men of Italy, Spain and Portugal*, v. 2, London.

Butts, Robert E. (1978). "Some Tactics in Galileo's Propaganda for the Mathematization of Scientific Experience," in R. E. Butts and J. C. Pitts, eds., *New Perspectives on Galileo*, Reidel, Boston/London.

Charon, Jean (1970). *Cosmology. Theories of the Universe*, trans. Patrick Moore, World University Library, McGraw-Hill, New York.

Cohen, I. Bernard (1979). Preface to Newton's *Opticks*, Dover, New York.

Cohen, Robert S. (1971). Introduction to B. Hessen, *Social and Economic Roots of Newton's Principia*, Howard Fertig Inc., New York.

Cook, Bruce (1982). *Brecht in Exile*, Holt, Rinehart and Winston, New York.

Dickson, David (1979). "Science and Political Hegemony in the Seventeenth Century," *Radical Science Journal*, no. 8, London, pp. 7–38

Donnington, Robert (1981). *The Rise of Opera*, Faber, London.

Drake, Stillman (1972). "Galileo Galilei," "Vincenzio Galilei," *Dictionary of Scientific Biography*, Charles C. Gillispie, ed., Scribners, New York.

——— (1980). *Galileo*, Oxford University Press, Oxford.

Eley, Geoff, and Hunt, William, eds. (1988). *Reviving the English Revolution,* Verso, London.

Fahie, John J. (1903). *Galileo: His Life and Work,* London.

Finocchiaro, Maurice A. (1989). *The Galileo Affair: A Documentary History,* University of California Press, Berkeley and London.

Fuller, Peter (1980). *Seeing Berger: A Reevaluation,* Writers and Readers, London.

Galilei, Galileo (1610). *Sidereus Nuncius,* trans. Albert Van Helden (1989). University of Chicago Press, Chicago and London.

Galilei, Galileo (1623). *Il Saggiatore,* trans. Stillman Drake and C. D. O'Malley (1961) in *The Controversy on the Comets of 1618,* University of Pennsylvania, Philadelphia.

Geymonat, Ludovico (1957). *Galileo Galilei,* McGraw-Hill, New York.

Gray, William M. (1990). "Strong Association Between West African Rainfall and U.S. Landfall of Intense Hurricanes," *Science,* v. 249, pp. 1251–56.

Griffin, Susan (1978). *Woman and Nature. The Roaring Inside Her,* The Woman's Press, London.

Hadjinicolaou, Nicos (1973). *Histoire de l'art et lutte des classes,* trans. Louise Asmal (1978), Pluto, London.

Hessen, Boris (1931). "The Social and Economic Roots of Newton's Principia," in *Science at the Crossroads,* New Edition with an Introduction by Gary Werskey (1971), Frank Cass, London.

Hill, Christopher (1940). *The English Revolution of 1640,* Lawrence and Wishart, London.

——— (1969). *Reformation to Industrial Revolution,* Penguin, London.

——— (1970). "Newton and His Society," in Robert Palter, ed., *The Annus Mirabilis of Sir Isaac Newton, 1666–1966,* MIT, Cambridge.

Hogben, Lancelot (1937). *Mathematics for the Million,* George Allen Ltd.; reprinted 1968, W.W. Norton, New York.

Kellenberg, Hermann (1974). "Technology in the Age of the Scientific Revolution 1500–1700," in Carlo M. Cipolla, ed., *The Fontana Economic History of Europe,* Fontana, London.

Kiernan, V. G. (1980). *State and Society in Europe 1550–1650,* Basil Blackwell, Oxford.

Kline, Morris (1980). *Mathematics: The Loss of Certainty,* Oxford University Press, London/New York.

Koyré, Alexander (1968). *Newtonian Studies,* University of Chicago Press, Chicago.

Levy-Leblond, Jean-Marc (1982). "Physics and Mathematics," in *Penser les Mathématiques,* Seuil, Paris.

Marx, Karl (1968). *The Mathematical Manuscripts,* New Park, London.

Merchant, Carolyn (1980). *The Death of Nature. Women, Ecology and the Scientific Revolution,* Harper and Row, San Francisco.

Merton, R. K. (1970). *Science, Technology and Society in Seventeenth-Century England*, Harper and Row, New York.

Moser, Jurgen (1972). "Stable and Random Motions in Dynamical Systems with Special Emphasis on Celestial Mechanics," *Annals of Mathematics Studies*, no. 77, Princeton University Press, Princeton, New Jersey.

Needham, Joseph (1959). *Science and Civilisation in China*, v. 3, *Mathematics and the Sciences of Heaven and Earth*, Cambridge University Press, Cambridge.

Newton, I. (1730). *Opticks*, Dover, New York.

Poincaré, Henri (1892). *La Mécanique Céleste*, Dover, New York.

Prigogine, I. (1981). *From Being to Becoming*, Freeman, San Francisco.

Procacci, Giuliano (1968). *History of the Italian People*, Penguin, London.

Redondi, Pietro (1983). *Galileo: Heretic*, trans. Raymond Rosenthal (1987), Penguin, London.

Robertson, Alec, and Stevens, Denis, eds. (1963). *The Pelican History of Music 2: Renaissance and Baroque*, Penguin, London.

Santillana, Giorgio de (1955). *The Crime of Galileo*, University of Chicago Press, Chicago.

Singer, Charles; Holinyard, E. J.; Hall, A. R.; and Williams, T. I., eds. (1952). *A History of Technology*, v. 3, Oxford.

Stewart, Ian (1989). *Does God Play Dice?: The New Mathematics of Chaos*, Penguin, London.

Struik, Dirk J. (1948). *A Concise History of Mathematics*, Dover, New York.

Wallerstein, Immanuel (1974). *The Modern World-System I: Capitalist Agriculture and the Origins of the European World Economy in the Sixteenth Century*, Academic, New York.

CHAPTER 2: Paris 1824/Berlin 1916

NOTES

We have forgotten how much of the industrial revolution was fueled by child labor. In 1789, in three Arkwright spinning mills in Derbyshire two-thirds of the 1,150-member work force were children. In the cotton industry as a whole, half the work force were children.

Contemporary reports are harrowing. Sir Frederic Eden wrote in his *State of the Poor*, 1797: "It may, perhaps, be worth the attention of the public to consider whether any manufacture, which in order to be carried on successfully requires that cottages and workhouses should be ransacked for poor children; that they should be employed by turns during the greater part of the night and robbed of the rest which though indispensable to all is most required by the young."

Although the owners of the mills justified their use of forced child labor by arguing that conditions in their mills were an improvement over the conditions the children had known in the orphanages and workhouses, contemporary accounts show that the actual conditions were horrific. Fielden wrote in 1836: "... overseers were appointed to see to the works, whose interest it was to work the children to the utmost, because their pay was in proportion to the quantity of work that they could exact. Cruelty of course was the consequence ... [they] were flogged, fettered and tortured in the most exquisite refinement of cruelty ... they were starved to the bone while flogged to their work and ... even in some instances ... were driven to commit suicide.

And as Eden noted:

> The ready communication of contagion to numbers crowded together, the accession of virulence from putrid effluvia, the injury done to young persons through confinement and to long continued labour are evils which we have lately heard ascribed to cotton mills by persons of first medical authority assembled to investigate the subject. To these must be added an evil which still brands with disgrace the practice of some cotton mills, the custom of obliging a part of the children employed there to work all night.

*

One of the least recognized aspects of the scientific literature is the aesthetic pleasure it can bring. Every serious student of the subject has his or her favorites. Here is Ludwig Boltzmann, a pioneer in statistical mechanics, commenting on his experience of reading nineteenth-century writers of mathematical physics.

> Even as a musician can recognize his Mozart, Beethoven or Schubert after hearing the first few bars, so can a mathematician recognise his Cauchy, Gauss, Jacobi, Helmholtz or Kirchoff after the first few pages. The French writers reveal themselves by their extreme formal elegance, while the English, especially Maxwell, by their dramatic sense. Who for example is not familiar with Maxwell's memoirs on his dynamical theory of gases. ... The variations of the velocities are, at first, developed majestically; then from one side enter the equations of state; and from the other side, the equations of motion in a central field. Ever higher soars the chaos of formulae. Suddenly we hear, as if from kettle drums, the four beats "put n = 5." The evil spirit V (the relative velocity of the two molecules) vanishes; and even, as in music, a hitherto dominating figure in the bass is suddenly silenced, that which has seemed insuperable has been overcome as if by a stroke of magic. ... One result after another follows in quick succession. We arrive at the conditions for ther-

mal equilibrium, together with the expressions for the transport coefficients. The curtain then falls!

Not every physicist is as thrilled as Boltzmann by Maxwell's derivation of expressions for the viscosity, thermal conductivity, and rates of diffusion of a gas. But all physicists have a smile of recognition at Boltzmann's response. All physicists know what Boltzmann means. And indeed, the aesthetic experience of comprehension, the mental transition from jumble to clarity, the beauty of understanding, are experiences that we all have had.

*

In 1989, according to figures supplied by British Gas, electric cookers comprised 40 percent of all cookers used in the UK consuming an estimated 1200 kwh each annually. With an estimated twenty million households in the UK, the annual consumption of electricity from electric cookers is 2.4×10^{10} kwh. In terms of coal consumption in therms, one therm equals 29.3 kwh. The annual energy consumption of electric cookers is $.8 \times 10^{9}$ therm. To generate this electric energy from coal-fired turbines at 40 percent efficiency requires 2×10^{9} therms. So the nominal energy wastage is 60 percent of 2×10^{9} therms = 1.2×10^{9} therms. But electric cookers are 25 percent more efficient than gas cookers so the wastage is more like 1×10^{9} therms. What does a billion therms cost?

Anthracite coal contains 315 therms per tonne. So the energy wastage is equivalent to three million tonnes of anthracite. Anthracite costs £110/tonne. The cost of the waste is then about £300 million, which is about 3 percent of the total annual energy costs of Great Britain.

*

The formula for the maximum efficiency of a heat engine, $e = 1\text{-}T_1/T_2$, made it plain that internal combustion engines would in principle be more far more efficient than steam engines. The idea is that the upper temperature instead of being the temperature of steam would be the very high temperatures of the burning fuel itself. In 1864 Nicholas A. Otto designed the modern four-stroke gasoline engine and by 1876 he constructed the first working model, the "silent Otto," with a compression ratio of 2.5 to 1 and a thermal efficiency of 14 percent. The four-stroke engine can be approximated by a cycle called the Otto cycle. A calculation of the efficiency of the Otto cycle, now given to undergraduates as an exercise, gives the formula $e = 1 - (V_2/V_1)^b$ where V_2 is the volume of the compressed gas at the top of the stroke, V_1 is the volume of the uncompressed gas at the bottom of the stroke, and b is a property of the fuel which for an air-gasoline mixture is about 0.4.

Now the designers could see that the thermal efficiency depended on so-called compression ratio, V_2/V_1, the ratio of the volumes of the compressed and uncompressed air-gasoline mixture. The modern automobile engine has a typical compression ratio of eight, and using a hand calculator one finds that the maximum theoretical efficiency of the Otto cycle is 56 percent. In practice the four-stroke internal combustion engine is no more than 15 percent–20 percent efficient, a major inefficiency arising from the explosive burning—knock—of the air gasoline mixture. The addition of 0.8 grams/liter of tetraethyl lead to the gasoline retards the combustion during the compression stroke of the engine so that less explosive, more uniform burning at high compression ratios can be achieved.

As has been known since Roman times, lead is an extremely hazardous chemical affecting the growth and functioning of the human central nervous system. A woodcut in Agricola's *De Re Metallica* (c. 1540) shows a lead worker eating butter to protect himself from lead fumes. Nevertheless in 1922, when Thomas Midgely, Jr., chief of the fuel section of the General Motors Research Corporation, discovered that tetraethyl lead acted to promote more efficient burning of air-gasoline mixtures, General Motors and Standard Oil Company formed the Ethyl Gasoline Corporation, which has resulted in the introduction of hazardous levels of lead into our environment in the name of producing high-performance automobile engines.

Carnot was alive to the dangers that a restricted concentration on high performance would bring to the design of heat engines. He concluded his analysis in 1824 with this warning: "We should not expect ever to utilise in practice all the motive power of combustibles. The attempts made to attain this result would be far more hurtful than useful if they caused other important considerations to be neglected."

In the last fifteen years the oil companies have reduced the lead in gasoline from 0.8g/1 to .15g/1 because popular pressure on U.S. and Japanese automakers has forced them to introduce catalytic converters. The catalytic converter consists of a porous ceramic that offers a massive surface area to the outgoing exhaust. Coating the surface is a thin layer, two molecules thick, of either platinum or palladium. The platinum acts to hold unburnt hydrocarbons, nitrous oxides, and carbon monoxide in place where they can combine with the oxygen in the air to produce relatively harmless carbon dioxide, water, and nitrogen. According to industry spokespersons, the system can reduce emissions by 85 percent–95 percent. But the platinum surface is poisoned by lead. Thus the refining industry has been forced to produce lead-free gasoline so that the automotive industry can use the catalytic converter.

*

There is a further structure to skylight than its blue color. When the sun is on the horizon, either at sunrise or sunset, the character of the blue light from the sky directly overhead is very different from the blue light coming from the horizon. This effect can be made visible to the human eye with the aid of Polaroid sunglasses. If one rotates the glasses at the sky directly overhead, one can observe marked changes in the intensity of the light coming through the Polaroid. A similar rotation at the sky on the horizon will show no such effect. One says that the light scattered from the atmosphere at right angles to the sun's rays is polarized. Polarized light causes receiving charges to oscillate in a particular pattern: straight up and down (called plane-polarized light); in a circle; or in an ellipse. The overhead skylight is partially plane-polarized.

Erasmus Bartholinus in 1669 first reported the existence of polarized light in a study of the optical properties of a crystal known as Iceland spar. Both Huygens and Newton also studied the effect. In 1808 Malus accidentally observed polarized light in the glare of sunlight reflected from the windows of the Luxembourg Palace. In 1828 Nicol designed a prism to facilitate the production and study of polarization effects. The Nicol prism remained the only efficient tool for producing polarized light until Edwin Land developed his Polaroid filters in the mid-1930s.

Polaroid filters consist of thin sheets of nitrocelluose into which the manufacturer inserts microcrystals of an organic compound called iodosulphate of quinine, a substance discovered by a student of W. B. Herapath in 1852. In the first of Land's filters, Land stretched polyvinyl alcohol films to line up the long molecules of the film. He then dosed the films with the quinine crystals. The charges in the quinine were then constrained by the polyvinyl film to oscillate only in one direction. In subsequent patents, he improved upon quinine by replacing it with ultramicroscopic particles of what are called inorganic periodides, using in particular the thirty-seven-letter compound purpureocobaltchloridesulphateperiodide. Today Polaroid sunglasses are a cheap, safe, effective screen against glare, the effect discovered by Malus at the Luxembourg Palace.

It turns out that the tiger salamander is capable of perceiving polarized light. Within the framework of evolutionary biology, one says that the process of evolution must have conferred a reproductive advantage on salamanders who had acquired this capacity. One hypothesizes that the selective advantage may consist of the increased knowledge that an animal at the bottom of a pool has of the position of the sun—the polarization of the sky overhead is maximum at sunset, minimum at noon—knowledge which may be useful for the purpose of the twilight migrations that characterize this species.

One of the things that the physics of the nineteenth century makes inescapable is that the physical universe has structures that exist whether we are here to see them or not. We are too far down the road of industrial development to return to the dinner party idealism of Bishop Berkeley and his descendants and their fabulous theories of the world as mind and mind alone. Indeed, this view has not been treated with the ridicule it deserves. We are much too grown up to continue to deny the experience of Edwin Land and the tiger salamander.

SOURCES

Adler, Ronald; Bazin, Maurice; and Schiffer, Menahem (1975). *Introduction to General Relativity,* McGraw-Hill, New York.

Albury, David, and Schwartz, Joseph (1982). *Partial Progress: The Politics of Science and Technology,* Pluto, London.

Beaud, Michel (1984). *A History of Capitalism 1500–1980,* trans. Tom Dickman and Anny Lefebvre, Macmillan, London.

Bernal, J. D. (1964). *Extension of Man,* Palladin, London.

Biezunski, Michel (1981). *La diffusion de la théorie de la relativité en France,* thesis, University of Paris VII, Department of the Teaching of the Physical Sciences and Technology.

Blackburn, Robin (1988). *The Overthrow of Colonial Slavery 1776–1848,* Verso, London.

Braudel, Fernand (1967). *Capitalism and Material Life 1400–1800,* trans. Miriam Kochan, Harper, New York.

——— (1977). *Afterthoughts on Material Civilization and Capitalism,* trans. Patricia Ranum, Johns Hopkins, Baltimore and London.

Carnot, L. H. (1861). *Mémoires sur Carnot par son fils,* v. 1, Paquerre, Paris.

Carnot, Sadi (1960). *Reflections on the Motive Power of Fire,* ed. with an introduction by E. Mendoza, Dover, New York.

——— (1986). *Reflexions on the Motive Power of Fire,* trans. and ed. Robert Fox, Manchester University Press, Manchester.

Chandresekhar, S. (1987). *Truth and Beauty. Aesthetics and Motivations in Science,* University of Chicago Press, Chicago.

——— (1979). "Beauty and the Quest for Beauty in Science," in *Proceedings of the International Symposium in Honor of Robert R. Wilson,* April 27, 1979, Fermi National Accelerator Laboratory, Batavia, Illinois.

Crowther, J. G. (1969). *Scientific Types,* Barrie and Rockliffe, London.

Cunningham, Andrew, and Jardine, Nicholas, eds. (1990). *Romanticism and the Sciences,* Cambridge University Press, Cambridge, England.

Daumas, Maurice, and Gille, Paul (1980). "The Steam Engine," in Maurice Daumas, ed., *A History of Technology and Invention,* v. 3, J. Murray, London.

Dickinson, H. W. (1958). "The Steam Engine," in C. Singer, E. J. Holmyard, A. R. Hall, and T. I. Williams, eds., *A History of Technology,* Clarendon Press, Oxford.

Einstein, Albert (1952). *The Principle of Relativity,* Dover, New York.

Engels, Frederick (1844). "The Position of England: The Eighteenth Century," in Karl Marx and Frederick Engels, *Articles on Britain,* Progress Publishers, Moscow (1975).

Feynman, R. P.; Leighton, R. B.; and Sands, M. (1963). *The Feynman Lectures on Physics,* v. 1, Addison-Wesley, Reading, Mass.

Frankel, Eugene (1977). "J. B. Biot and the Mathematization of Experimental Physics in Napoleonic France," *Historical Studies in the Physical Sciences,* v. 8, pp. 33–72.

Gillispie, Charles Coulson (1971). *Lazare Carnot, Savant,* Princeton University Press, Princeton.

Hafele, J. C., and Keating, Richard E. (1972). "Around-the-World Atomic Clocks: Observed Relativistic Time Gains," *Science* v. 177, pp. 168–70.

Hill, Christopher (1967). *Reformation to Industrial Revolution,* Penguin, London.

Hobsbawm, E. J. (1962). *Age of Revolution 1789–1848,* Abacus, London.

Howard, D., and Stachel, J., eds. (1989). *Einstein and the History of General Relativity,* Birkhauser, Boston.

Jennings, Humphrey (1985). *Pandemonium 1660–1886: The Coming of the Machine as Seen by Contemporary Observers,* Andre Deutsch, London.

Landau, L., and Lifshitz, E. (1951). *The Classical Theory of Fields,* Addison-Wesley, Reading, Mass.

Levy, Jacques R. (1972). "Leverrier," in Charles C. Gillispie, ed., *Dictionary of Scientific Biography,* Simon and Schuster, New York.

Marx, Karl (1967). *Capital, v. 1: A Critical Analysis of Capitalist Production,* International Publishers, New York.

Pais, Abraham (1982). *"Subtle is the Lord ..." The Science and the Life of Albert Einstein,* Oxford University Press, New York.

Pyenson, Lewis (1982). "Audacious Enterprise: The Einsteins and Electrotechnology in Late Nineteenth Century Munich," *Historical Studies in the Physical Sciences,* v. 12, pp. 373–92

——— (1985). *The Young Einstein: The Advent of Relativity,* Adam Hilger, Bristol.

Rudé, George (1964). *Revolutionary Europe 1783–1815,* Fontana, London.

Schwartz, Joseph, and McGuiness, Michael (1979). *Einstein for Beginners,* Pantheon, New York.

Stachel, John, ed. (1987). *The Collected Papers of Albert Einstein, v. 1: The Early Years, 1879–1902,* Princeton University Press, Princeton.

Tredgold, Thomas (1838). *The Steam Engine,* London.

Weinberg, Steven (1972). *Gravitation and Cosmology,* John Wiley, New York.

CHAPTER 3: Munich 1919/Alamogordo 1945

NOTES

The self-understanding physicists had of their activity on the bomb project was that the Nazis must be beaten. Thirty and forty years after the event the threat of the Nazis still dominates the recollections of the physicists who participated in the Manhattan Project. "The Germans had Hitler and the possibility of developing an atomic bomb was obvious and the possibility that they would develop it before us was very much of a fright," said Feynman at a lecture in 1975. Victor Weisskopf, a former director-general of CERN, said in 1985: "Nuclear weapons in the hands of Hitler could well have meant his victory; there was no choice but to develop them on our side as fast as possible." Theoretical physicist Rudolph Peierls recalled in 1985: "For all we knew the Germans could already be working on such a weapon, and the idea of Hitler getting it first was most frightening."

But Germany surrendered on May 7, 1945, two months before the Alamogordo test shot on July 16. Why, as Brian Easlea asks, if fear of the Nazis was the overriding concern, did they not stop work as Joseph Rotblat did and go home? "We stopped thinking," said Feynman. But stopping thinking is a complex act. Peierls has addressed the question with some sensitivity.

> Given all the wisdom of hindsight, what should we have done? Should we have refrained from working on the atom bomb from the beginning, or stopped work after the defeat of Germany? The first would have meant an intolerable risk; at the later stage there was still a bloody and cruel war going on, which could have been and was shortened by the new weapon....
>
> Or should we have insisted on keeping control over the way the results of our work were being used? This would have implied an arrogant assumption that we were better qualified than others to make the right political and military decisions, and in any case it could never have been achieved. My regrets are that we did not insist on more dialogue with the military and political leaders, based on full and clear scientific discussions of the consequences of possible courses of action. It is not clear of course that such discussions would have made any difference in the end.

The lack of confidence that made the physicists feel that they were not qualified to challenge their superiors and made them accept with little question that the bomb must be completed to use against Japan stemmed partially from a lack of political vision. These men had seen the

Russian Revolution, socialist revolutions in Germany and Hungary, Red Clyde in Scotland, the 1926 General Strike in Britain, and the shelling by the Austrian government of workers' housing in Red Vienna. For many of them the threat of socialist revolution was more fearsome than the rise of the Nazi Party. For others the Nazis were an inconvenience that stopped them from doing physics. Einstein was always being told to stop making so much fuss. "The soup is never eaten as hot as it is cooked," Planck said to him in the early 1930s. Schroedinger felt that both the Nazis and their socialist and Communist opposition were ridiculous. "What is the difference between a Nazi and a Sozi?" he used to joke. Bohr, until corrected by Rosenfeld, thought Heisenberg was perhaps right, that the Nazis would bring order to Germany. Amaldi recalled that in the depths of Fascist Italy, "physics as soma" was the response of Fermi's group in Rome. The physicists did not have the political experience that could have given them the confidence to recognize when they and their betters in the U.S. military and political establishments had come to a parting of the ways.

But there is an additional dynamic at work. The physicists of the 1920s and 1930s were men who had found intense satisfaction in the direct sensuous engagement with physical reality. The excitement of the detection of the passage of a previously invisible cosmic ray, the excitement of successfully building equipment that could detect the magnetic moment of the neutron, the sensitive tuning of the cyclotron to permit the appearance of new nuclear isotopes, the profound experience of understanding the specific heat of hydrogen were experiences that, in the social turmoil of the 1920s and 1930s, they could share with few others. These were men who to a significant degree found in their relationship with nature the intimacy, connection, and sensitivity that most of us associate with human relationships.

But even though their relationship with nature was profoundly human, the physicists of the 1920s and 1930s were driven in their work. As Luis Alvarez described the work at Berkeley in the 1930s: "People who did not work eighty hours a week were considered to be not very interested in physics."

Many of them were teased and ridiculed for being bookish, for being eggheads, for tinkering endlessly by themselves with equipment in the family garage, for being too good in school, for being precocious, for being in the end not as socialized or integrated into the normal heterosexual male identity as other boy children of their cohort. Their relationships with women would have been strained, as young women would not have been able to place or understand these awkward, socially unskilled youths. They would have been eager to answer the call of physics, and disappointed that others could not or would not appreciate what they found so appealing. And they would have grown into adulthood with a certain sense of failure in terms of the standard images of male behavior.

These were men who perhaps more than most had something to prove. Alvarez, with a record of outstanding accomplishment before the war, recalled of his work on radar and the bomb: "We went away boys and came back men." Not only did the 1930s physicists participate in the building of the bomb, they pursued it with such a passion that even now many describe it as the most fulfilling time of their lives. When Fermi arrived in Los Alamos in September 1944, he was amazed at the intensity of feeling he found. "You people act as if you actually *want* to build this bomb," he said.

This commitment to succeed is difficult to understand with real accuracy because the participants themselves have been unwilling to question themselves sufficiently closely. An exception is Victor Weisskopf, who, in his memoirs published in 1991, has given more thoughtful attention to the nuances of his motivation at the time than he has in the past.

> Today I am not quite sure whether my decision to participate in the awesome—and awful—enterprise was solely based on the fear of the Nazis beating us to it. It may have been more simply an urge to participate in the important work my friends and colleagues were doing. There was certainly a feeling of pride in being part of a unique and sensational enterprise. Also, this was a chance to show the world how powerful, important and pragmatic the esoteric science of nuclear physics could be.

Robert Jay Lifton, who has had extensive experience in analyzing the experiences of people involved in highly destructive events, has concluded that the participants in nuclear weapons development and the perpetrators of the Nazi crimes suffered a similar genocidal mentality, a transcendence offered by the act of creating powerful destructive capabilities that blots out awareness of the fate of the human species as a whole.

Such an interpretation may appear extreme. But it is clear that both the Holocaust and the atomic bomb were marking points in the history of the human race. In the interwar years, the intersection of the historical/social dynamics of capitalism and the social/interpersonal dynamics of patriarchy was such that two projects causing unparalleled human agony could be brought into existence. We will probably never be able to understand the experience of the Nazi doctors. But it would be good if Philip Morrison, Robert Wilson, Owen Chamberlain, and the numerous other surviving participants in the Manhattan Project could share their reflections on their involvement in the light of recent evidence and analyses.

SOURCES

Interviews

The oral history archive of the Niels Bohr Library at the American Institute of Physics is an invaluable source for any person wishing to understand the physics of the 1920s and 1930s. Credit goes to the American Institute of Physics for housing and maintaining the archive; to Thomas Kuhn, who recognized thirty years ago how valuable the experiences of the physicists of the 1920s would prove to be; and to the skill of the interviewers, of whom Charles Weiner may be particularly mentioned. The level of preparation of the interviewers has produced an archive at a high technical and historical level.

Luis Alvarez, by Charles Weiner, February 7, 1967.
Hans Bethe, by T. S. Kuhn, January 17, 1964.
Hermann Bondi, by David DeVorkin, March 20, 1978.
Richard Courant, by T. S. Kuhn and M. Kac, May 9, 1962.
P. P. Ewald, by T. S. Kuhn, March 29, 1962, and by Charles Weiner, May 17–24, 1968.
Phillip Frank, by T. S. Kuhn, July 9, 1962; July 12, 1962.
Maurice Goldhaber, by Gloria Lubkin and Charles Weiner, January 10, 1966.
Werner Heisenberg, by T. S. Kuhn, November 30, 1962; February 7, 1963; February 11, 1963; February 13, 1963; February 15, 1963; February 19, 1963; February 27, 1963.
Samuel A. Goudsmit, by T. S. Kuhn, December 5, 1963; December 7, 1963.
Philip Morrison, by Charles Weiner, February 7, 1967.
Frank Oppenheimer, by Charles Weiner, February 9, 1973.
Leon Rosenfeld, by T. S. Kuhn and J. L. Heilbron, July 1, 1963.
E. E. Salpeter, by Spencer Weart, March 30, 1978.
Dirk Struik, by Charles Weiner, November 17, 1983.
George Uhlenbeck, by T. S. Kuhn, March 30, 1962.
Clyde Wiegand, by Bruce Wheaton, September 26, 1977.

Other Sources

Abendroth, Wolfgang (1972). *A Short History of the European Working Class*, New Left Books, London.
Alvarez, Luis W. (1987). *Adventures of a Physicist*, Basic Books, New York.
Anderson, Evelyn (1945). *Hammer or Anvil. The Story of the German Working-Class Movement*, Gollancz, London.
Anderson, Herbert (1973). "Three Questions About the Sustained Nucle-

ar Chain Reaction," *The University of Chicago Magazine*, March/April, pp. 3–7.

Badash, Lawrence; Hirschfelder, Joseph O.; and Broida, Herbert P. (1980). *Reminiscences of Los Alamos, 1943–1945*, Studies in the History of Modern Science 5, Reidel, London.

Berger, John (1969). *The Cubist Moment*, Weidenfeld & Nicolson, London.

Beyerchen, Alan D. (1977). *Scientists Under Hitler*, Yale, New Haven.

Boller, Paul F., Jr. (1982). "Hiroshima and the American Left, 1945," *International Social Science Review*, Winter 1982.

Born, Max (1926). *Problems of Atomic Dynamics*, M.I.T. Press, Cambridge, Mass.

———(no date). *Atomic Physics*, fifth ed. (first ed., 1936), Hafner, New York.

——— (1971). *The Born-Einstein Letters*, Macmillan, London.

Bradley, John (1978). *The Illustrated History of the Third Reich*, Magma Books, Leicester.

Byelorusfilm & Mosfilm (1985). *Come and See*.

Casimir, Hendrik B. G. (1983). *Haphazard Reality. Half a Century of Science*, Harper and Row, New York.

Cohen, K. P.; Runcorn, S. K.; Suess, H. E.; and Thode, H. G. (1983). "Harold Clayton Urey," in *Biographical Memoirs of the Fellows of the Royal Society*, v. 29.

Davis, Nuel, Pharr (1968). *Lawrence and Oppenheimer*, Simon & Schuster, New York.

Deighton, Len (1988). *Winter. A Berlin Family 1899–1945*, Grafton, London.

Ehrenfest, P. (1932). *"Einige die Quantenmechanik betreffende Erkungdigungsfragen," Zeitschrift für Physik*, v. 78, pp. 555–59.

Einstein, Albert; Schroedinger, Erwin; Planck, Max; and Lorentz, H. A. (1967). *Letters on Wave Mechanics*, ed. K. Przibram, Philosophical Library, New York.

Forman, P. (1972). "Weimar Culture, Causality and Quantum Theory, 1918–1927: Adaptation by German Physicists to a Hostile Intellectual Environment," *Historical Studies in the Physical Sciences*, pp. 1–115.

——— (1974). "The Financial Support and Political Alignment of Physicists in Weimar Germany," *Minerva*, v. 12, pp. 39–66.

———, and Hermann, A. (1972). "Sommerfeld," in C. C. Gillispie, ed., *Dictionary of Scientific Biography*, Scribners, New York.

Gilbert, Martin (1986). *The Holocaust. The Jewish Tragedy*, Fontana/Collins, London.

Groves, Leslie A. (1962). *Now It Can Be Told. The Story of the Manhattan Project*, Harper & Row, New York.

Heilbron, J. L. (1983). "The Origins of the Exclusion Principle," *Historical Studies in the Physical Sciences*, v. 13, part 2, pp. 261–311.

Heisenberg, Werner (1971). *Physics and Beyond. Encounters and Conversations*, Harper & Row, New York.

——— (1976). *Across the Frontier*, Harper & Row, New York.

Hermann, Armin (1979). *The New Physics. The Route into the Atomic Age*, Inter Nationes, Bonn/Bad Godesberg.

——— (1976). *Werner Heisenberg 1901–1976*, Inter Nationes, Bonn/Bad Godesberg.

Heyck, T. W. (1982). *The Transformation of Intellectual Life in Victorian England*, Croom and Helm, London.

Hobsbawm, E. J. (1968). "The Fabians Revisited," in E. J. Hobsbawm, *Labouring Men: Studies in the History of Labour*, Weidenfeld & Nicolson, London, pp. 250–71.

Jones, R. V. (1978). *Most Secret War. British Scientific Intelligence 1939–1945*, Hamish Hamilton, London.

——— (1987). "A Merchant of Light" (review of Kramish [see below]), *Nature*, v. 325, pp. 203–204.

——— (1987). Telephone interview with J. Schwartz, May 19.

Kangro, Hans (1972). "Planck," in C. C. Gillispie, ed., *Dictionary of Scientific Biography*, Scribners, New York.

Kedrov, B. M. (1972). "Mendeleev," in Gillispie, ed., *op cit.*

Kirchoff, G. (1863). "Contributions Towards a History of Spectrum Analysis and of the Analysis of the Solar Atmosphere," *Philosophical Magazine*, v. 25, pp. 250–63.

Kramish, Arnold (1986). *The Griffin: The Greatest Untold Espionage Story of World War II*, Houghton Mifflin, New York.

Lifton, Robert Jay, and Markusen, Eric (1990). *The Genocidal Mentality. Nazi Holocaust and Nuclear Threat*, Basic Books, New York.

Lock, Grahame (1973). Introduction to Karl Liebknecht, *Militarism and Anti-militarism*, Rivers Press, Cambridge, England.

Maier, Charles S. (1975). *Recasting Bourgeois Europe*, Princeton University Press, Princeton, New Jersey.

McCormmach, Russell (1982). *Night Thoughts of a Classical Physicist*, Harvard University Press, Cambridge, Mass.

McGucken, William (1969). *Nineteenth Century Spectroscopy. Development of the Understanding of Spectra 1802–1897*, Johns Hopkins, Baltimore.

Noble, David F. (1977). *America by Design. Science, Technology, and the Rise of Corporate Capitalism*, Knopf, New York.

Pais, Abraham (1982). *"Subtle is the Lord ..." The Science and the Life of Albert Einstein*, Oxford University Press, New York.

Pauli, Hertha (1972). *Break of Time (Der Riss der Zeit geht durch mein Herz)*, Hawthorn Books, New York.

Pauli, Wolfgang (1933). *"Einige die Quantenmechanik betreffende Erkungdigungsfragen," Zeitschrift für Physik*, v. 80, pp. 573–86.

——— (1945). In *The Nobel Lectures 1942–1962,* Elsevier, Amsterdam, pp. 27–43.

———, ed. (1955). *Niels Bohr and the Development of Physics,* McGraw-Hill, New York.

Pearson, Karl (1901). *The Ethic of Freethought,* 2nd ed., London, pp. 303–11.

Peierls, Rudolph (1985). *Bird of Passage,* Princeton University Press, Princeton.

Reissner, Larissa (1977). *Hamburg at the Barricades,* trans. and ed. Richard Chappell, Pluto, London.

Rhodes, Richard (1986). *The Making of the Atomic Bomb,* Penguin, London.

Roizen, Ron (1986). "Herschel Grynszpan: The Fate of a Forgotten Assassin," *Holocaust and Genocide Studies,* v. 1, pp. 217–28.

Rosenfeld, L. (1972). "Kirchoff," in Gillispie, ed., *op cit.*

Rotblat, Joseph (1985). "Leaving the Bomb Project," *Bulletin of the Atomic Scientists,* August.

——— (1989). Interview with J. Schwartz, June 22, London.

Schacher, Susan G. (1972). "Bunsen," in Gillispie, ed., *op cit.*

Schorske, Carl E. (1955). *German Social Democracy 1905–1917. The Development of the Great Schism,* Harvard University Press, Cambridge, Mass.

Schuster, A. (1910). Spectroscopy in *Encyclopaedia Britannica,* 11th ed., v. 25, pp. 619–33.

Segré, Émilio (1970). *Enrico Fermi. Physicist,* University of Chicago, Chicago.

Serwer, Daniel (1977). "*Unmechanischer Zwang:* Pauli, Heisenberg and the Rejection of the Mechanical Atom 1923–1925," *Historical Studies in the Physical Sciences,* v. 8, pp. 189–256.

Sherwin, Martin J. (1973). *A World Destroyed/The Atomic Bomb and the Grand Alliance,* Knopf, New York.

Shirer, William L. (1984). *20th Century Journey. A Memoir of a Life and the Times. Volume II. The Nightmare Years 1930–1940,* Bantam, New York.

Smith, Alice Kimball (1965). *A Peril and a Hope. The Scientists Movement in America 1945–1947,* University of Chicago Press, Chicago.

———, and Weiner, Charles, eds. (1980). *Robert Oppenheimer. Letters and Recollections,* Harvard University Press, Cambridge, Mass.

Snow, C. P. (1966). *Variety of Men,* Scribners, New York.

Stoner, E. C. (1924). "Suggested Distribution of Electrons Among Atomic Levels," *Philosophical Magazine,* v. 48, pp. 719–36.

Tash, Tony (1989). "The New Music," part 6 of the series *Man and Music,* Granada Television, made for Channel Four Television, London.

Thomas, L. H. (1926). "The Motion of the Spinning Electron," *Nature,* v. 117, p. 514

Thomson, G. P. (1966). *J. J. Thomson. Discoverer of the Electron,* Anchor, New York.

Thomson, J. J. (1903). *The Conduction of Electricity Through Gases*, Cambridge University Press, Cambridge, England.

Uhlenbeck, G. E., and Goudsmit, S. (1926). "Spinning Electrons and the Structure of Spectra," *Nature*, v. 117, pp. 264–65.

van der Waerden, B. L. (1960). "Exclusion Principle and Spin," in M. Fierz and V. F. Weisskopf, eds., *Theoretical Physics in the Twentieth Century. A Memorial Volume to Wolfgang Pauli*, Interscience, New York.

——— (1967) Intro. and ed., *Sources of Quantum Mechanics*, Classics of Science, v. 5, Dover, New York.

Walker, F. A. (1887). *Lectures Delivered Before the Students of Phillips Exeter Academy 1885–1886*, Boston.

Weart, Spencer R. (1982). "The Road to Los Alamos," in "International Colloquium on the History of Particle Physics. Some Discoveries, Concepts, Institutions from the Thirties to Fifties," *Journal de Physique*, Tome 43, Colloque C-8, supplément au no. 12, pp. 301–21.

——— (1988). *Nuclear Fear. A History of Images*, Harvard University Press, Cambridge, Mass.

Weisskopf, V. (1972). *Physics in the Twentieth Century*, M.I.T. Press, Cambridge, Mass.

——— (1991). *The Joy of Insight. Passions of a Physicist*, Basic Books, New York.

Willett, John (1978). *The New Sobriety. Art and Politics in the Weimar Period 1917–1933*, Thames and Hudson, London.

CHAPTER 4: Cold Spring Harbor 1946

NOTES

The references to the critical literature on the heritability of IQ performance are:

Leon Kamin, *The Science and Politics of IQ* (New York, 1974).
Stephen Jay Gould, *The Mismeasure of Man* (New York, 1981).
F. S. Fehr, *Harvard Educational Review 39* (1969), 57.
D. Layzer, *Science 183* (1974), 1259.
Hilary Putnam, *Cognition 2* (1973), 131.
P. A. P. Moran, *Annals of Human Genetics 37* (1973), 217.
R. C. Lewontin and R. Feldman, *Science 190* (1975) 1163.
A. Vetta, *Nature 263* (1976), 263.
D. J. Cohen and colleagues, *Archives of General Psychiatry 29* (1973), 465.
B. Tizard, *Nature 247* (1974), 316.
M. Schwartz and J. Schwartz, *Nature 248* (1974), 84.

M. Ghodsian and K. Richardson, *Nature 263* (1976), 314.
D. D. Dorfman, *Science 201* (1978), 1177.

*

The literature of intelligence testing contains numerous references to the concept of inherited intelligence in the writings of Plato and Aristotle. Plato, a wealthy Athenian aristocrat, wrote *The Republic* to secure a court appointment as tutor to Dionysius II, Tyrant of Syracuse. Plato saw human intelligence as the ability to grasp the concept of eternal category: those who cannot see the platonic ideal are less intelligent than those who can.

> I can understand, Socrates, how a person could see a table or a cup but you are saying that there is an ideal cup or a universal table. And Tableness is something I don't see.
>
> This is natural, since you have the eyes wherewith to see the table and with which to see the cup, but you do not have the intelligence wherewith to see tableness and cupness.

When cited superficially, the reference to ancient Greek conceptions of intelligence conveys a timeless quality to the concept of inherited intelligence. But in fact the intervening one thousand years of medieval society were predicated on a fundamental human equality rather than a fundamental inequality.

The breakup of classical Greek and Roman civilization is conventionally dated to the reign of Hadrian (117–138 A.D.). The slave-run Roman latifundia and central Roman authority evolved into self-sufficient manorial holdings and a relatively decentralized political structure. The serfs were not free but neither were they the personal property of the landlord. The system developed into a set of mutual rights and obligations, much to the landlord's benefit.

The prevailing view of human capacity in the medieval period was equality between individuals and classes based on the myth of Adam and Eve as the common ancestors of all humanity. The Church argued that social inequality on earth was only temporary—an expression of God's will. True equality would be found in the hereafter. On earth liberty and servitude were only relative. True liberty in earthly life consisted in being free from earthly passions. True servitude was being enslaved to vice and therefore being unable to follow the Scriptures. And since all were equal before God, all were equally capable of obeying God's will. "Whoever thinks that either the status of (true) liberty or servitude is due to any innate cause is in error, since mankind upon the earth has a similar origin, consists of and is nourished by the same elements, breathes the same air and lives and dies with others of his kind," wrote John of

Salisbury in 1159 in *Policraticus,* a guide to feudal behavior.

The feudal hierarchy was challenged from below with claims that equality meant equality in the here and now. The English peasant revolt of 1381 based its claims for tax relief, a ceiling on rents, freedom to buy and sell in the cities, and manumission of the serfs on the human equality preached in the Bible. The voice of the movement was John Ball, a provincial chaplain: "At the beginning all were created equal. It is the tyranny of perverse men that has caused servitude to arise, in spite of God's law; if God had willed that there should be serfs, He would have said at the beginning who should be serf and who should be lord."

Far from being a cultural universal, the concept of a differentially inherited intelligence is very much an artifact of certain kinds of class societies unable to respond to pressures to develop more democratic forms of social life and interaction.

*

The retrospective of nineteenth-century American painting mounted at the Smithsonian Institution in Washington, D.C., by William Treuttner in June 1991 shows clearly the racism and class antagonisms roused in established society by the development of monopoly. Paintings of last stands in the Old West were eagerly snapped up by patrons in high society as metaphors for Anglo-Saxons holding the fort against the floodgates of immigration. Frederic Remington, the most famous painter of these nostalgic evocations of Old America, was similar to Francis Galton in his racism and in his hatred of the working class. "You can't glorify a Jew—coin lovin' puds—nasty humans. I've got some Winchesters and when the massacreing begins ... I can get my share of 'em and what's more I will ... Jews, injuns, Chinamen, Italians, Huns, the rubbish of the earth I hate." In his coverage of the famous Pullman strike of 1894, Remington wrote: "... a malodorous crowd of anarchistic foreign trash ... vicious wretches with no blood circulating above the ears ... will follow any demagogue with revolutionary tendencies."

The attitudes expressed by the Nazis were not unique to Germany. They were widespread in every advanced country in the West. It is true, of course, that it was in Germany, to its everlasting shame, that action on these feelings was carried out in an unprecedented way.

SOURCES

The Galton Archive, University College, London.

Walker, F. A. *Memorabilia,* a collection of clippings housed at the New York Public Library.

Adams, Jad (1989). *Aids: The HIV Myth,* Macmillan, London.

Albury, David, and Schwartz, Joseph (1982). *Partial Progress. The Politics of Science and Technology,* Pluto, London.

Allen, Garland (1975). *Life Science in the Twentieth Century,* Cambridge University Press, Cambridge.

Ann Arbor Science for the People Collective (1977). *Biology as a Social Weapon,* Burgess Publishing Company, Minneapolis.

Applebury, Meredithe L. (1990). "News and Views: Insight into Blindness," *Nature,* v. 343, pp. 316–17.

Baltimore, David, and Feinberg, Mark B. (1989). Editorial: "HIV Revealed. Toward a Natural History of the Infection," *New England Journal of Medicine,* v. 321, pp. 1673–75.

Blattner, W.; Gallo, R. C.; and Temin, H. (1988). Policy Forum: "HIV Causes AIDS," *Science,* v. 241, pp. 515–16.

Brown, Michael Barrett (1988). "Away with All the Great Arches: Anderson's History of British Capitalism," *New Left Review,* 167, January/February, pp. 22–51.

Cairns, J.; Stent, G. S.; and Watson J. D. (1966). *Phage and the Origins of Molecular Biology,* Cold Spring Harbor Laboratory of Quantitative Biology, Cold Spring Harbor, New York.

Chargaff, Erwin (1971). "Preface to a Grammar of Biology," *Science,* v. 172, pp. 637–42.

Concar, David (1990). News: "AIDS Research Funding. Budget Division Disputed," *Nature,* v. 344, p. 803.

Cowan, Ruth S. (1977). "Nature and Nurture: The Interplay of Biology and Politics in the Work of Francis Galton," *Studies in the History of Biology,* v. 12, pp. 133–208.

Crick, Francis (1988). *What Mad Pursuit. A Personal View of Scientific Discovery,* Basic Books, New York.

———, *et al.* (1974). "Molecular Biology Comes of Age," *Nature,* v. 248, pp. 766–88.

Delbrück, Max (1972). "Signal Transducers: Terra Incognita of Molecular Biology," *Angewandte Chemie,* International Edition, v. 2, January, pp. 1–6.

——— (1978). "Mind from Matter?," *American Scholar,* v. 47, pp. 339–53.

——— (1986). *Mind from Matter. An Essay on Evolutionary Epistemology,* Blackwell, Oxford.

Duesberg, Peter H. (1987). "Retroviruses as Carcinogens and Pathogens: Expectations and Reality," *Cancer Research,* v. 47, pp. 1199–1220.

——— (1988). Policy Forum: "HIV is Not the Cause of AIDS," *Science,* v. 241, pp. 514–17. And see following correspondence with Duesberg reply on November 18, pp. 997–98.

——— (1989). "Human Immunodeficiency Virus and Acquired Immunodeficiency Syndrome: Correlations but Not Causation," *Proceedings of the National Academy of Sciences, USA,* v. 86, pp. 755–64.

——— (1990). "AIDS: Non-infectious Deficiencies Acquired by Drug Consumption and Other Risk Factors," *Research in Immunology*, v. 141, pp. 5–11.

Eigen, Manfred (1989). "The AIDS Debate," *Naturwissenschaften*, v. 76, pp. 341–50.

Evans, Alfred S. (1989). Review: "Does HIV Cause AIDS? An Historical Perspective," *Journal of Acquired Immune Deficiency Syndrome*, v. 2, pp. 107–13.

Gallo, R. C. (1985). Introduction for P. H. Duesberg, *Haematology and Blood Transfusion*, v. 29, pp. 7–8.

Galton, Francis (1908). *Memories of My Life*, London.

Geison, Gerald L. (1972). "Pasteur," in C. C. Gillispie, ed., *Dictionary of Scientific Biography*, Scribners, New York.

Gould, Stephen Jay (1981). *The Mismeasure of Man*, W.W. Norton, New York.

——— (1989). *Wonderful Life. The Burgess Shale and the Nature of History*, Hutchinson Radius, London.

Hayes, William (1968). *The Genetics of Bacteria and Their Viruses. Studies in Basic Genetics and Molecular Biology*, 2nd ed., Wiley, New York.

Ho, David D.; Moudgil, Tarsem; and Alam, Masud (1989). "Quantitation of Human Immunodeficiency Virus Type I in the Blood of Infected Persons," *The New England Journal of Medicine*, v. 321, pp. 1622–25; following report, same issue, Robert W. Coombs, *et al.*, Plasma Viremia in Human Immunodeficiency Virus Infection," pp. 1626–31; and ensuing correspondence from Duesberg with replies from Ho, Coombs, and Baltimore, *ibid.*, v. 322, pp. 1466–68.

Hobsbawm, E. J. (1964). "The Fabians Reconsidered," in *Labouring Men. Studies in the History of Labour*, Weidenfeld & Nicolson, London.

Jacob, Francois (1988). *The Statue Within. An Autobiography*, Basic Books, New York.

Kamin, Leon J. (1974). *The Science and Politics of IQ*, Lawrence Erlbaum Associates, Potomac, Maryland. Distributed by the Halsted Division of John Wiley, New York.

Kion, Tracy A., and Hoffman Geoffrey W. (1991). "Anti-HIV and Anti-Anti-MHC Antibodies in Alloimmune and Autoimmune Mice," *Science*, v. 253, pp. 1138–1140.

Lane, Harlan (1976). *The Wild Boy of Aveyron*, Palladin, London.

Levidow, Les, ed. (1986). *Science as Politics*, Free Association, London.

Lewontin, Richard C. (1968). Review of Cairns, *et al.* (1966), *Phage and the Origins of Molecular Biology*, in *Journal of the History of Biology*, v. 1, pp. 155–61.

Lewontin, R. C. (1990). Letter: "Are We Robots?," *New York Review of Books*, May 31, p. 45, with reply by John Maynard Smith, pp. 45–46.

Levy, Jay A. (1988). "Mysteries of HIV: Challenges for Therapy and Prevention," *Nature,* v. 333, pp. 519–22.

Luria, S. E. (1973). *Life. The Unfinished Experiment,* Scribners, New York.

——— (1984). *A Slot Machine, a Broken Test Tube. An Autobiography,* Harper & Row, New York.

Luzzatto, L., and Goodfellow, P. (1989). News and Views: "A Simple Disease with No Cure, *Nature,* v. 337, pp. 17–18.

Maddox, John (1991). News and Views: "AIDS Research Turned Upside Down," *Nature,* v. 353, p. 297.

Mayr, Ernst (1988). *Toward a New Philosophy of Biology. Observations of an Evolutionist,* Harvard University Press, Cambridge, Mass.

Olby, Robert (1974). *The Path to the Double Helix,* Macmillan, London.

Orbach, Susie; Schwartz, Laura; Schwartz, Mike; and Schwartz, Joe (1978). "The Myth of Intelligence," *Science for the People,* v. 10, March/April, pp. 7–14.

Pearson, Karl (1914–1930). *The Life, Letters and Labours of Francis Galton,* 3 vols., Cambridge University Press, Cambridge, England.

Petersen, J. (1925). *Early Conceptions and Tests of Intelligence,* New York.

Root-Bernstein, Robert S. (1990). "Do We Know the Cause(s) of AIDS?," *Perspectives in Biology and Medicine,* v. 33, pp. 480–500.

Rose, Steven; Lewontin, R. C.; and Kamin, Leon J. (1984). *Not in Our Genes,* Pelican, London.

Rubin, Harry (1988). Letters: "Etiology of AIDS," *Science,* June 10, p. 1389. And see critical letter, July 22, *ibid.,* V. De Gruttola and S. W. Lagakos, "AIDS Risk," p. 399.

——— (1988). Scientific Correspondence: "Is HIV the Causative Factor in AIDS?," *Nature,* v. 324, p. 201.

Sayre, Anne (1975). *Rosalind Franklin and DNA,* W.W. Norton, New York.

Schroedinger, Erwin (1956). *What Is Life?,* Doubleday, New York.

Schwartz, Michael, and Schwartz, Joseph (1974). "Evidence Against a Genetical Component to Performance on IQ Tests," *Nature,* v. 248, pp. 84–85.

Stott, E. J. *et al.* (1991). Scientific Correspondence: "Anti-cell Antibody in Macaques," *Nature,* v. 353, p. 393.

Wagner, Robert P.; Judd, Burke H.; Sanders, Bob G.; and Richardson, Richard H. (1980). *Introduction to Modern Genetics,* John Wiley, New York.

Thomson, George (1972). *The First Philosophers,* Lawrence and Wishart, London.

Watson, James D. (1968). *The Double Helix,* New American Library, New York.

Weber, Jonathan (1988). "AIDS and the 'Gulity' Virus," *New Scientist,* May 5, pp. 32–33.

Weiss, Robin A., and Jaffe, Harold W. (1990). Commentary: "Duesberg, HIV and AIDS," *Nature*, v. 345, pp. 659–60.

Winn, Marie (1990). "New Views of Human Intelligence," *New York Times Magazine*, part 2, "Good Health," p. 16.

Wright, Logan (1968). *Bibliography on Human Intelligence. An Extensive Bibliography*, U.S. Department of Health, Education and Welfare, Public Health Service Publication No. 1839, Superintendent of Documents, U.S. Government Printing Office. Washington, D.C. 20402.

Wyatt, H. V. (1974). "How History Has Blended," *Nature*, v. 249, pp. 803–805.

Young, Robert M. (1985). *Darwin's Metaphor*, Cambridge University Press, Cambridge, England.

Yoxen, Edward (1986). *Unnatural Selection. Coming to Terms with the New Genetics*, Heinemann, London.

Chapter 5: Berkeley 1963/Geneva 1984

NOTES

The remoteness of particle physics makes it easy to forget that the outlines of the subject as we know it today took shape in the 1950s in the United States, a decade marked by McCarthyism. The political climate of the times was a contributing factor to the loss of the criterion of comprehensibility as the definition of a successful theory.

The case of J. Robert Oppenheimer has come to symbolize what are called the excesses of the McCarthy period. But numerous other, less well-known, persecutions succeeded in destroying left-wing opposition in the United States in the 1950s. Physicists were not exempt. Melba Phillips was blacklisted from 1952 to 1957 for her refusal to cooperate with the McCarran Committee. Philip Morrison was nearly jailed on charges of subversion. Joseph Weinberg was suspended in 1951 by the president of the University of Minnesota and subsequently accused of perjury for which he had to stand trial, to be acquitted in March 1953. David Bohm was acquitted in 1951 for contempt of court, a charge routinely brought against those who refused to cooperate with the investigating committees.

Berkeley lost its entire theoretical physics faculty over the issue of loyalty oaths. Gian Carlo Wick refused to sign and was banned from the Radiation Laboratory by its director Ernest Lawrence. Wick and Harold Lewis were fired by the president of the university, Robert Sproull. Geoffrey Chew and Howard Wilcox resigned.

The experimentalist Wolfgang Panofsky put up a fuss. His aunt had been an ardent socialist in the Weimar Republic and had been the first woman police commissioner in Germany. His father, the noted art historian Erwin Panofsky, had been dismissed from his post at the University of Hamburg in 1934 under the Nazi anti-Jewish laws. Panofsky's boss, Luis Alvarez, argued with him. If you are not a Communist, why do you object to signing? Panofsky felt it was precisely because he was not a Communist that he should not sign. Raymond Birge, chairman of the physics department, later recalled in wonderment that Panofsky had had a "psychotic hatred of loyalty oaths." It was Berkeley's loss. Panofsky went to Stanford, a private university more circumspect in its exclusion of left-wing persons. Others were not so lucky in finding other jobs. One of them was Frank Oppenheimer, Robert Oppenheimer's younger brother. The case of Frank Oppenheimer symbolizes what was lost to physics in the political purges of the 1950s.

Frank Oppenheimer joined the Communist Party in 1937 when he was a graduate student at Cal Tech. He was not a parlor Red. Along with pianist Ruth Tolman, wife of Cal Tech relativist E. C. Tolman, he organized benefit concerts and parties in support of the Spanish Republic. He helped organize a federation of architects, engineers, chemists, and technicians ("sort of a trade union"), which took up the issue of fingerprinting on license plate applications, as well as trying to establish political connections to the growing U.S. trade union movement. He worked hard for the political arm of the militant Congress of Industrial Organizations (CIO), and by 1939 he was "very involved."

After Cal Tech refused him a postdoctoral fellowship, he got a seventy-five-dollar-a-month research job at Stanford, where he embarrassed the university authorities by his political work. He helped organize the first teachers' union. He wrote a monthly bulletin for the Labor Non-partisan League of Palo Alto. His organization was banned from meeting in the Palo Alto Civic Center. It was mainstream activity, very much part of the vibrant political organizing that characterized Communist Party political work in the mid- and late 1930s.

By 1940 Oppenheimer found party membership a less useful tool to express his political concerns. He let his connection with the party fade. Beginning in 1941 he worked on the atomic bomb, first at Berkeley, where Ernest Lawrence did not care about his politics as long as Oppenheimer did not embarrass the laboratory, then at Westinghouse in Pittsburgh, and then at Oak Ridge for work on the separation of the fissile isotope, U-235, from the more abundant U-238, ending up working for his brother at Los Alamos, where he helped with the organization of the Trinity Test at Alamogordo.

Oppenheimer's involvement with the Communist Party was similar to that of the majority of party members of the period. He found party support of practical political work valuable and not in contradiction with his work as a physicist. It was part of the times. Indeed it was the best part of the times as dedicated rank-and-file party members changed the political face of the United States. As Berkeley physicist Edwin McMillan recalled in 1968: "I sympathized very well with some of these points of view, when you saw how things were in the world."

After the war, in the spring of 1949, Oppenheimer appeared before the House Committee on Un-American Activities (HUAC). In the previous three years he had been refused a job at Berkeley and had been subjected to FBI harassment at the University of Minnesota in Minneapolis, where he had been hired as an assistant professor of physics. At the HUAC hearings he refused to name names. Under FBI pressure, the president of the University of Minnesota fired him. The universities of Washington and Chicago and Cornell University expressed interest in his services. But the FBI successfully discouraged them from making an offer. The FBI sent their agents around to talk to him. "Don't you want to get a job at a university? If you do, you'll have to cooperate with us."

Oppenheimer continued to refuse to cooperate. In this decision, Oppenheimer again was similar to most members of the party, who, no matter what their feelings were about the party's fatal mistakes, refused to cooperate with the witch hunt. This was particularly true of those who had experienced at first hand the successes of the organizing drives of the 1930s. After all, for them the party was a tool to be used in order to be politically effective; when it no longer became so, they left. They were disappointed in many cases, but they had no need to acquire identities as informers. At age thirty-seven, Oppenheimer was forced out of physics and took up ranching in New Mexico.

The case of Frank Oppenheimer represented a denial of the basic rights of freedom of speech. Oppenheimer's "crime" was real. He was not innocent of the charge of being a Communist. He had been a Communist. When right-wing U.S. officialdom succeeded in drumming him out of physics, they succeeded in diminishing the range of opinion that the First Amendment was designed to protect.

The expulsion of Frank Oppenheimer and other left-wing physicists contributed to the marginalization of the sensibility that had made physics a crown jewel of the bourgeois culture of the nineteenth century, a sensibility that the world was understandable. This sensibility has remained alive on the margins of physics, most notably in the San Francisco Exploratorium, created by Frank Oppenheimer late in his career after his release from internal exile.

Most science museums are spectacles. They entertain through a combination of mystery and awe. Whether it is a gigantic reconstruction of diplodocus or the impressive complexity of microelectronic circuitry, we shake our heads at "the wonders of science," the truly amazing results of scientific exploration. The Exploratorium, however, is different. Oppenheimer sought to communicate a different reality about science, the opposite of awe and mystery. For Oppenheimer, science in general, and physics in particular, show not that the world is a mysterious place, but, on the contrary, that through effort the world is knowable. From this perspective have flowed all the special hands-on design touches that have given the Exploratorium its well-deserved popularity and worldwide reputation. Other museums have responded and the Exploratorium concept is now a standard feature in the design of the modern science museum.

*

Uranium-lead dating has had an unexpected side effect. In the 1960s, during a routine investigation of the age of the earth from deep-sea sediments using the uranium-238/lead-206 method, Cal Tech geochemist Clair Patterson noticed that there was a marked lead influx into the top layer of the sediments. Suspecting that the influx might be evidence for lead pollution on a global scale, he used the facilities of the ultra-clean lunar rock laboratory at Cal Tech to explore the effect. In 1980 he and collaborator Dorothy Settles published results showing that there was a global pattern of elevated lead levels in plants and animals and that in particular the concentrations of lead in lead-soldered tins of tuna was over ten thousand times higher than those reported by governmental agencies.

The hazard is nontrivial. A diet of tinned tuna fish added to the routine intake of airborne lead in conurbations is sufficient to bring an individual up to the retained lead levels shown by industrial workers with classic symptoms of lead poisoning. Aside from the obvious health consequences of this pattern (Patterson has concluded that it is immoral to continue to mine lead), the controls used to test for lead in food have themselves become contaminated with lead. Thus government agencies measured lead in tinned versus fresh tuna and concluded that while there was about twice as much lead in tinned tuna as fresh tuna, the difference did not constitute a hazard. Patterson and Settles, on the other hand, by analyzing carefully the tissues of fresh-caught tuna so as to eliminate contamination by ambient levels of lead, found the horrific effect of a ten-thousandfold increase and concluded their report with the recommendation that lead-soldered tins should be removed from the market.

Most tins are lead-soldered. The sheet metal is formed into a cylinder. It is soldered down the side. And the top and bottom are crimped on. After the report of Patterson and Settles, some manufacturers, notably Chicken of the Sea, responded positively by converting to a two-piece manufacture where the cylinder and bottom are formed from a single piece by a punch press and the top is crimped on as before. You can look for this difference in manufacture in your local supermarket. The reader may wish to buy the two-piece nonsoldered tin, particularly for food to be given to children.

*

The mendacious attitudes of high-ranking scientific spokespersons on the nuclear issue was perhaps most clearly revealed in the mid-1980s when the failure of the nuclear establishment to make any provision for the safe disposal of nuclear waste became public knowledge. For over thirty years we had been told that disposal of radioactive waste from nuclear reactors constituted no great problem. Public hearings had been dominated by confident-sounding government physicists who assured impressionable civil authorities that all was well. Those with technical training waited in vain for some concrete evidence that the problems of the safe disposal of plutonium-contaminated waste were close to being solved. As the plutonium burden on the earth increased year by year, one heard about salt mines, about rockets to dump the waste into the sun, about glass vitrification—but no concrete plan had been forthcoming.

In 1984 a study committee of the International Council of Scientific Unions (ICSU) on the geological disposal of radioactive waste confirmed what many have suspected all along. Research on the problem of the disposal of radioactive waste was in fact virtually nonexistent.

Wastes had only been studied in the laboratory with no on-site geological studies. There was no work on the question of stability of possible sites with respect to the motion of the earth's tectonic plates, with respect to long-term permeability, or with respect to climatic changes. The analysis of rock fractures was "quite inadequate." In particular, it seemed that hard rock, such as granite, could permit flow rates to the surrounding environment of up to ten thousand times greater than that of loose rock such as shale. The idea was that fractures in granite, although on average ten meters apart compared to ten centimeters apart in shale, have an average width of one centimeter compared to an average width of one-tenth of a millimeter in shale. Since the rate of fluid flow is proportional to the cube of the crack width, the difference, contrary to superficial first estimates, meant that shale with many small fractures could retard the flow of water ten thousand times better than granite with far fewer but much larger cracks. The image of immense, secure rock caverns safely holding radioactive wastes for 25,000 to 100,000 years had been only a public relations exercise conducted by chief government scientists. The ICSU study concluded "of all waste disposal problems, understanding the hydrological characteristics of fracture systems is one of the most urgent areas for study."

Furthermore, no work had been done on the research and development of the tools and equipment necessary to actually construct caverns to hold the waste even if possible sites could be found. No work had been done on the effect of cold temperatures on the stability of the wastes, of the effects of chemical reactivity with the surrounding environment, or of the effects of fluid flow and rock alteration on the stability of the storage site. Nor had there been any work done on constructing adequate safety protocols. How might a leak from a repository be detected and corrected? When asked whether they had received any feedback from the authorities about their report, one of the authors said: "Not a bit."

*

The conditions under which the criterion of understanding might again be a main motivating force in the creation of theory in physics are by no means clear. (See Paul Forman [1974] for a classic analysis of how the social uncertainties of Weimar influenced physicists to think along probabilist rather than determinist lines in their development of quantum mechanics.) Historically, the great creative consolidations in understanding have tended to follow periods of great overall social innovation. Newton's mechanics was a consolidation of the physics of the Renaissance; Carnot's second law of thermodynamics a consolidation of the experience of steam following the early phase of the industrial revolution; the theory of relativity a consolidation of the physics of electricity following the later stages of the industrial revolution. Quantum mechanics, although incomplete, is also a consolidation of the experience of materials gained also in the later stages of the industrial revolution.

The attempts to create an understanding of the experience of nuclear matter have occurred in a period marked not by great innovation but by great destruction. Except for the brief period of the sixties, there has not been a widespread creative social sensibility that could generate creative sparks within physics.

What might such a sensibility look like? The sixties offered a possible hint of the conditions under which we might expect physicists to want to create new ways of understanding rather than simply reproduce old understandings at a higher level of abstraction. The sixties was a decade of challenge and confrontation. Professional societies all birthed challenges to the status quo, most visibly as disruptions at professional meetings and in the appearance of critical journals in every discipline. The guardians of the English language fought over the legitimacy of Black English. The criminologists fought over the definition of crime, the psychologists over the definition of personality. The psychiatrists were forced to demedicalize homosexuality. The sociologists began dealing not with the problem of poverty, but with the problem of wealth. Radical historians resituated the presumed timeless categories of sexuality, motherhood, and intelligence as historically specific, changing entities subject to human influence and direction. In science, activists challenged the establishment on the issues of race and IQ, sociobiology, sexism in science, the teaching of school science, corporate control of science, and U.S. involvement in Vietnam.

The deepest expression of this prerevolutionary current in Western societies occurred in May 1968 in France. *Les événements* produced a situation where the government had formulated plans to leave the country, where martial law was in place, and where mass demonstrations could have taken over the ministries of government. Among the institutions centrally involved in a potential transformation of French society was the Center for Nuclear Research (CEN) at Saclay, an organization of ten thousand research workers and support staff similar to CERN in Geneva and the U.S. national laboratories at Berkeley, Stanford, and Batavia.

On May 3, the dispute between students and the government spread from Nanterre to the Latin quarter. Barricades were built. A member of the CRS, the French riot police, was hit by a *pavée.* On May 6, people at Saclay were still unconcerned. It was a disturbance, but not very important, they thought. On the evening of the sixth, there was more violence by the state—this time, tear gas and truncheons. The students charged the police. Cars were left burning in the street. There was a public outcry against the arsonists.

Nevertheless, at Saclay, as in the rest of France, there were discussions. Why such violence? Why was the regime responding in this way to student criticism? The next day, May 7, came the first petition at Saclay supporting the students.

A week later, on the morning of May 13, after the violent repression of the students on the nights of May 11 and 12, the French trade unions called for a general strike. At Saclay, a contingent of two thousand workers was organized to take part in the massive 800,000-person demonstration in Paris that afternoon. Inside and outside the unions at Saclay there were hectic discussions. The colleges of France were in occupation.

In the next days the factories went on strike. Following the example of the students, the French work force occupied the factory buildings. Nine million people were on strike. The country had stopped working.

At Saclay on May 17 came the first meetings. By eleven o'clock, three hundred people were meeting. The discussion topic was, Who was to control the laboratory, and how?

A mass meeting was called for the afternoon. Five thousand people showed up, half of the Saclay work force. The unions were unable to contain the discussions within the customary framework of bureaucratic rules of procedure and precedence. The astounding turnout had everyone confused. The discussion foundered. The five hundred people from the morning meeting decided to stay all night and then all weekend.

In the apparent structurelessness of the new participation, the discussions circled over the entire terrain of social life at Saclay: bureaucracy, entry passes, armed guards, the unions. Everyone spoke, sometimes all at once. After three days of up to fifteen hundred people meeting continuously, themes began to emerge: the established structure of the laboratory must fall—from individual research groups all the way up to the level of directorial control of the laboratory. The atmosphere was electric, fatiguing, creative. In the country at large ten million people were on strike. It was time to do things differently.

A two-part set of proposals for laboratory reorganization was created, the first part for democratization of the laboratory and "humanization of labor relations," the second part a set of economic demands. The text was placed before an assembly of six thousand people on the morning of May 20. Its tone, its language, its reasonableness electrified the audience.

I. PREAMBLE

The workers of CEN Saclay and of the outside companies who held the meeting during the weekend have analyzed the present situation in France. The student movement has lifted the curtain on a deeply rooted crisis in French society and had been the fuse which permitted a massive mobilization of the working class to get under way. As a movement of struggle submitting to scrutiny all means whereby bureaucracy, the state, and capitalism operate; as a movement objectively directed toward human liberation, the student movement must receive our respect and our support.

II. DEMOCRATIC DEMANDS

Instead of the absolute power of the administration we demand a committee of the work unit elected and subject to recall in whole, or in part, by the workers and having power of supervision and decision.

Instead of the discretionary power of the service and department heads, we demand the power of elected councils for each service department.

An end must be made to all coercive and oppressive measures submitted to in the name of security controls. We accept the pass system solely for access to areas where there is a real danger of radioactivity.

We demand to have freedom of expression and of assembly for every class of activity, including political and trade unions, equally for the personnel of CEA and (including agents of the security services) for the outside companies.

The local union branch must receive recognition; it may also summon any individual, including political and union leaders.

Finally, we state we have the right to strike without notice.

Economic demands included new demands for permanent vocational training during working hours, a one-month education leave for all workers, and "control over the hiring of labor by the workers and their representatives."

The meeting proposed for immediate action an indefinite on-the-spot strike, occupation of the center, and an indefinite go-slow. A central action committee was set up consisting of five representatives, one from each of the unions, fifteen members elected by workers at Saclay, and eight elected by contract workers of the outside companies.

Throughout the month of May the central action committee coordinated the operation of the laboratory. The internal telephones were restored, food was organized, news letters published, public address systems installed, negotiations with management conducted. Work was restarted to provide radioisotopes for the hospitals. Gasoline was obtained from the Finac picket at Nanterre. Medical supplies—rubber gloves, oxygen bottles, white overalls, alcohol—were made available to injured students at the mini-hospital in the Sorbonne.

The strike action spread to the rest of the French atomic energy commission. Seventeen other labs elected action committees and formulated demands for joint control of their workplaces. At Fontenoy aux Roses the staff general assembly by a nearly unanimous vote established a committee elected by the whole body of workers of CEN/FAR and called for participation in the scientific, technical, administrative, financial, and social decision-making. "The aim of this committee is by democratic means, and by exchange of ideas with the staff of the other centers, to build a new organizational structure and oblige the management to accept joint control."

Other laboratories echoed the demand for democratically-run workplaces. French physicists were attempting the first reorganization of their social relationships since the French Revolution.

One can suggest then, along with Pierre Bourdieu, that attempts to create new ways of understanding can really be expected to occur only when new ways of doing things in general are the order of the day. New approaches must find an environment strong and self-sustaining enough to support, at the earliest stages of preperception, an alternative sensibility. Otherwise the requirements of social existence produce reflexive responses to experience that reproduce what has gone before rather than creating the new ways of understanding that we customarily call breakthroughs.

The drive to create a new physics has been frustrated since the 1920s. If one believes in the theory of genius we are waiting for a new Einstein. But if one believes that great discoveries are made one year before they are absolutely inevitable, we are waiting for a popular involvement in physics and in everything else to create the tidal swell that nourishes individual creative effort.

SOURCES

American Institute of Physics Oral History Archive Interviews

Luis Alvarez, by Charles Weiner and Barry Richman, February 14–15, 1967.

Paul Dirac, by T. S. Kuhn, April 1, 1962; May 6, 1963; May 7, 1963; May 10, 1963; May 14, 1963.

James Franck, by T. S. Kuhn, July 12, 1962.

F. E. Low, autobiography, July 30, 1965.

E. M. McMillan, by Charles Weiner, n.d.

W. K. H. Panofsky, by Charles Weiner, May 15, 1973.

Melba Phillips, by K. R. Sopka, December 5, 1977.

E. E. Salpeter, by Spencer Weart, March 30, 1978.

Additional archive material

R. T. Birge, *History of the University of California Physics Department*, unpublished manuscript on file at the Niels Bohr Library of the American Institute of Physics, New York.

Other sources

Albury, David, and Schwartz, Joseph (1982). *Partial Progress. The Politics of Science and Technology*, Pluto, London.

Alvarez, Luis W. (1969). "Recent Developments in Particle Physics," *Science*, v. 165, pp. 1071–91.

Bertolotti, Mario (1983). *Masers and Lasers. An Historical Approach*, Adam Hilger, Bristol.

Beyer, Robert T., ed. (1949). *Foundations of Nuclear Physics*, Facsimiles of Thirteen Fundamental Studies as They Were Originally Reported in the Scientific Journals, Dover, New York.

Brown, Laurie M., and Hoddeson, Lillian, eds. (1983). *The Birth of Particle Physics*, Cambridge University Press, New York.

Caudwell, Christopher (1939). *The Crisis in Physics*, John Lane, London.

Cahn, Robert N., and Goldhaber, Gerson (1989). *The Experimental Foundations of Particle Physics*, Cambridge University Press, Cambridge, England.

Chew, Geoffrey F. (1961). *S-Matrix Theory of Strong Interactions*, Benjamin, New York.

——— (1983). "Bootstrapping the Photon," *Foundations in Physics*, v. 13, pp. 217–46.

Ellis, John (1990). "Holy Grail or Snark?" (Review of J. F. Gunion, H. E. Haber, G. Kane, and S. Dawson, *The Higgs Hunter's Guide: Frontiers in Physics*), *Nature*, v. 348, p. 359.

Feynman, Richard P. (1962). *Quantum Electrodynamics*, Benjamin, San Francisco.

——— (1985). *QED. The Strange Theory of Light and Matter*, Princeton University Press, Princeton, N.J.

———; Leighton, Robert B.; and Sands, Matthew (1963). *The Feynman Lectures on Physics*, v. 3, Addison-Wesley, Reading, Mass.

Forman, Paul (1974). "Weimar Culture, Causality and Quantum Theory, 1918–1927: Adaptation by German Physicists and Mathematicians to a Hostile Intellectual Environment," *Historical Studies in the Physical Sciences*, v. 18, pp. 1–115.

Fyfe, W. F.; Babuska, V.; Price, N. J.; Schmid, E.; Tsang, C. F.; Uyeda, S.; and Velde, B. (1984). "The Geology of Nuclear Waste Disposal," *Nature*, v. 310, pp. 537–541.

Guth, Alan H.; Huang, Kerson; and Jaffe, Robert L. (1983). *Asymptotic Realms of Physics. Essays in Honor of Francis E. Low*, M.I.T. Press, Cambridge, Mass.

Iliopoulos, J. (1976). *An Introduction to Gauge Theories*, Lectures Given in the Academic Training Program of CERN 1975–1976, Geneva.

Kemmer, N. (1982). "Isospin," in "International Colloquium on the History of Particle Physics," *Journal de Physique*, Tome 43, Colloque C-8, supplément au no. 12, December.

Kline, Morris (1980). *Mathematics. The Loss of Certainty*, Oxford University Press, Oxford, England.

Lodge, David (1988). "L'Uni Left in a State" (review of Pierre Bourdieu, *Homo Academicus*, December 9, trans. Peter Collier, Polity Press, London), *The Guardian*, p. 27.

Miller, Jonathan, and Van Loon, Borin (1982). *Darwin for Beginners*, Writers and Readers, London.

Pauli, Wolfgang (1921). *Theory of Relativity*, trans. George Field, Dover Publications, New York (1981).

Penrose, Roger (1989). *The Emperor's New Mind. Concerning Computers, Minds and the Laws of Physics*, Vintage, London.

Perkins, Donald H. (1982). *Introduction to High-Energy Physics*, 2nd ed., Addison-Wesley, Reading, Mass.

Pickering, Andrew (1984). *Constructing Quarks. A Sociological History of Particle Physics*, University of Chicago Press, Chicago.

———, and Trower, W. Peter (1985). Commentary: "Sociological Problems of High-Energy Physics," *Nature*, v. 318, pp. 243–45.

Polkinghorne, John (1989). *Rochester Roundabout. The Story of High-Energy Physics*, W.H. Freeman, New York.

Purcell, Edward M. (1963). *Electricity and Magnetism*, Berkeley Physics Course, v. 2, McGraw-Hill, New York.

Quigg, Chris (1983). *Gauge Theories of the Strong, Weak and Electromagnetic Interactions*, Benjamin, Reading, Mass.

Schwinger, Julian, ed. (1958). *Selected Papers on Quantum Electrodynamics,* Dover, New York.
Weinberg, Steven (1970). "Dynamic and Algebraic Symmetries," in *Lectures on Elementary Particles and Quantum Field Theory.* 1970 Brandeis University Summer Institute in Theoretical Physics, v. 1, M.I.T. Press, Cambridge, Mass.
——— (1973). "Where We Are Now," *Science,* v. 180, pp. 273–78
Yang, Chen Ning (1983). *Selected Papers 1945–1980 with Commentary,* Freeman, San Francisco.

CHAPTER 6: London 1991

NOTES

The problem with postmodern intellectuals is that they know little about science. Their critiques of epistemology—the certainty of knowledge, the sanctity of science, the value and knowability of truth—are accurate. Truth *is* constructed, not discovered. Claims for objectivity *do* disguise invidious, unequal power relationships. Knowledge is a text, no more and no less. These statements are valuable contributions to our intellectual life. The more we can take their critique on board the more we will be able to free ourselves from the immobilized modernism of the past.

But even though the postmodernists have beautifully expressed the failures of modernism, they have nowhere to go. The accuracy with which they have skewered the pompous certainties of establishments everywhere starts to read more like a whine rather than being the basis of a new beginning. The postmodern intellectuals seem to give up just where the analysis needs to begin—with a critical appreciation of the achievements of the modern movement, including its science. There is a laziness here, a shooting from the hip, which one suspects has to do with a fear to engage the relevant texts. A good start might be a detailed postmodern critique of the strengths and weaknesses of the theory of relativity.

SOURCES

Anon. (1990). *Report of the Advisory Committee on the Future of the U.S. Space Program,* U.S. Government Printing Office, Washington, D.C., December.
Anon. (1990). "Guilty Manslaughter Verdict," *Hazards,* Bulletin Number 28, April, pp. 2–3.
Bell, John (1978). "An Unstable Enterprise," *New Scientist,* March 12, pp. 13–15.
Berger, John (1980). *About Looking,* Writers and Readers, London.

Berman, Marshall (1984). "The Signs in the Street," *New Left Review*, no. 114, March/April, pp. 114–23.

Braverman, Harry (1989). "The Degradation of Work," *Monthly Review*, v. 41, October, pp. 35–47.

Donovan, Patrick (1990). "Safety Fears in the Shadow of Zeebrugge," *The Guardian*, October 20, p. 3.

Feynman, Richard P. (1988). *What Do You Care What Other People Think? Further Adventures of a Curious Character*, W.W. Norton, New York.

Foster, Hal, ed. (1985). *Postmodern Culture*, Pluto, London.

Graham, William (1990). Telephone interview, October 16.

Hamer, Mick (1987). "A Ferry Designed for Disaster," *New Scientist*, July 23, pp. 23–25.

Pike, Dag (1987). "Herald of Disaster," *New Scientist*, March 12, p. 12.

Soper, Kate (1991). "Postmodernism, Subjectivity and the Question of Value," *New Left Review*, no. 186, March/April, pp. 120–28.

Index